IMAGES
of America

SHREVEPORT

IMAGES
of America

SHREVEPORT

Eric J. Brock

ARCADIA
PUBLISHING

ISBN 978-0-7385-9001-1

Published by Arcadia Publishing
Charleston, South Carolina

Printed in the United States of America

For all general information contact Arcadia Publishing at:
Telephone 843-853-2070
Fax 843-853-0044
E-mail sales@arcadiapublishing.com
For customer service and orders:
Toll-Free 1-888-313-2665

Visit us on the Internet at www.arcadiapublishing.com

For Cristina Walker

Contents

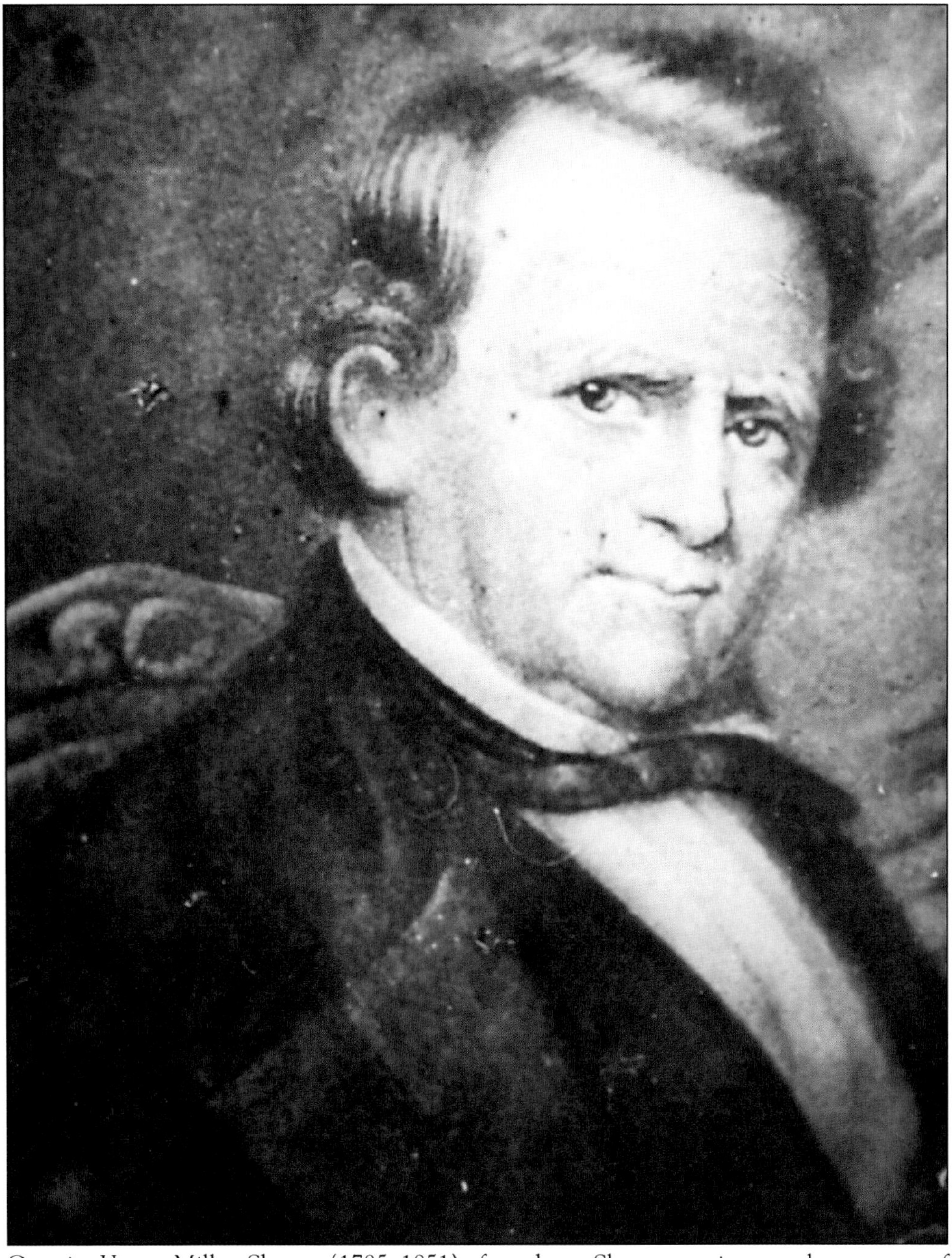

Captain Henry Miller Shreve (1785–1851), for whom Shreveport is named, was one of the most influential navigators of the nineteenth century. His work with the U.S. Army Corps of Engineers in removing the 180 mile-long logjam on Red River known as "The Great Raft" resulted in opening the river to traffic and the land along the river to settlement. In 1836 the Shreve Town Company, a land venture established by Shreve and seven others, laid out the village of Shreve Town. In 1839 the name was changed to Shreveport. Though the town was named in his honor, Shreve never lived in Shreveport, making his home instead in St. Louis, Missouri.

Introduction

Shreveport was born about the same time as photography. Unfortunately, the citizens of the new town were so busy building a community, making a living, and carving out a niche for themselves that few photographic images of the city's first few years were made.

By the 1850s there were a few photographers here. Some of the city's nineteenth-century photographers signed their works, while others did not. Consequently, it is often, even usually, impossible to tell who took a particular photograph. Star Studios, Kaufman Studios, Dambley Studios, T.M. Elliott, and a handful of others made excellent images from the mid-nineteenth century to the early twentieth century that have come down to us. In the twentieth century the outstanding name among photographers who chronicled the development of Shreveport is Grabill Studios, established by Burch Grabill in 1918 and later operated by his son William for many years.

The late Bill Grabill had a great deal to do with this book. It was he, or rather his enormous collection of historic images of the Shreveport area, that sparked the interest of this writer in Shreveport history. From a few old prints given to the author as a child by Mr. Grabill has grown a substantial collection of historic images, a popular weekly newspaper column on the area's history, and a career in historical research, historic preservation, and the applications of these areas to city planning.

This book is a gathering of photographs, largely from the writer's own collection. It does not pretend to be a complete history of the city by any means, nor does it attempt to chronicle every event, building, person, or institution that has had a role in shaping the city of Shreveport. Rather, it is intended to be a sampling of little-known views of our city's past, showing just a few slices of where we come from, what we have been, what we have lost, and what we can yet preserve. We are all well aware of what we have and who we are, but are we really aware of where we have been and why we are as we are?

Shreveport is a wonderful city. It is a physically beautiful place, filled with lush foliage at any time of the year, blessed with a moderate climate that borders on the semi-tropical, and endowed with resources both natural and man-made that have made it the second city in Louisiana in importance almost from its very beginning. Indeed, Shreveport started as an economic venture, laid out precisely where the Red River, which connects the area to New Orleans, South Louisiana, and the Gulf of Mexico, meets the old Texas Trail (now U.S. Highway 80 and roughly the route of Interstate 20 through this area today), a major overland route from the United States to the Republic of Texas at the time Shreveport was founded.

Shreveport, in fact, was the westernmost city in the United States when laid out in 1836 by Captain Henry Miller Shreve and the Shreve Town Company, of which he was a member. Because of its location on the river and its proximity to Texas, then a newly-independent nation, the investors in the company were certain they could not miss in planning a town at this point; and they were correct. They, and the pioneers who followed and settled here, built this city: "If you seek their monument, look about you."

Shreveport has been a rough and rowdy river town, a railroad center, a center for cotton, lumber, and oil and gas. It has been the capital of Louisiana, the headquarters of a mighty army during the Civil War, and the home of several institutions of higher learning, including the oldest in the Louisiana. It is a community where Old and New South mingle quite well, where old gentility and new industry coexist and where, despite a great deal of racial tension in its past, a remarkable degree of racial harmony and cooperation has become the rule of the day.

Shreveport is also a city full of contradictions: It has been a community strongly influenced by religion and one whose religious leaders have exerted much influence nationally, yet it was also once the location of the largest red-light district of any city its size in the nation (and a legal one at that), and is today a major center for casino gambling in the South.

More than anything, Shreveport is a city full of stories. There is no singular story of Shreveport, but rather an exquisite, fascinating, often amusing, sometimes tragic, always riveting collection of stories that, taken as whole, make up its history. The history of Shreveport continues to be written; we, its citizens, are creating it just as our predecessors did before us. This book is a celebration of our city's past, a collection of stories in visual form. It is a rich past upon which we are building even at this very moment.

Eric J. Brock

One

Early Years

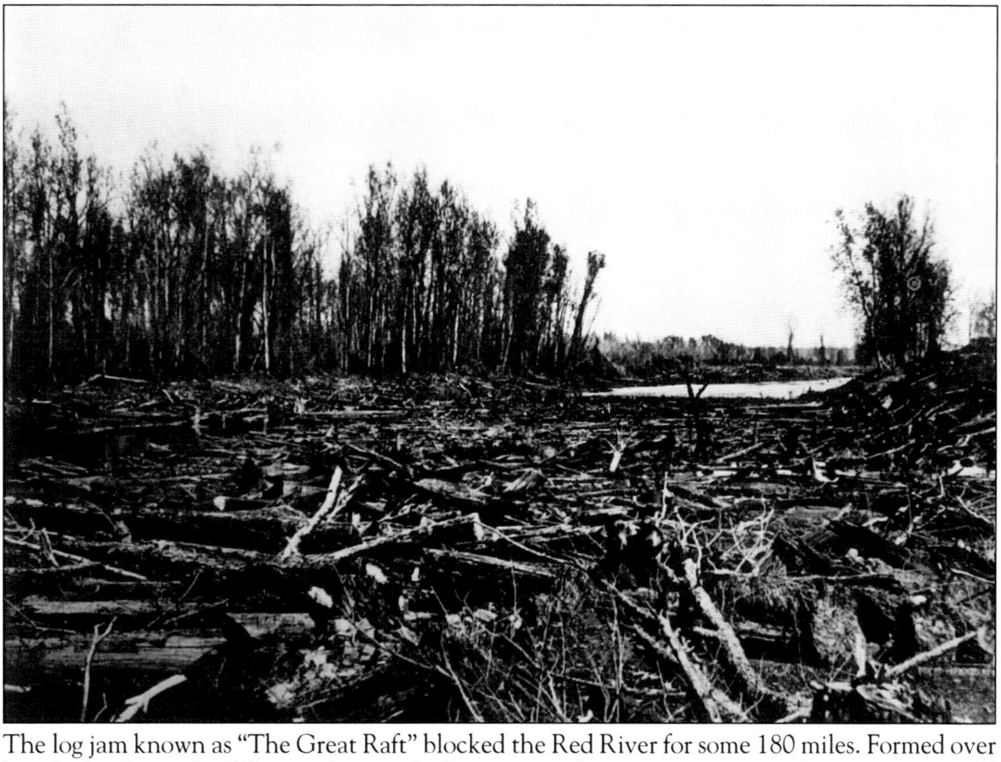

The log jam known as "The Great Raft" blocked the Red River for some 180 miles. Formed over hundreds of years by fallen timbers and silt, it was so dense in many areas that a person could ride safely across it on horseback.

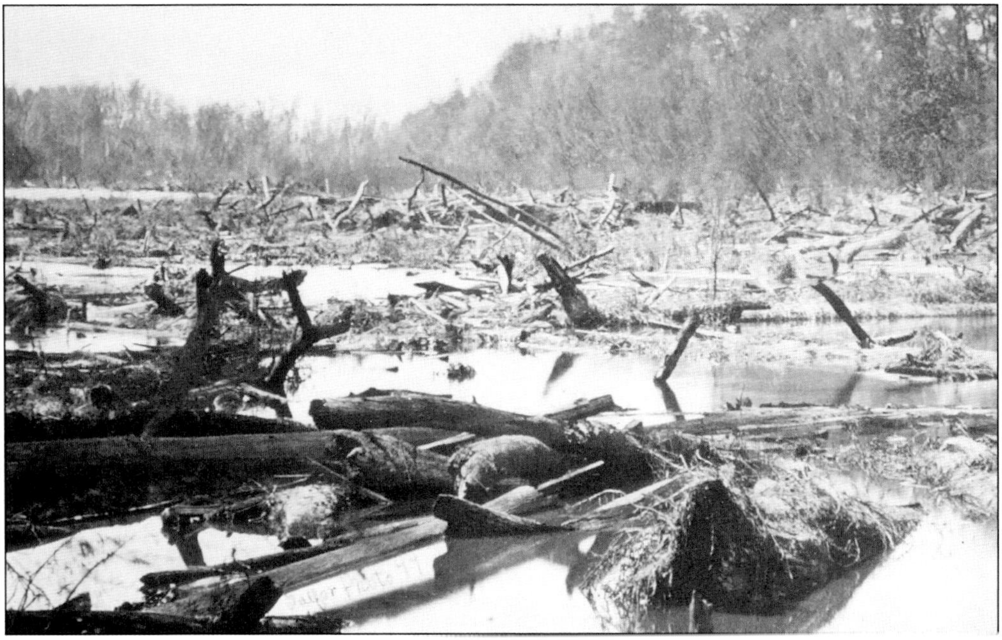

Captain Shreve, using a craft of his own invention, the snagboat, was able to successfully clear the river from its mouth, where it meets the Mississippi, to the site of Shreveport. In some places the Raft continued to re-form as late as the Civil War, creating swampy, impassable places where the river should have flowed (above). Snagboats, double hulled steamboats with cranes mounted on them to remove the logs from the water, continued to be used to keep Red River clear as late as 1873 (below).

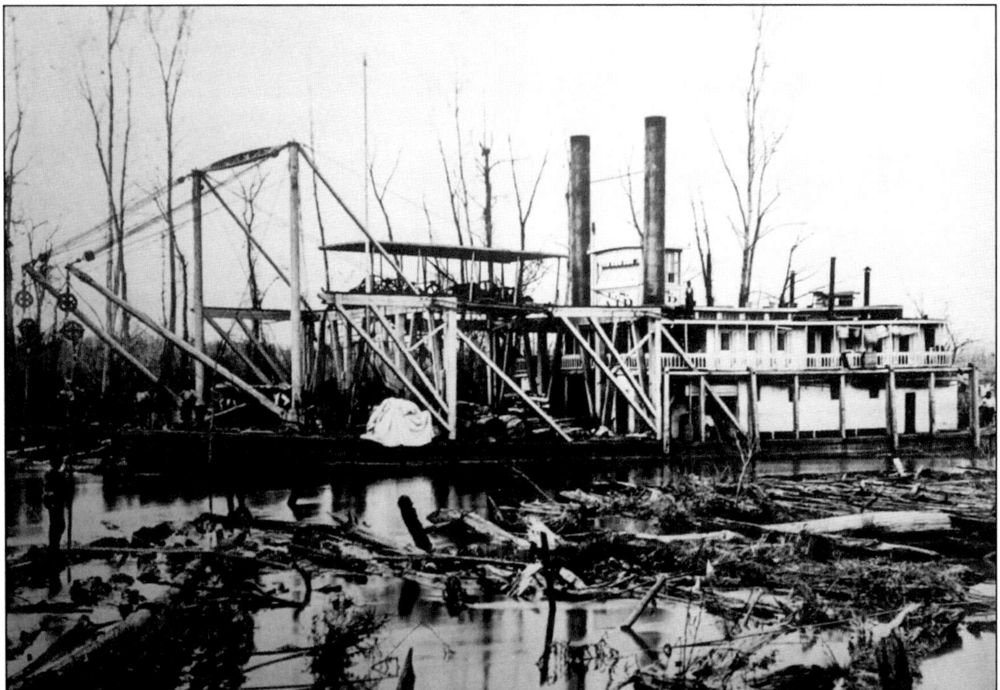

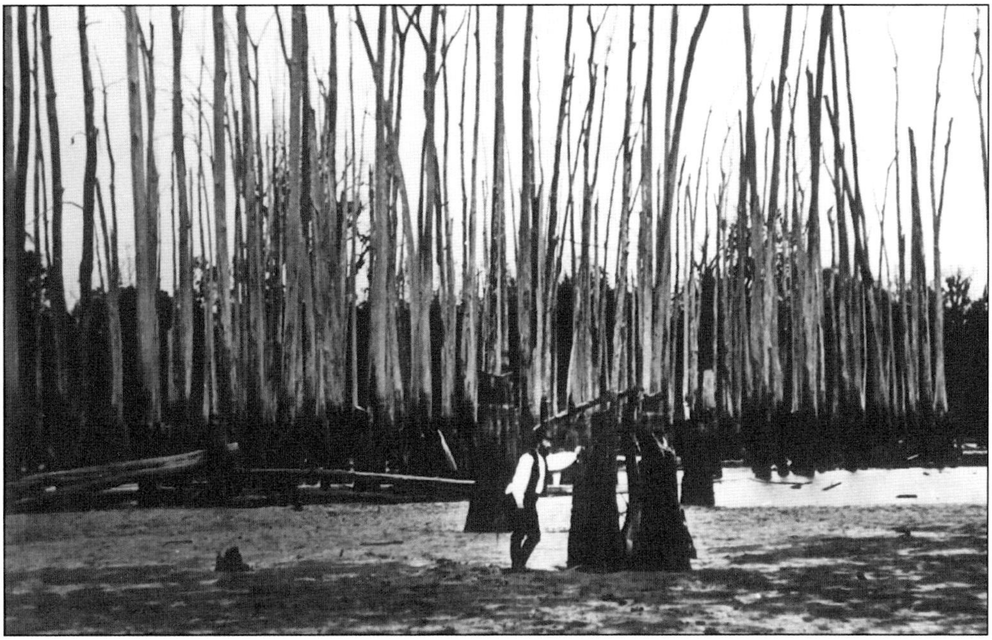

Here is a dramatic view (above) of the banks of the Red River near Shreveport during the clearing of the Great Raft. On May 16, 1873, the *R.T. Bryarly* became the first steamboat to traverse the length of the Red River past Shreveport without encountering obstructions (below). In 1876 the *Bryarly* sank on the Red River after striking a snag. During the decades that saw commerce on the Red, the river was called "the steamboat graveyard" and not without good reason.

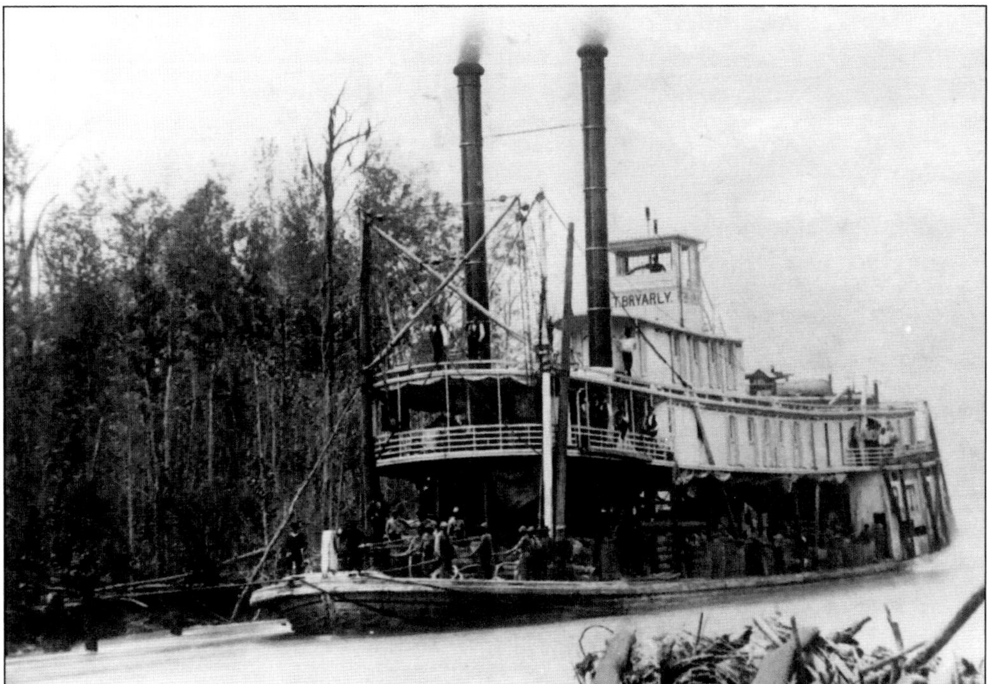

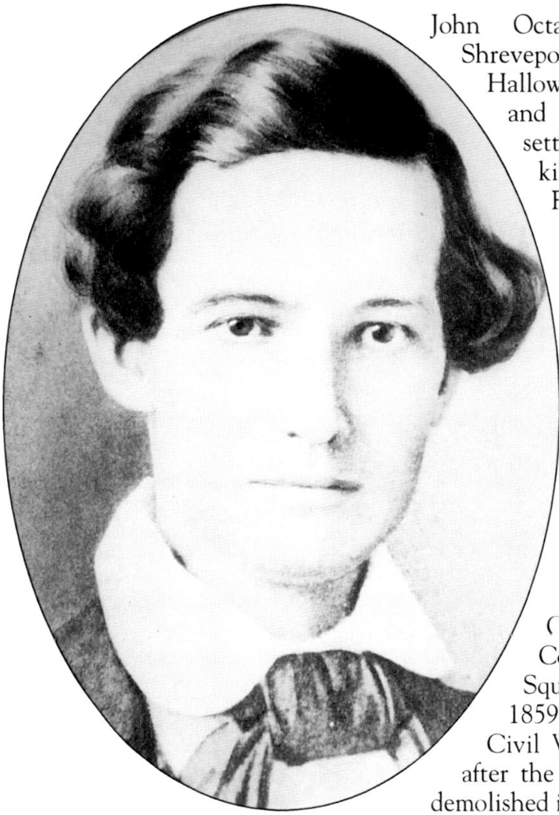

John Octavius Sewall (1806–1840) became Shreveport's first mayor in 1839. A native of Hallowell, Maine, he and his brothers Charles and Rufus were among the city's earliest settlers. In January 1840, Sewall was killed in a duel fought at nearby Elysian Fields, Texas.

Construction of the first Caddo Parish Courthouse to occupy the Courthouse Square on Texas Street was begun in 1859 and completed in 1860. During the Civil War it served as Louisiana's Statehouse after the government fled to Shreveport. It was demolished in 1890.

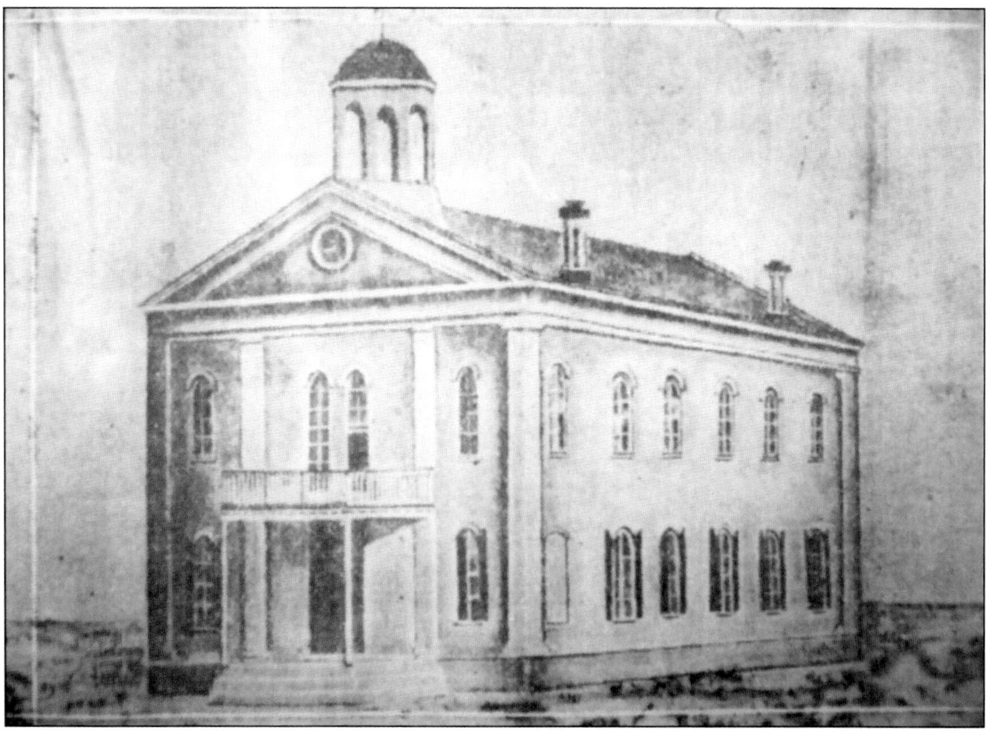

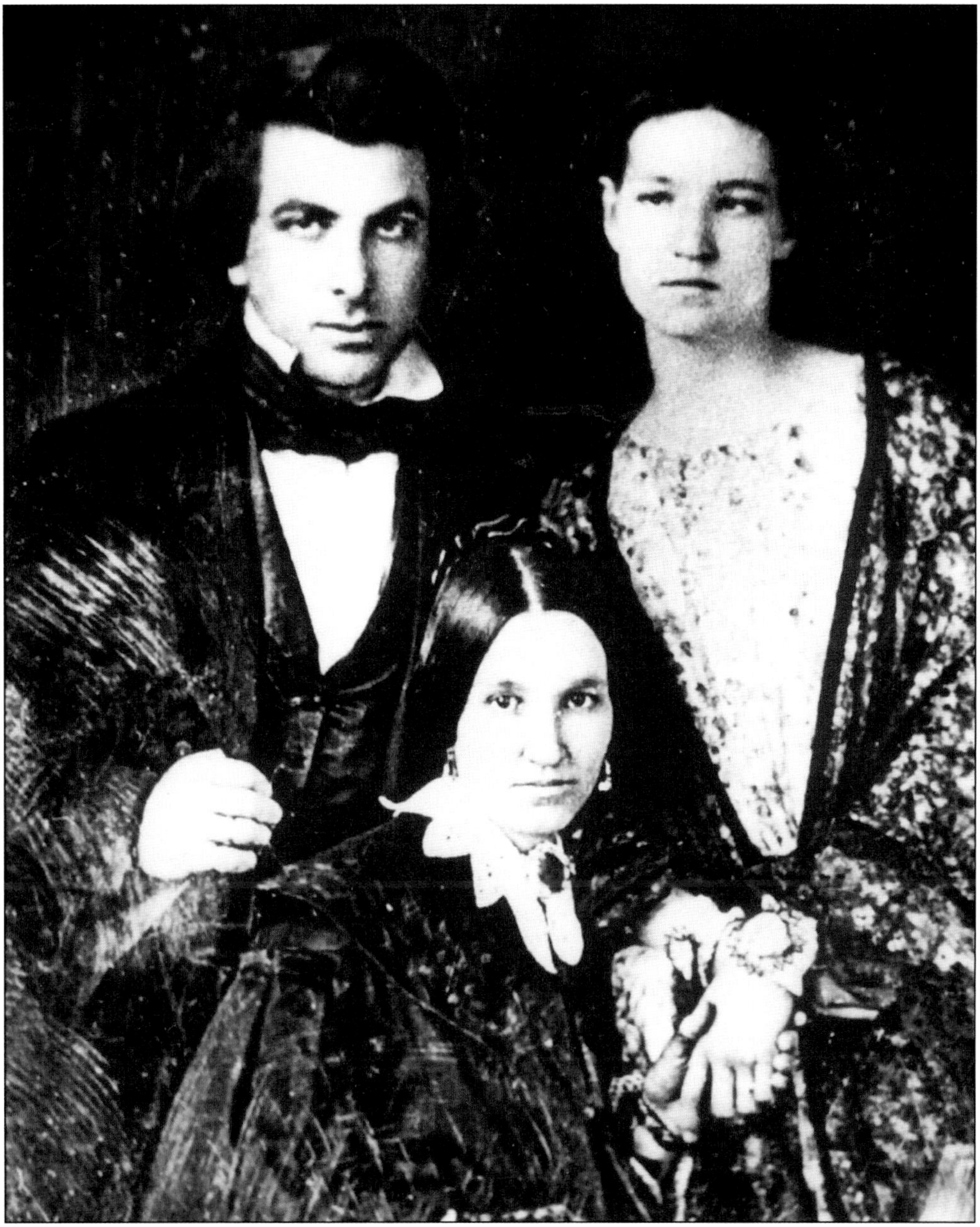

One of the city's most prominent pioneer merchants was Ed Jacobs (1822–1896), born Ephraim Jacobi in Pomerania, Germany. He came to Shreveport with his brother, Ben, in 1844, and the two became successful dry goods merchants and bankers. Ed is seen here with his wife, Palestine (1830–1918), who is seated, and her sister, later Ben's wife, Amaza (1839–1880), in 1852.

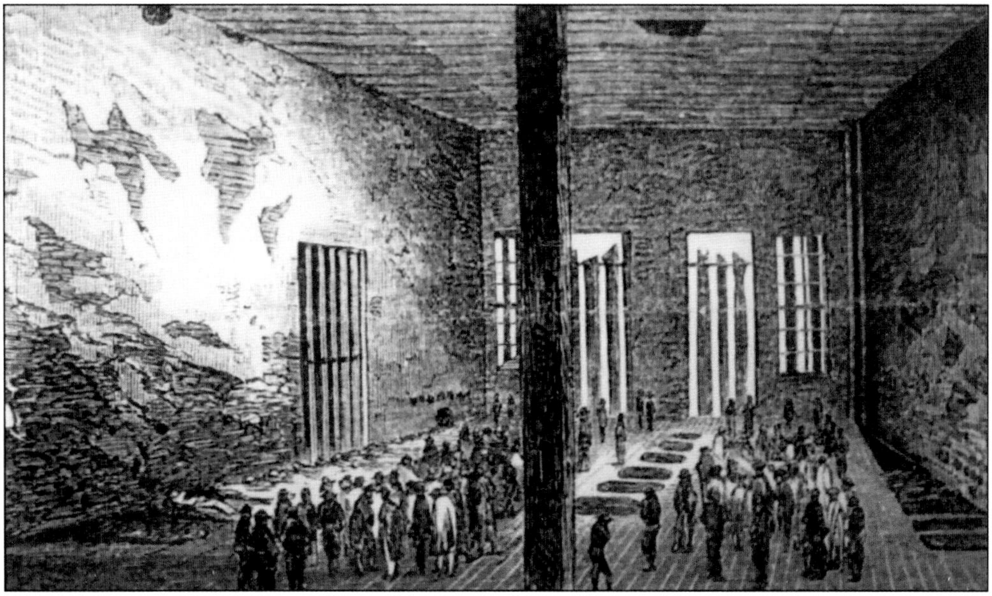

During the Civil War Shreveport was the headquarters of the Trans-Mississippi Department of the Confederate Army, as well as serving as state capital from 1863 to 1865. Once when Union prisoners were being marched through the city, a little boy in the crowd of observers was overheard asking his father if they were the legislators on their way to work.

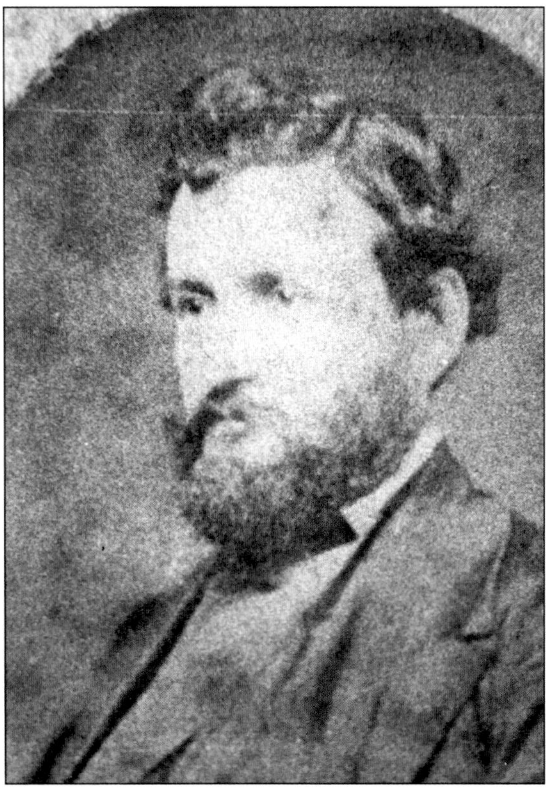

Colonel Leon D. Marks (1829–1863), a Shreveport attorney before the Civil War, commanded the 27th Louisiana Infantry during that conflict. He was mortally wounded at Vicksburg, where a monument to him now stands. He is buried in Shreveport's Oakland Cemetery.

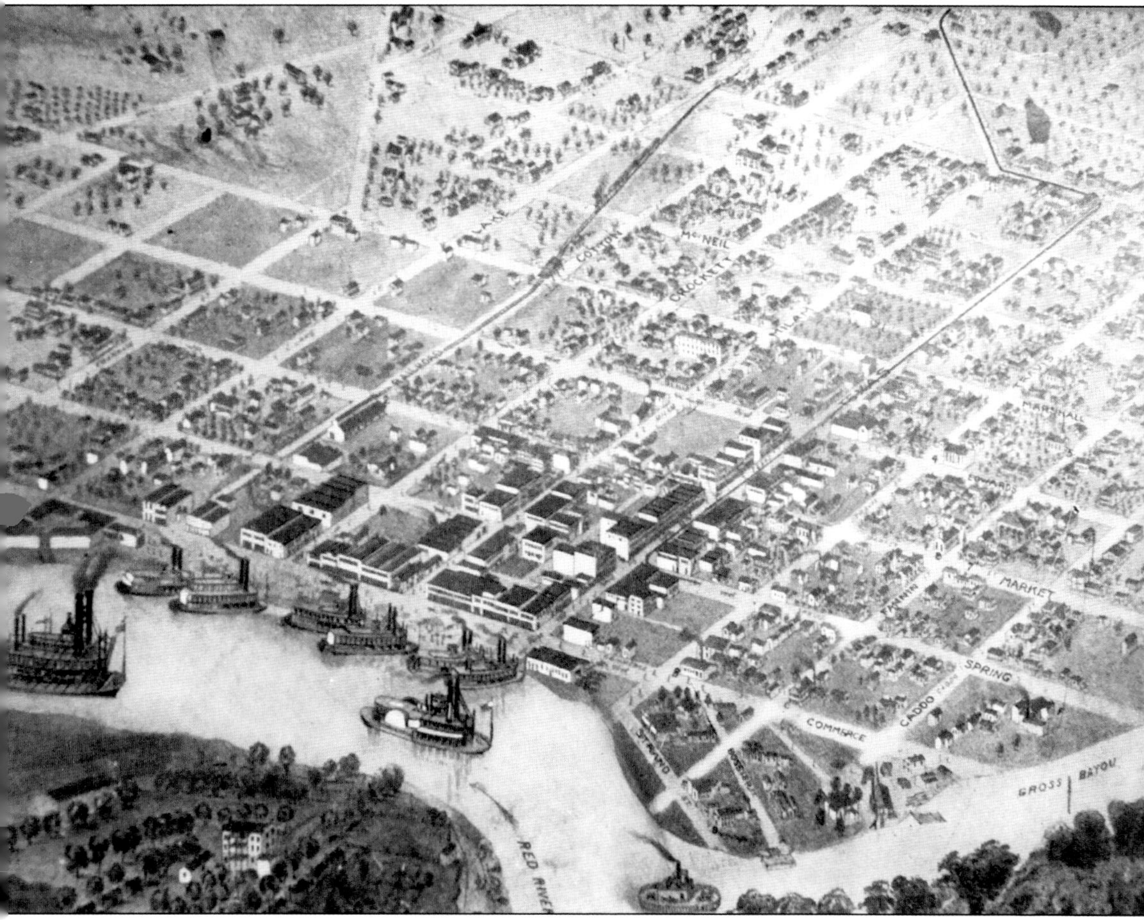

The famous "Bird's Eye View" of Shreveport was drawn by Herman Brossius and published in 1872. Only 300 original color lithographs of the map were printed, and very few are known to exist today. The area shown on the map is today's downtown central business district.

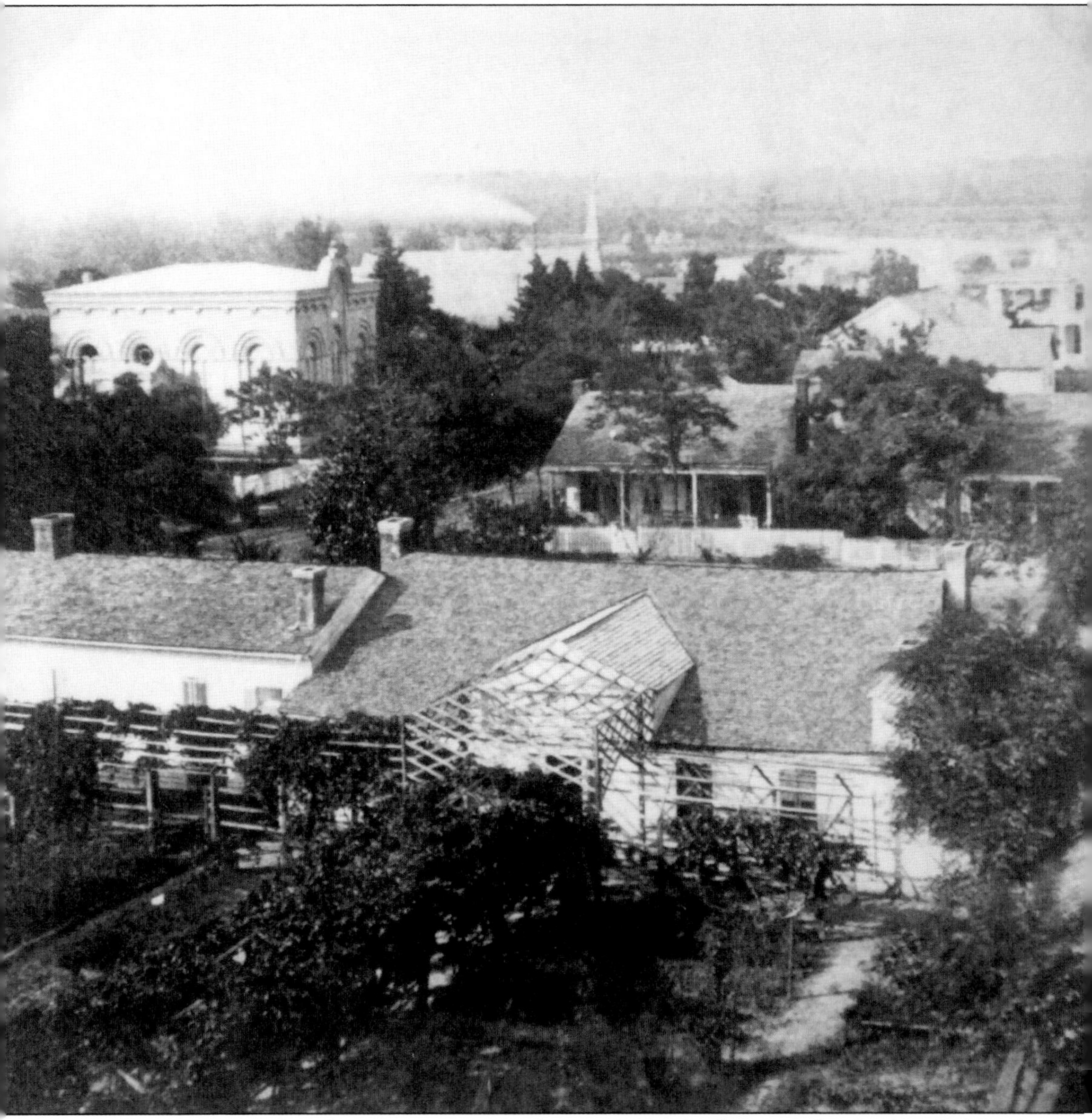

Shown here are Edwards at Fannin Streets, about 1870. In the foreground is the first St. Mary's Convent, at left center is B'nai Zion Temple, and behind it (with smoke coming from a stovepipe) is St. Mark's Episcopal Church. At right center, just above the two houses, can be seen the rear gable of the first home of First Methodist Church.

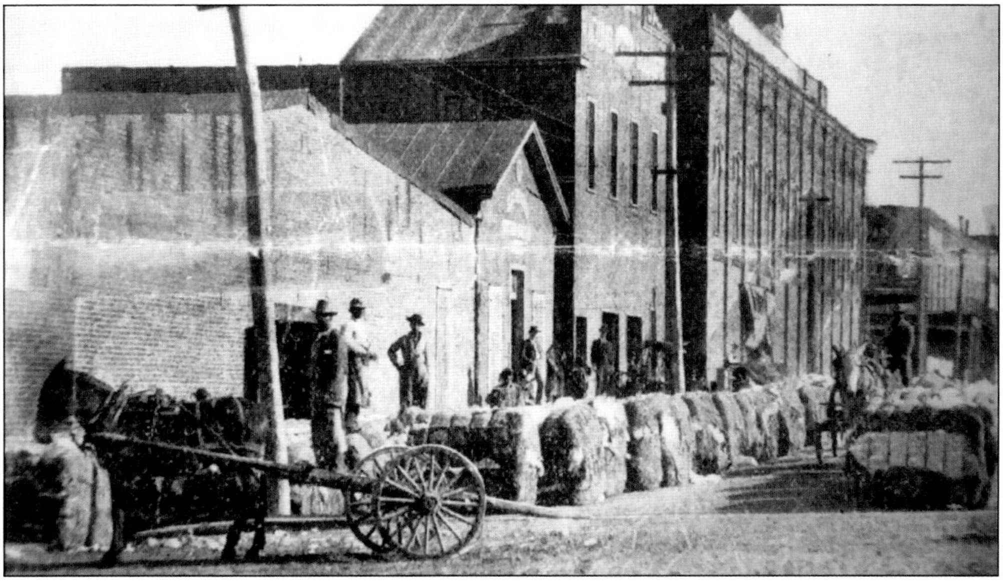

This view of the 400 block of Spring Street looking south from Travis Street was taken c. 1880. Bales of Caddo Parish–grown cotton are piled up ready for transfer to nearby steamboats and on to the markets of New Orleans. For many years during the nineteenth century Caddo Parish was the largest producer of cotton in Louisiana.

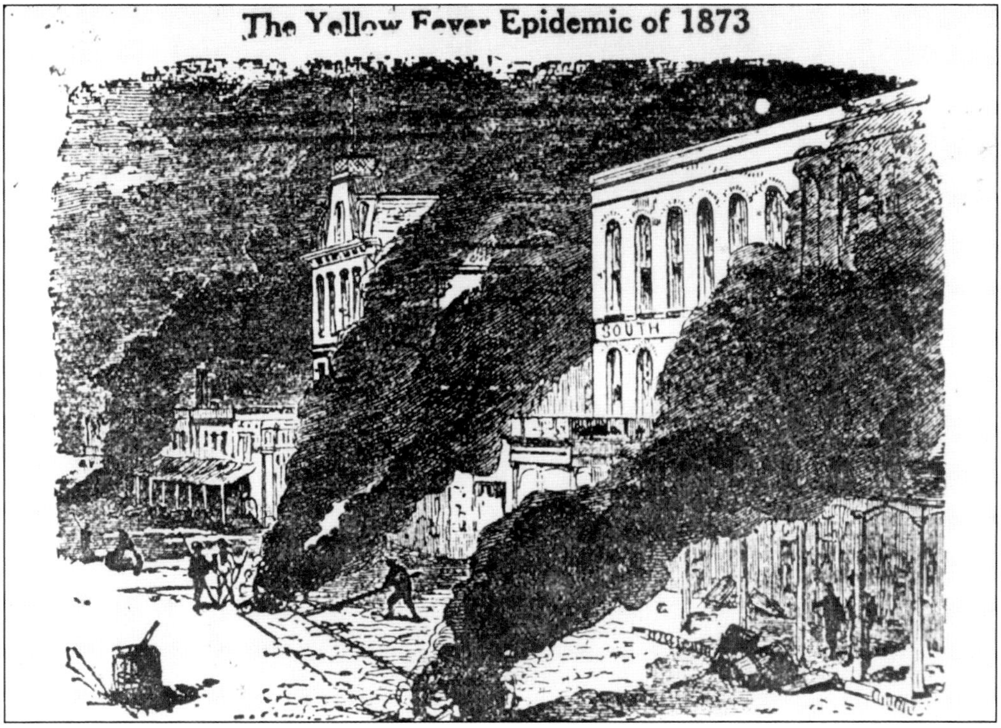

This is an engraving showing tar being burned on Texas Street in an effort to halt the spread of yellow fever in 1873. Epidemics struck the city in 1853, 1858, 1867, and 1873, all with devastating results. The 1873 yellow fever epidemic was the third worst in American history in terms of per capita loss of life. All told, the city's population was reduced by some 25 percent.

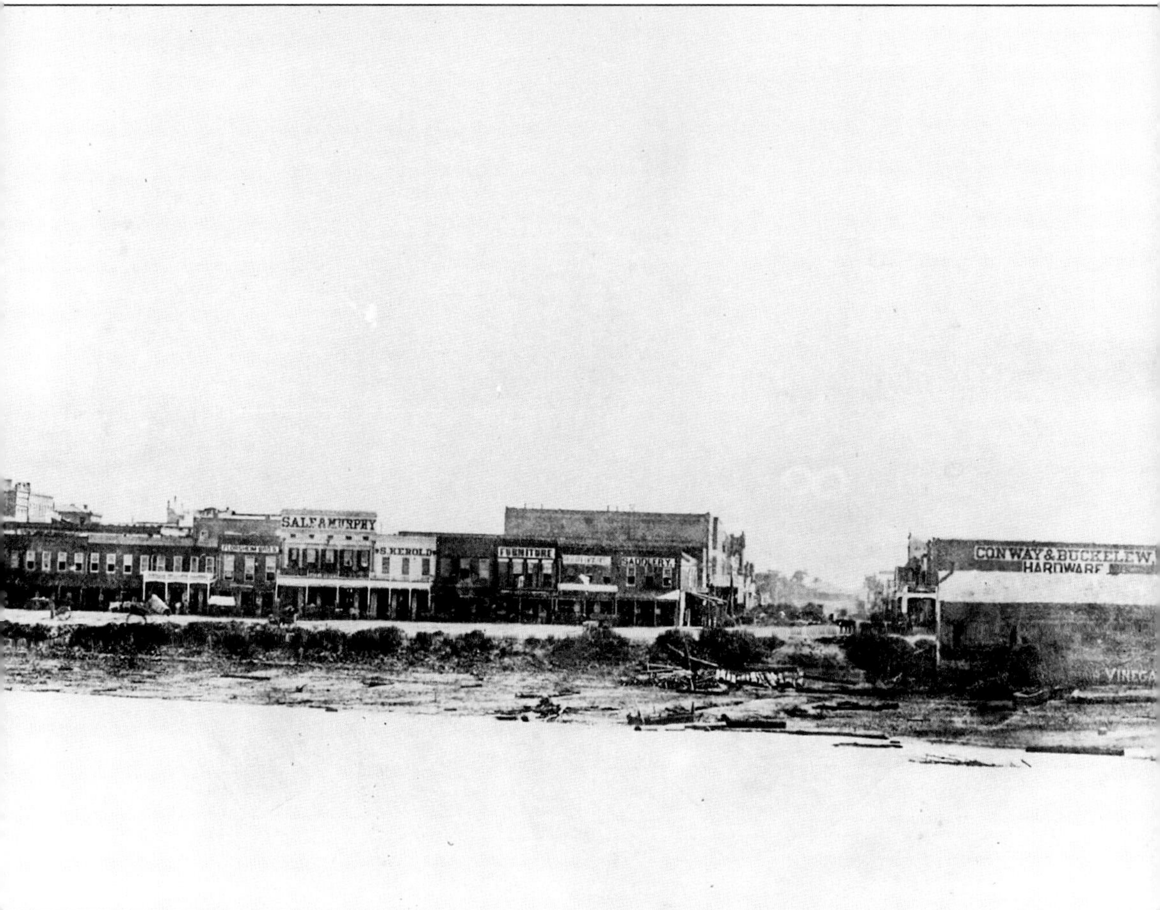

This is the riverfront as seen from the middle of the river, August 1873. Lt. Eugene Woodruff, who took this photograph, died only a month later of yellow fever. The view shows the city's mercantile district from Texas to Milam Streets virtually deserted. Several of the buildings shown in this photograph still stand.

One of the heroes of the yellow fever epidemic of 1873 was Rev. William T.D. Dalzell (1827–1899), rector of St. Mark's Episcopal Church, seen here with is wife, Estelle Logan Daizell (1839–1910), about the time of the epidemic. Reverend Dalzell, also a medical doctor, opted to stay in the stricken city rather than flee, risking his own life.

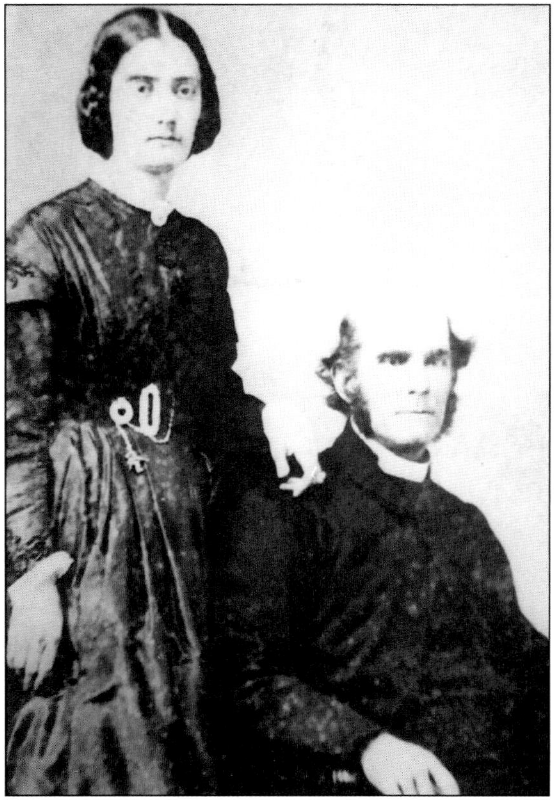

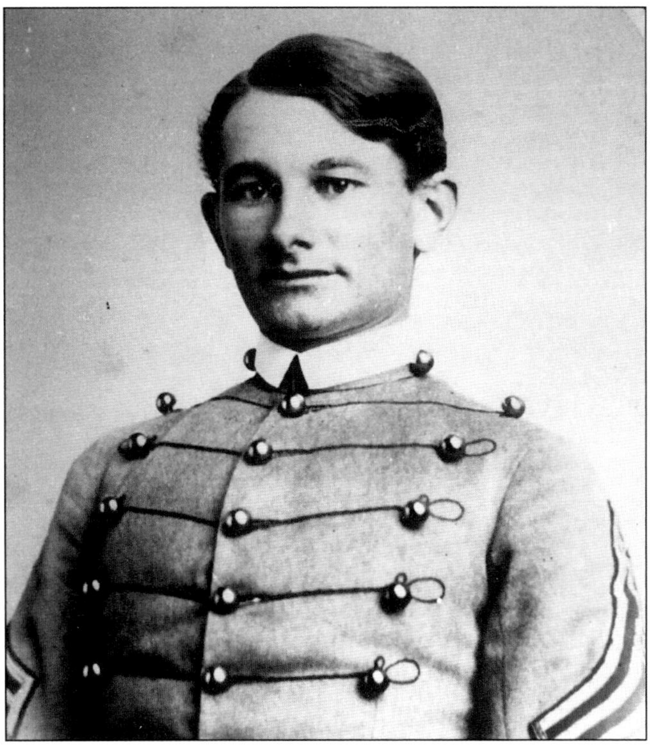

Another hero of the epidemic of 1873 was Lt. Eugene A. Woodruff (1841–1873) of the U.S. Army Corps of Engineers. A graduate of West Point, he was in Shreveport working with the Corps to remove the constantly re-forming log jam on Red River. Rather than leave the stricken city, he helped organize a relief society but lost his own life in the process.

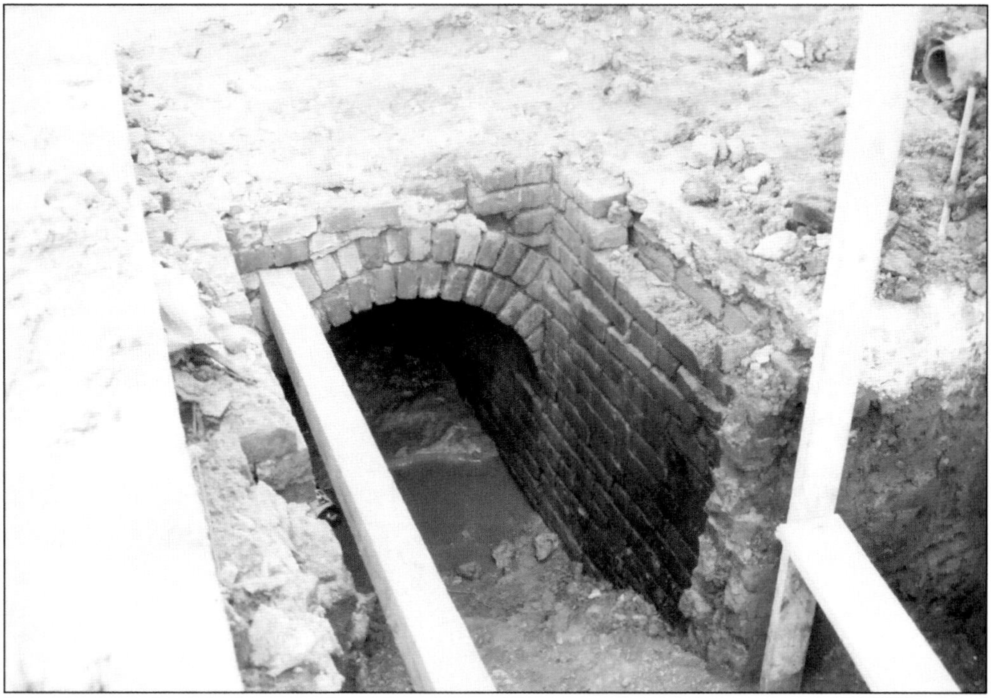

Shown here is a remnant of Shreveport's first major public works project: a sewerage culvert from the 1870s at Travis and Commerce Streets, briefly unearthed during road work in 1995. Many blamed the yellow fever on unsanitary conditions in the city, prompting efforts to clean up Shreveport after the epidemic subsided.

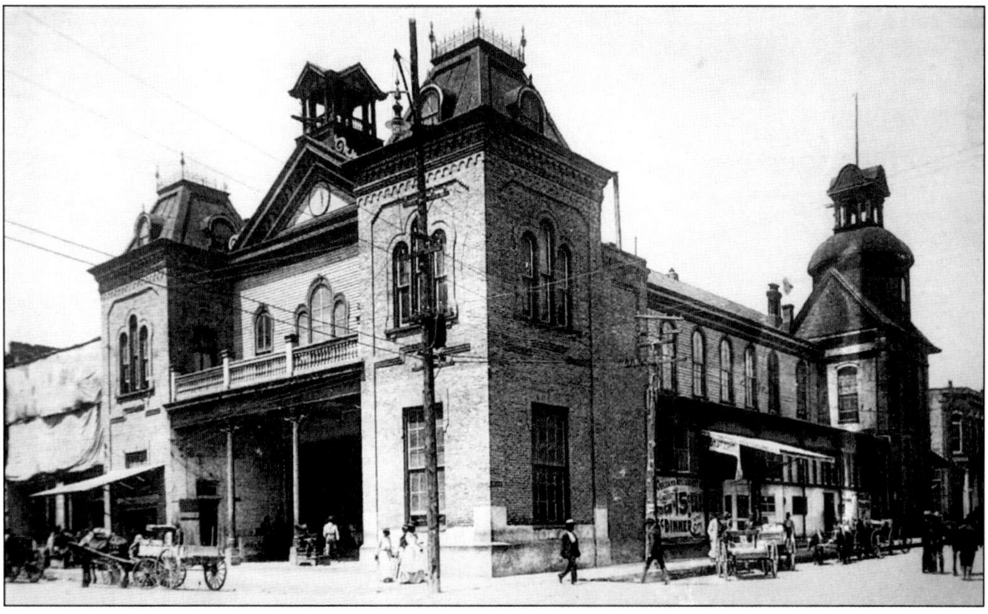

Shreveport's City Hall was located above the City Market, built in 1872 at Milam and Louisiana Streets. The 24-hour market was an open-air affair similar to the French Market in New Orleans. The city jail was in the rear tower at the right-hand side of the photo. In 1905 the imposing structure burned down, with the loss of one life.

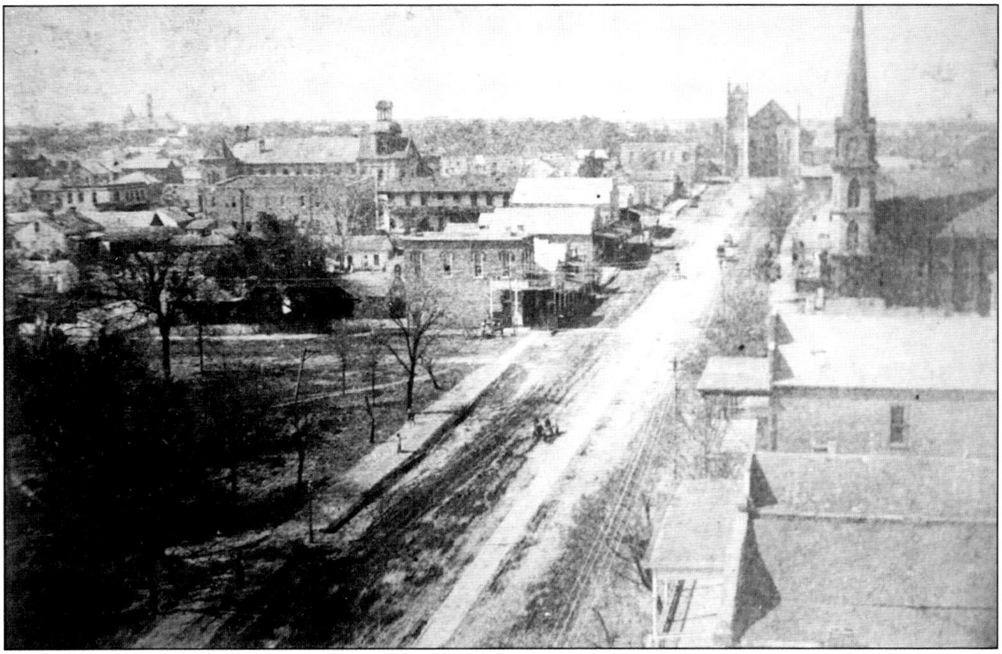

This photograph of Texas Street looking west from the Customhouse tower was taken in 1899. At right is the First Baptist Church steeple, and at the end of the street is First Methodist's. At left is the Courthouse Square and at left center can be seen the Market House roof. In the distance at left, the roof of Shreveport High School can be seen on the horizon.

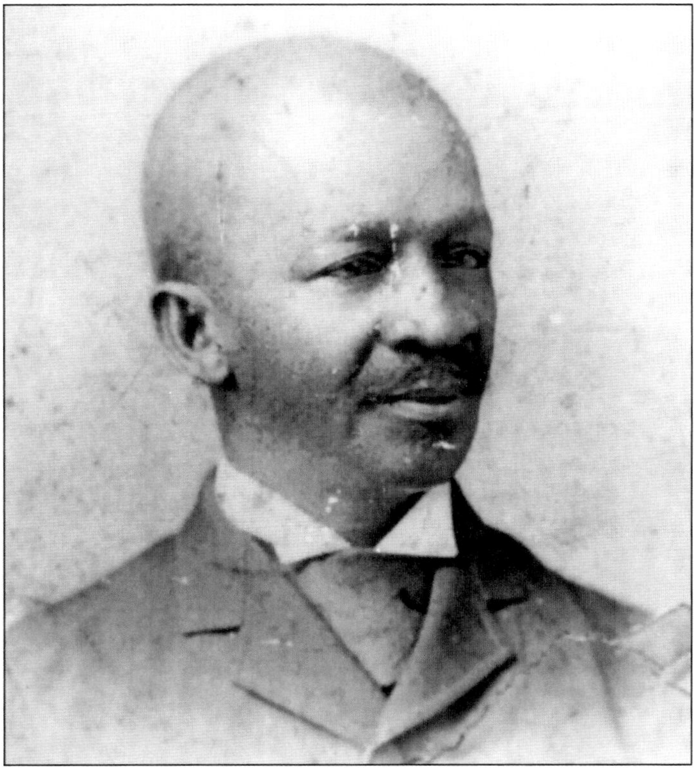

Caesar C. Antoine (1836–1921) was the first influential black Shreveporter. A New Orleans native and Union veteran, Antoine was a prominent figure in Reconstruction politics. Lieutenant governor under W.P. Kellogg, he served briefly as acting governor when Kellogg was impeached in 1876. In 1871, as a state senator, he authored the bill that incorporated Shreveport as a city.

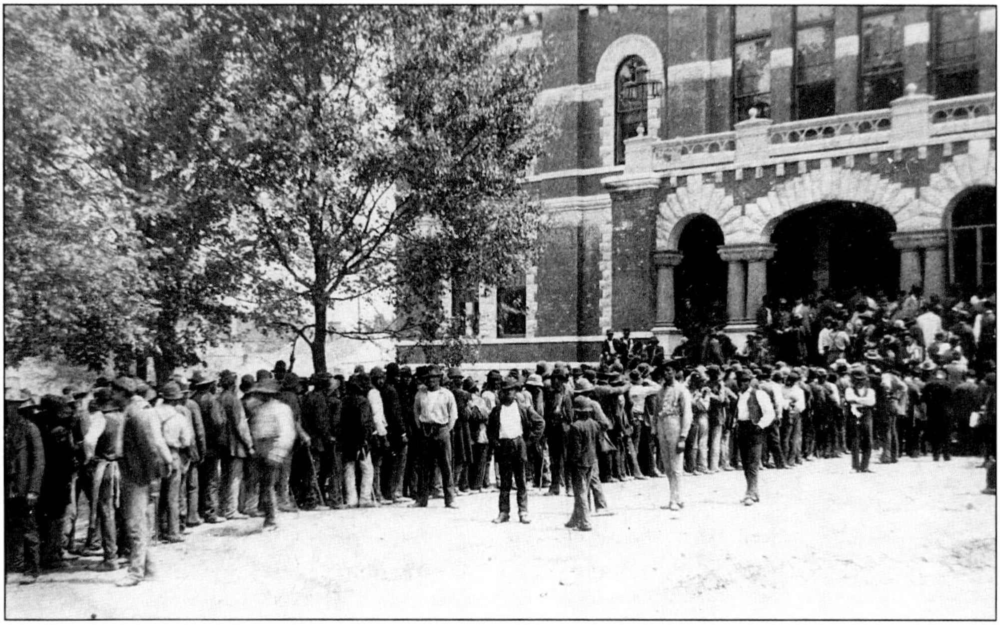

Black Shreveporters lined up to vote at the Caddo Parish Courthouse in 1897. Although Reconstruction ended in Louisiana in 1877, blacks continued to vote in significant numbers until disenfranchised by the Constitution of 1898, largely due to their support of Republican candidates.

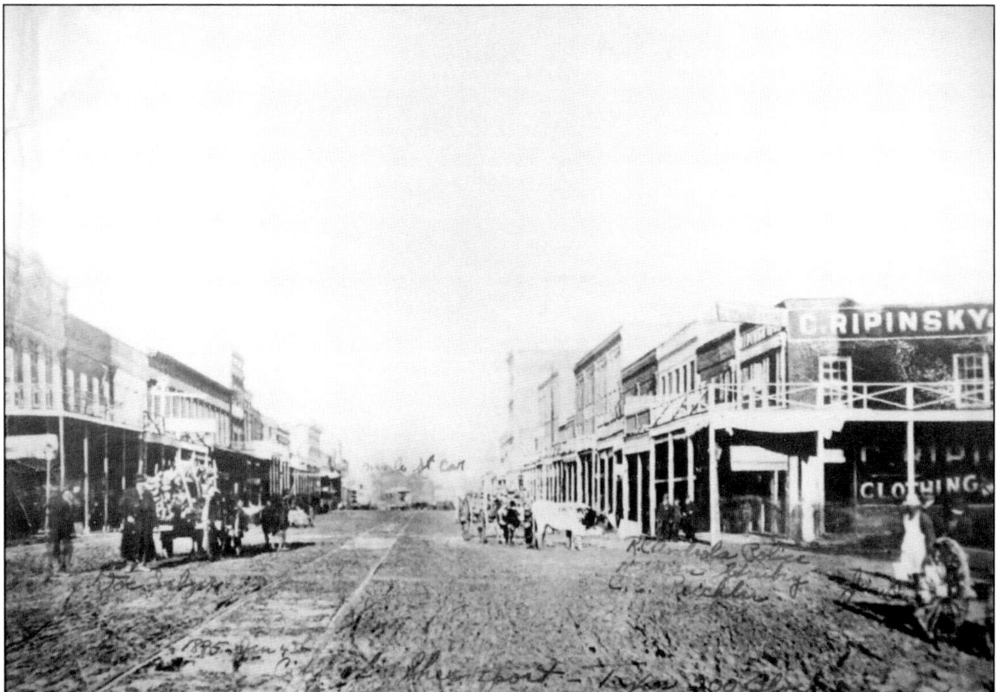

Shown here is Texas Street looking east from Market Street on January 4, 1885. Ripinsky's, one of the city's first department stores, is at right; nearby an ox pulls a wagon. In the distance can be seen a mule-drawn streetcar.

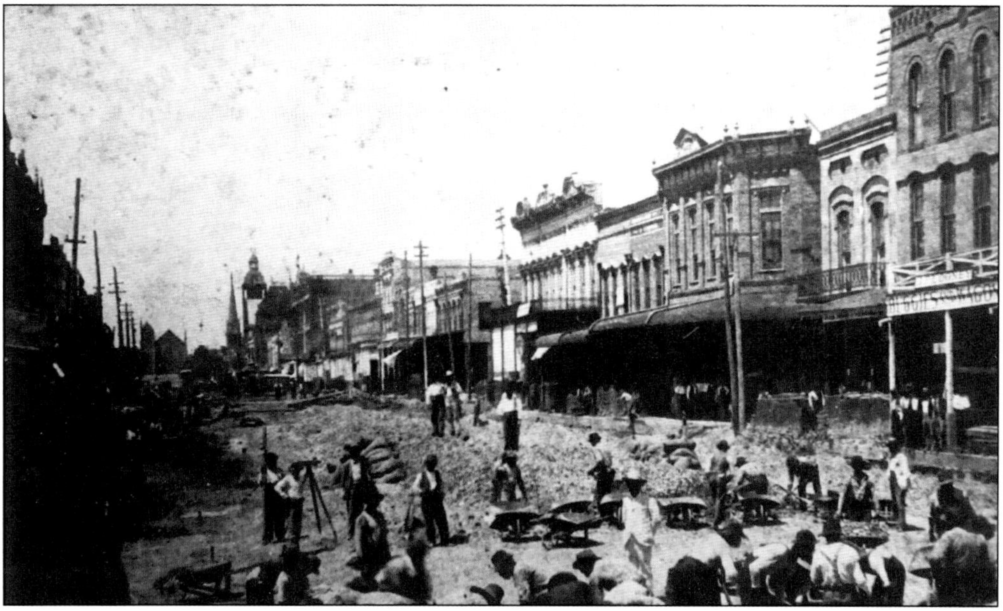

This is the 100 block of Texas Street looking west, in 1897, with Spring Street crossing at center. Every building to the right of the center of the photograph still stands. Here, Texas Street is being paved with bricks (it had been planked since 1872).

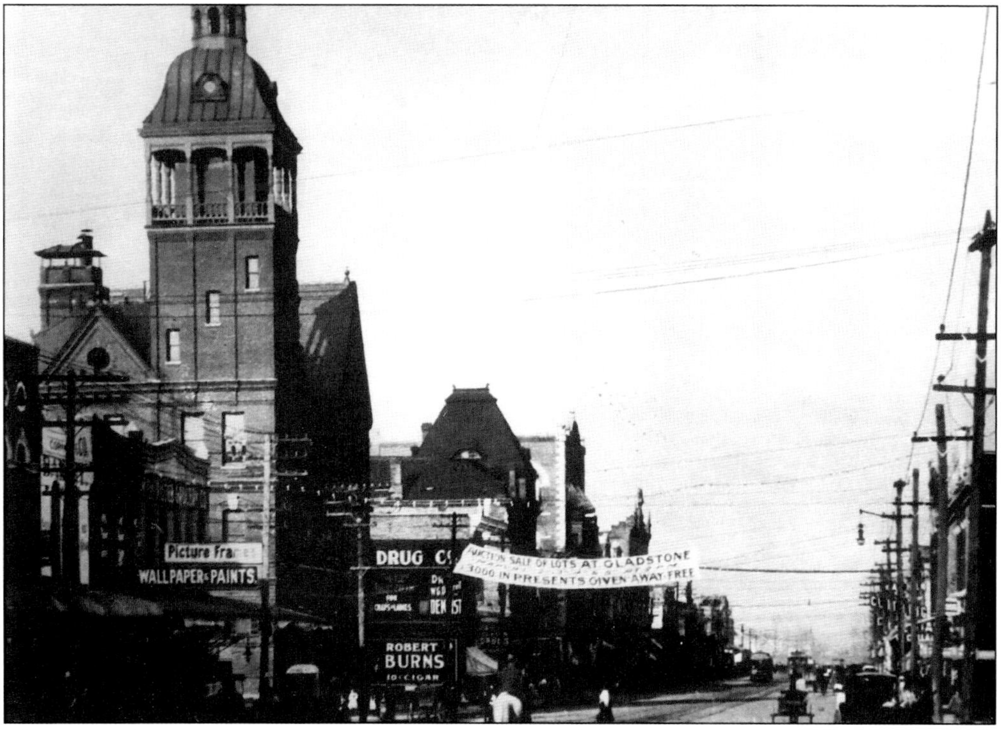

This view of Texas Street looking east from in front of the Courthouse was taken about 1900. The tall building at left is the Customhouse, which housed the post office and federal court from 1887 to 1910. Beyond is the roof of the Grand Opera House and just past it, the upper floors of M. Levy's Department Store are visible.

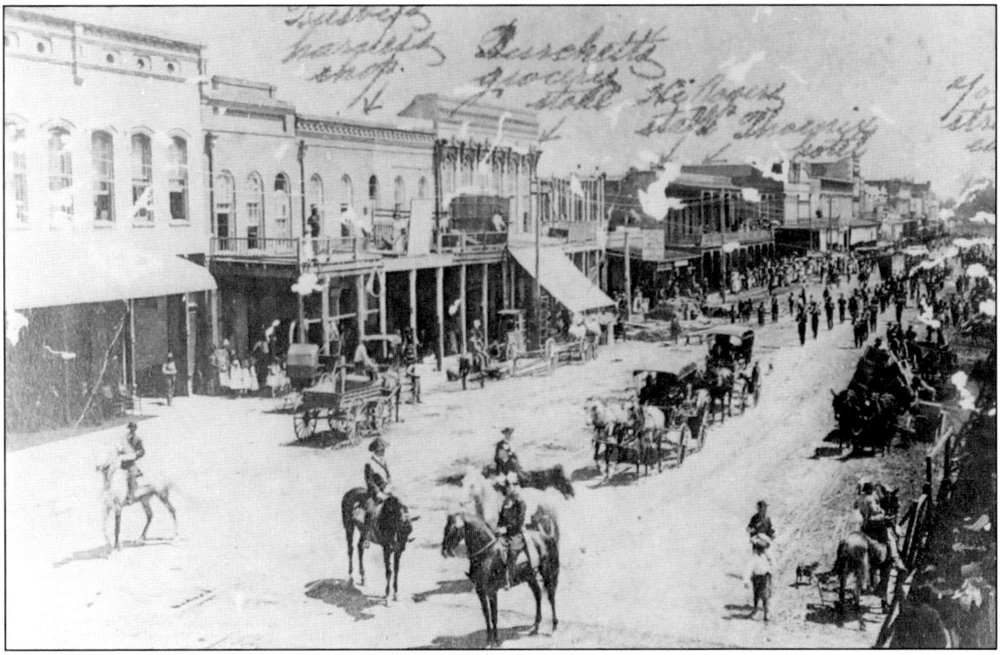

This is a rare early photograph of a parade on Texas Street in the mid-1880s (though the scene would have been much the same anytime from 1850 to 1900). Shown is the north side of the 300 block, looking east, with traffic going about their business as usual despite the approaching parade.

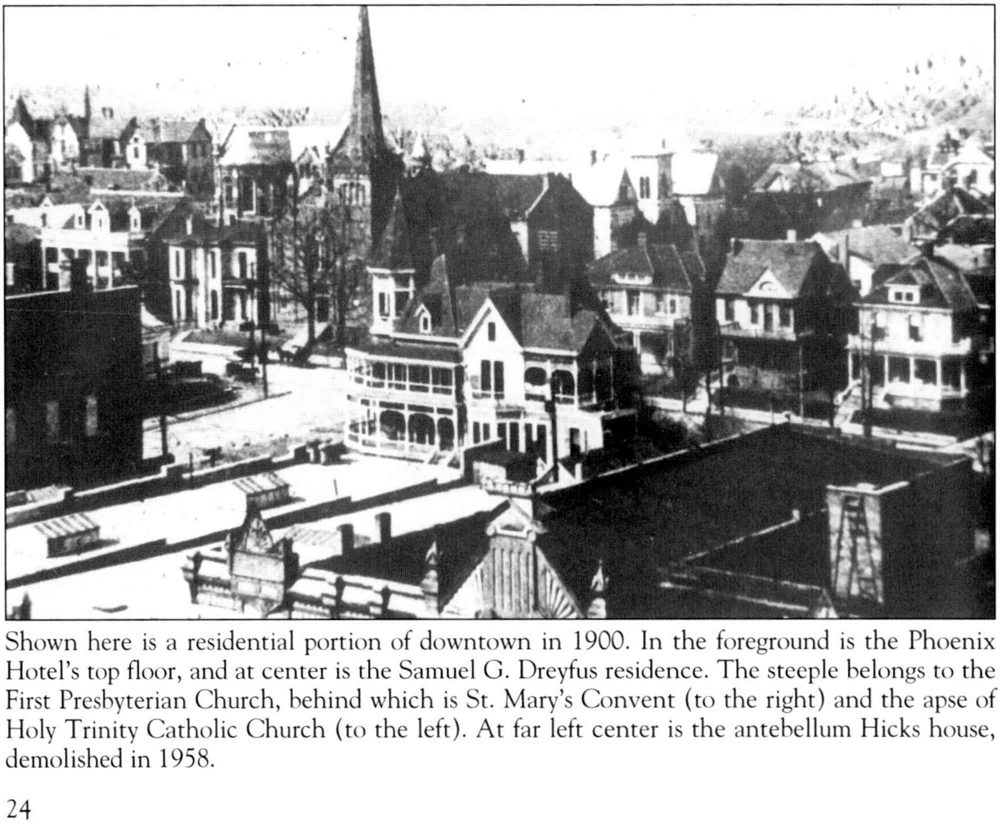

Shown here is a residential portion of downtown in 1900. In the foreground is the Phoenix Hotel's top floor, and at center is the Samuel G. Dreyfus residence. The steeple belongs to the First Presbyterian Church, behind which is St. Mary's Convent (to the right) and the apse of Holy Trinity Catholic Church (to the left). At far left center is the antebellum Hicks house, demolished in 1958.

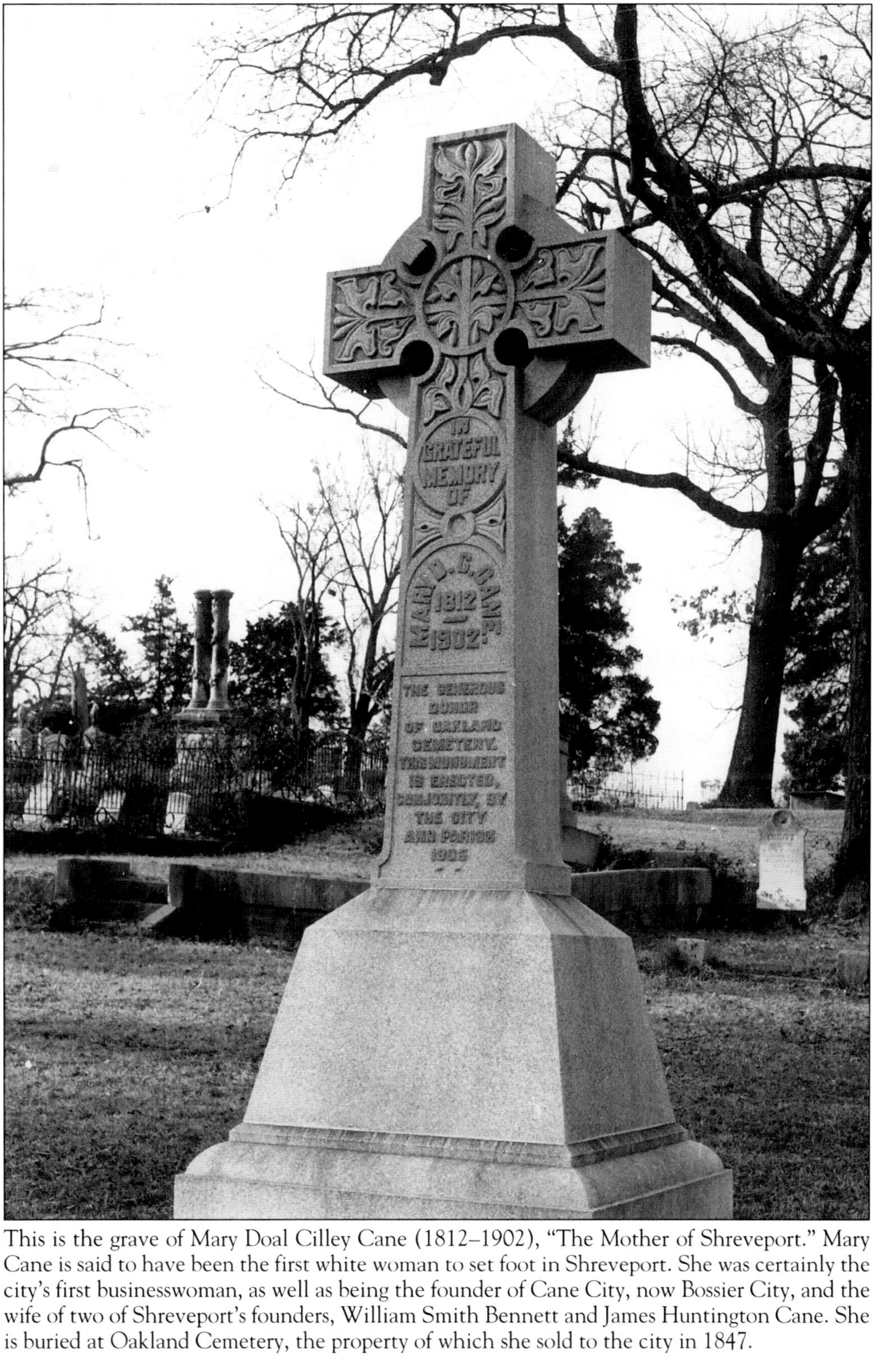

This is the grave of Mary Doal Cilley Cane (1812–1902), "The Mother of Shreveport." Mary Cane is said to have been the first white woman to set foot in Shreveport. She was certainly the city's first businesswoman, as well as being the founder of Cane City, now Bossier City, and the wife of two of Shreveport's founders, William Smith Bennett and James Huntington Cane. She is buried at Oakland Cemetery, the property of which she sold to the city in 1847.

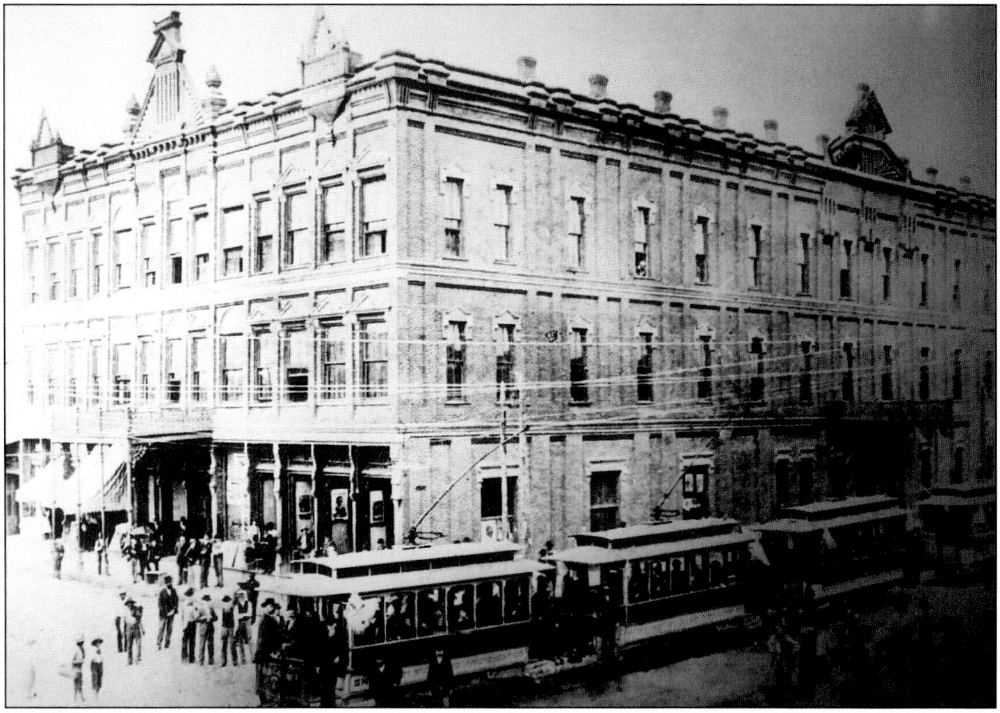

On October 4, 1890, Shreveport became the first city in Louisiana to inaugurate an electric streetcar system. Not until 1893 did New Orleans follow suit. Here we see the streetcars lined up beside the Phoenix Hotel at Texas and Market Streets on their first day of service.

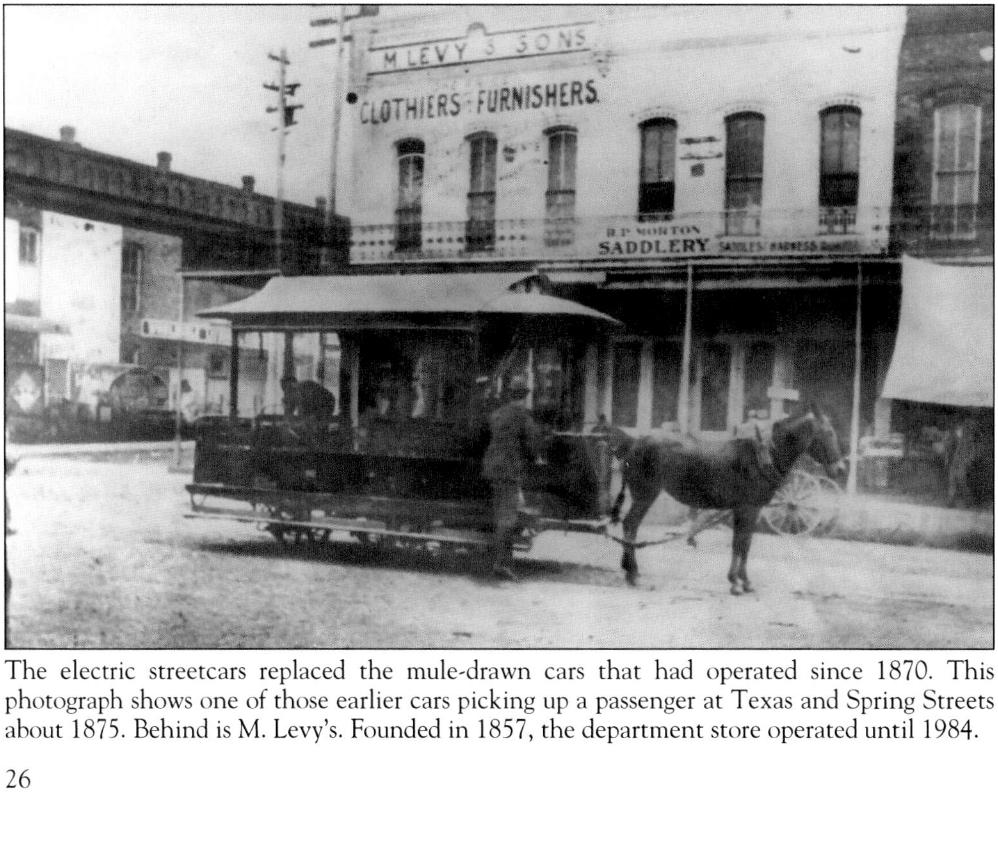

The electric streetcars replaced the mule-drawn cars that had operated since 1870. This photograph shows one of those earlier cars picking up a passenger at Texas and Spring Streets about 1875. Behind is M. Levy's. Founded in 1857, the department store operated until 1984.

Two

Civic Heritage

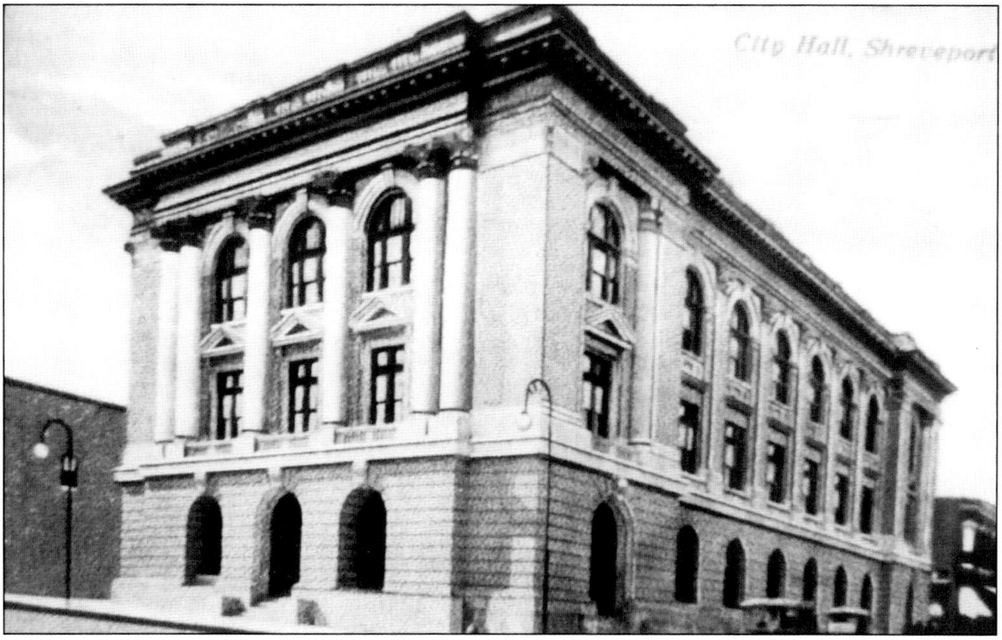

Shreveport's City Hall, at Milam and Louisiana Streets, was built in 1906 on the site of the old City Market House, which burned a year earlier. The new City Hall was already inadequate in size by the early 1920s and a new police station and city courts building had to be constructed at McNeill and Cotton Streets in 1924. Both buildings were closed in 1958 when City Hall moved to its present site.

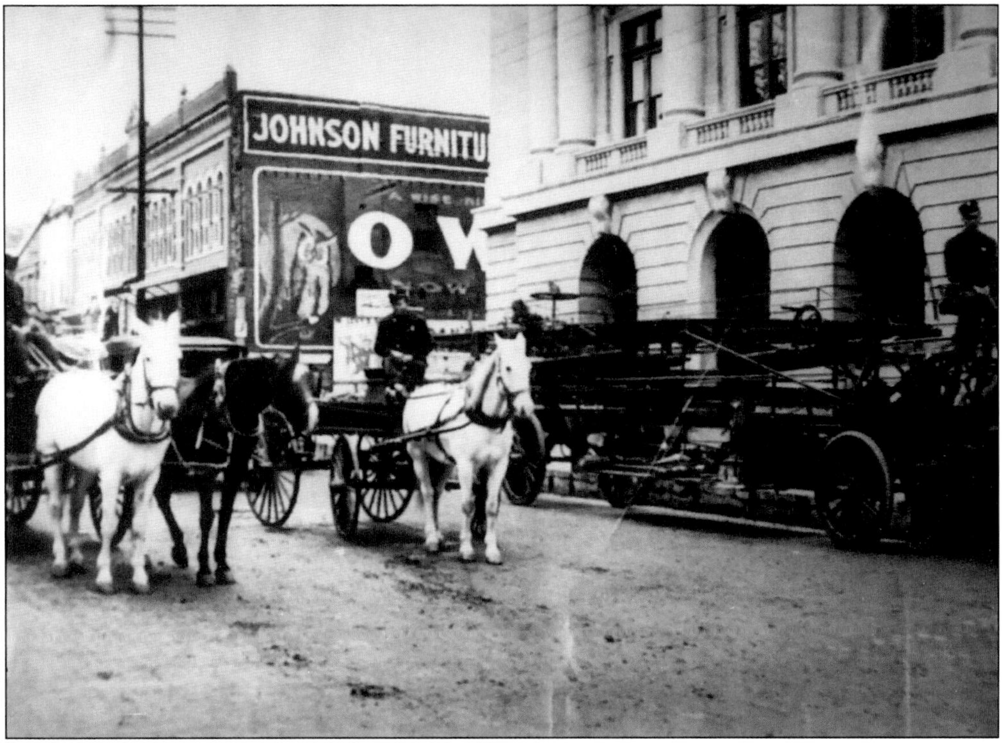

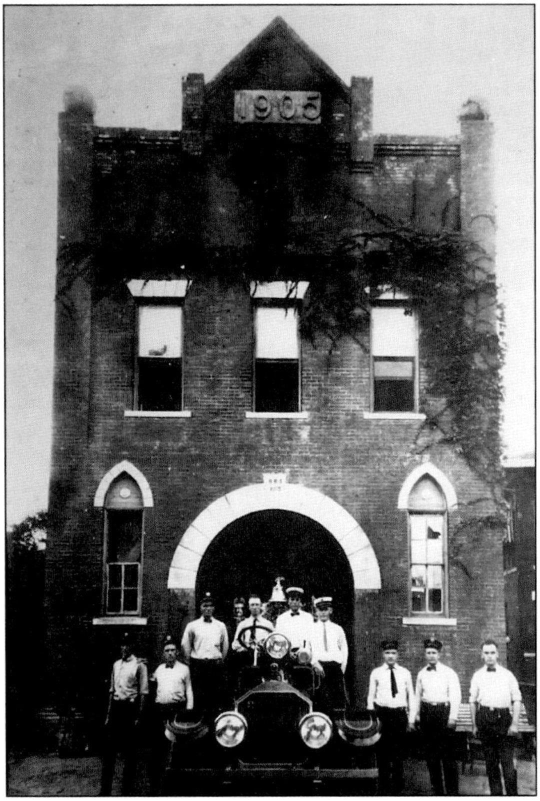

Pictured here is horse-drawn firefighting equipment on Milam Street in front of City Hall, 1910. The Central Fire Station was located in the 700 block of Milam, just opposite the Harkey Building (with the Johnson's Furniture sign), which still stands.

Fire Station Number Five, built in 1905 at Stoner Avenue and Nutt Street, shows off its new motorized engine about 1920. This building, no longer a fire station, still stands, though greatly remodeled.

Governor Newton Crain Blanchard (1849–1922), of Shreveport, held the state's highest office from 1904 to 1908. Blanchard is known as one of the early twentieth century's most progressive governors. Eight governors have resided in Shreveport.

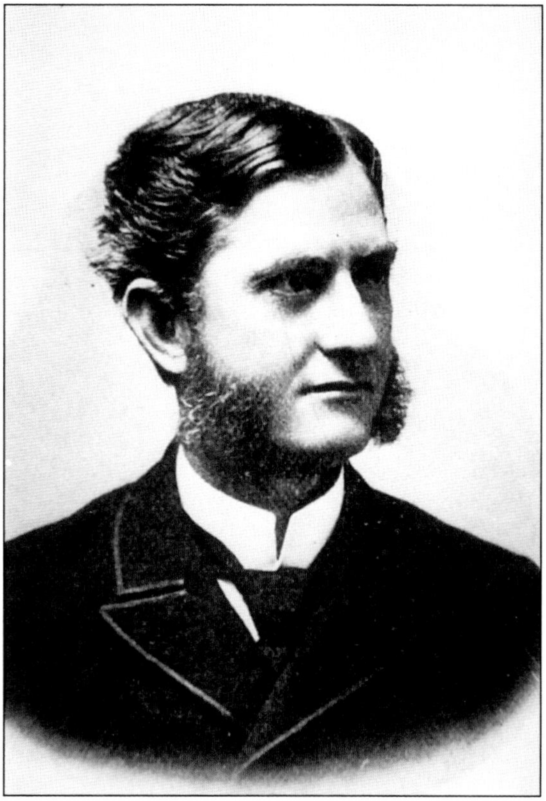

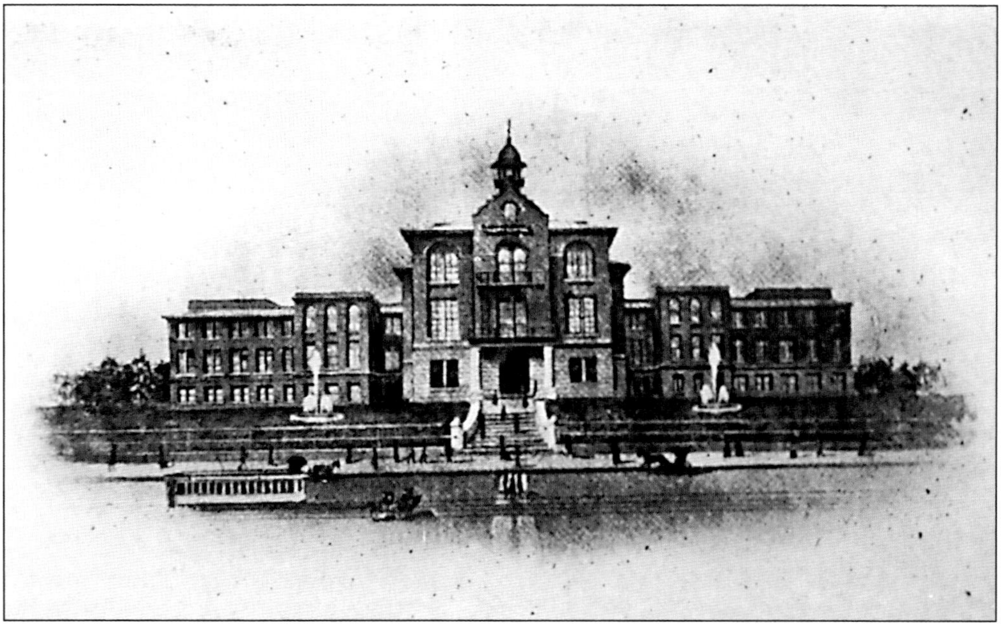

Charity Hospital was built in 1889 on Texas Avenue, between Murphy and Hope Streets. Over the years it was enlarged and remodeled several times before moving in 1953 to Kings Highway at Linwood Avenue, where it was re-named Confederate Memorial Medical Center. Today it is known as the LSU Medical Center.

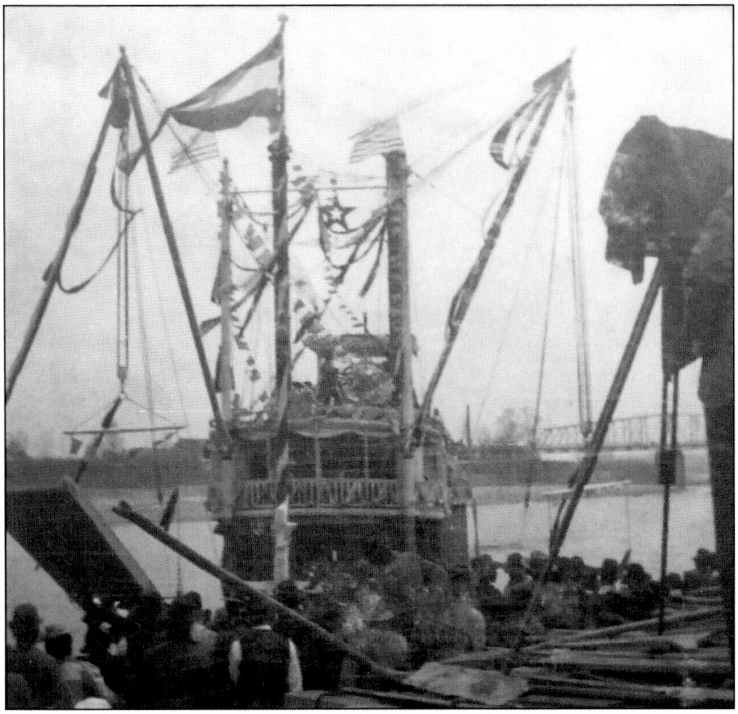

Many political candidates have visited Shreveport through the years. Once upon a time they came by steamboat as William Jennings Bryan did in 1900. Here a photographer (right) captures the arrival of Bryan's boat at the Commerce Street wharf. The old Vicksburg, Shreveport, and Pacific Railroad Bridge is in the background.

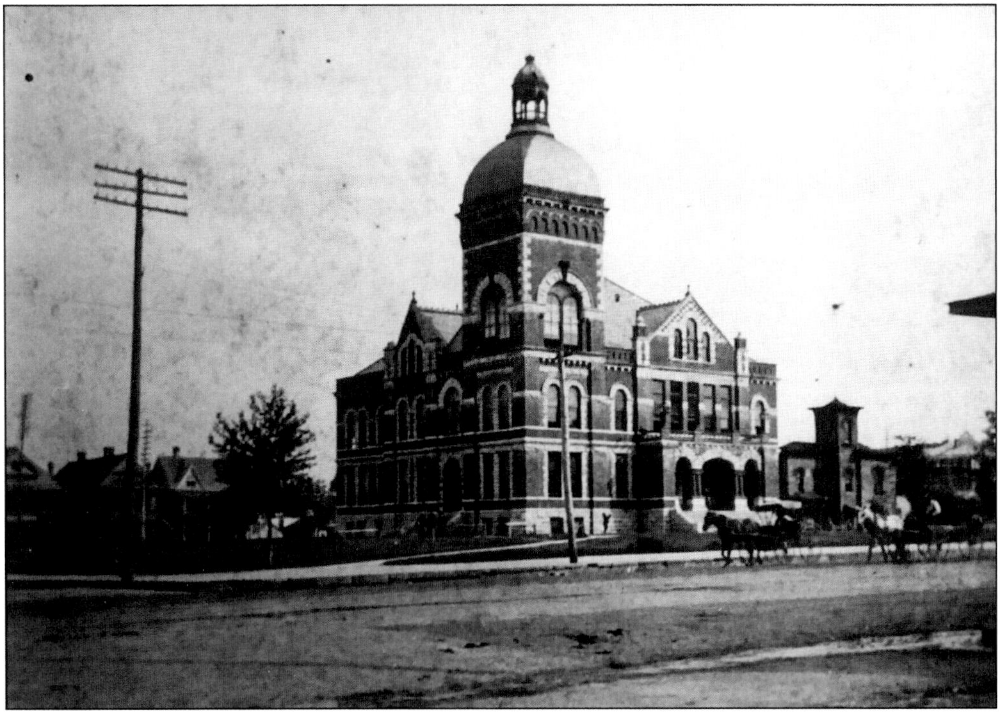

The second Caddo Parish Courthouse to occupy the Courthouse Square was completed in 1891. Seen here from the corner of Texas and Marshall Streets shortly after completion, the Courthouse is connected at left to the much older jail, which was replaced in 1910 when a more modern facility was built on Milam Street.

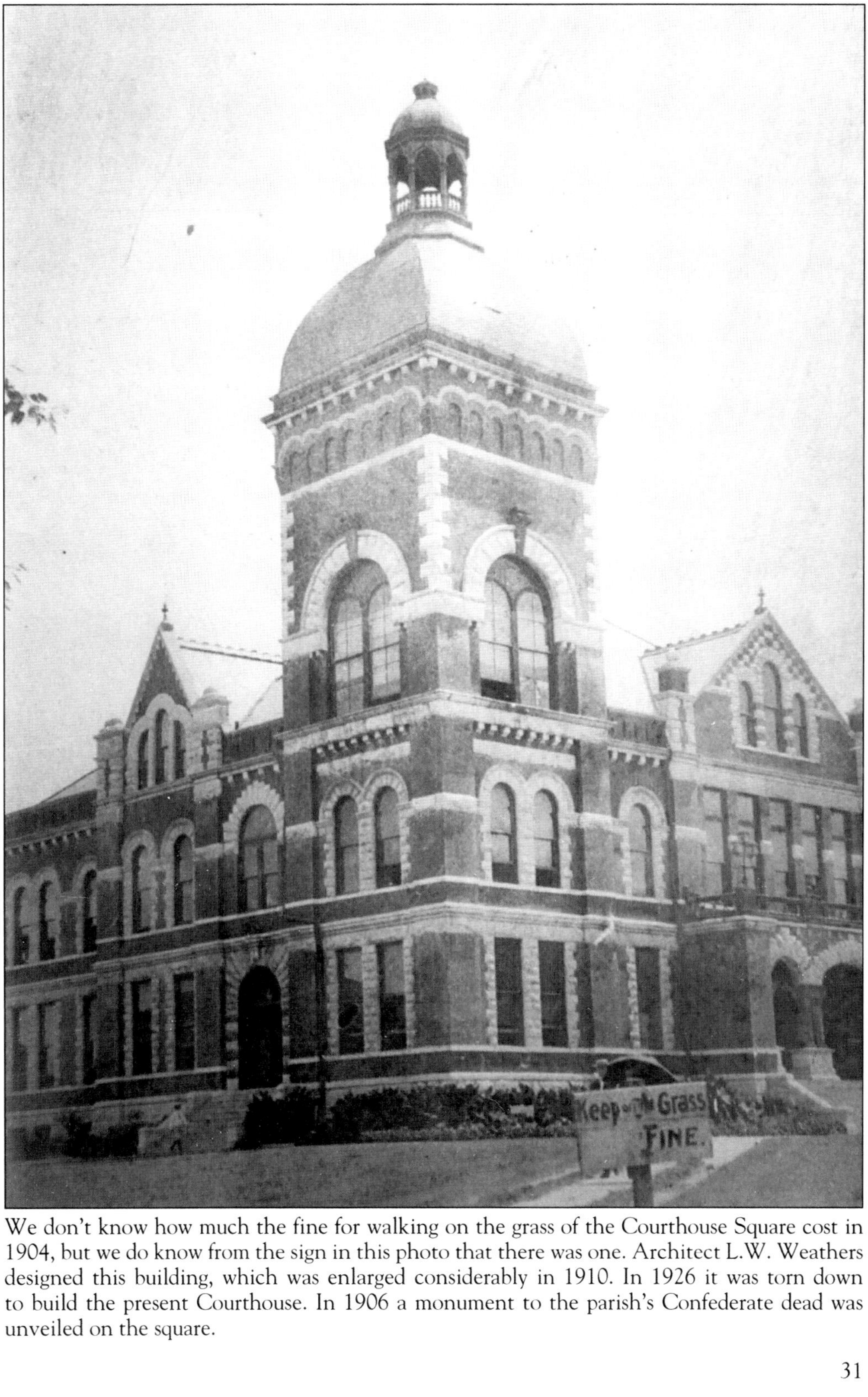

We don't know how much the fine for walking on the grass of the Courthouse Square cost in 1904, but we do know from the sign in this photo that there was one. Architect L.W. Weathers designed this building, which was enlarged considerably in 1910. In 1926 it was torn down to build the present Courthouse. In 1906 a monument to the parish's Confederate dead was unveiled on the square.

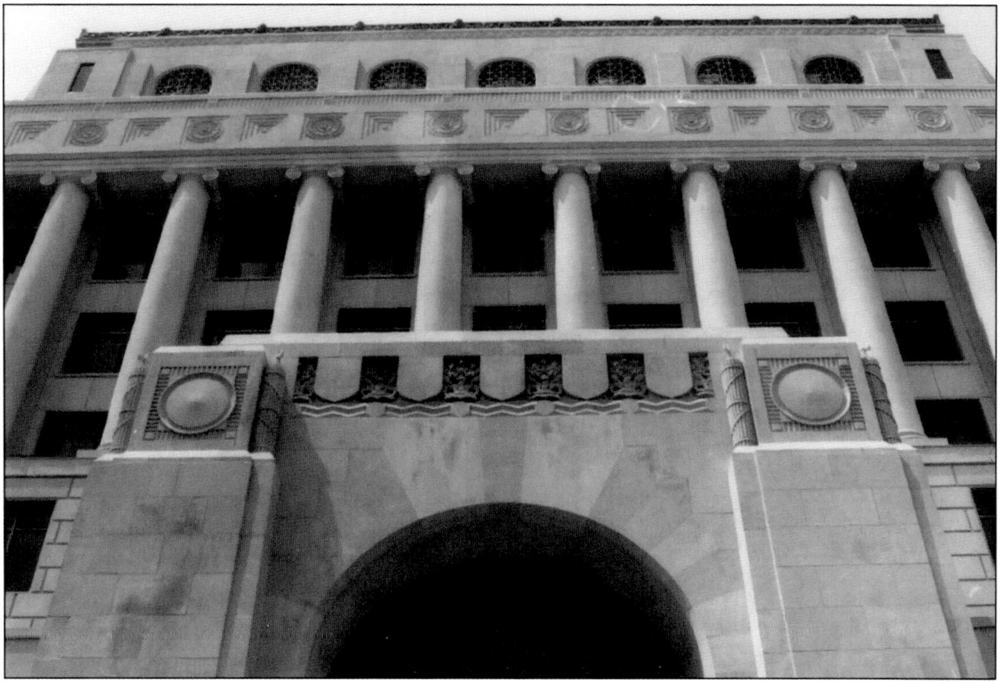

The Caddo Parish Courthouse in use today is the third to occupy the Courthouse Square. Designed by architect Edward F. Neild, it was the model for numerous other county courthouses around the nation, including similar structures by Neild in Phoenix and Kansas City. It was completed in 1928.

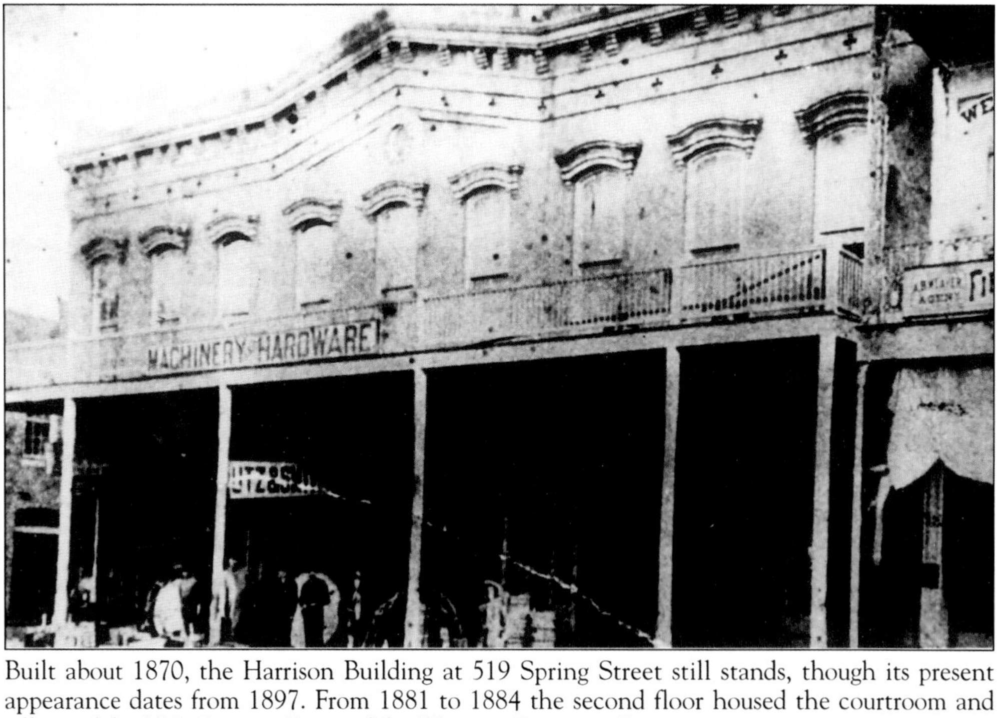

Built about 1870, the Harrison Building at 519 Spring Street still stands, though its present appearance dates from 1897. From 1881 to 1884 the second floor housed the courtroom and offices of the U.S. District Court of the Western District of Louisiana.

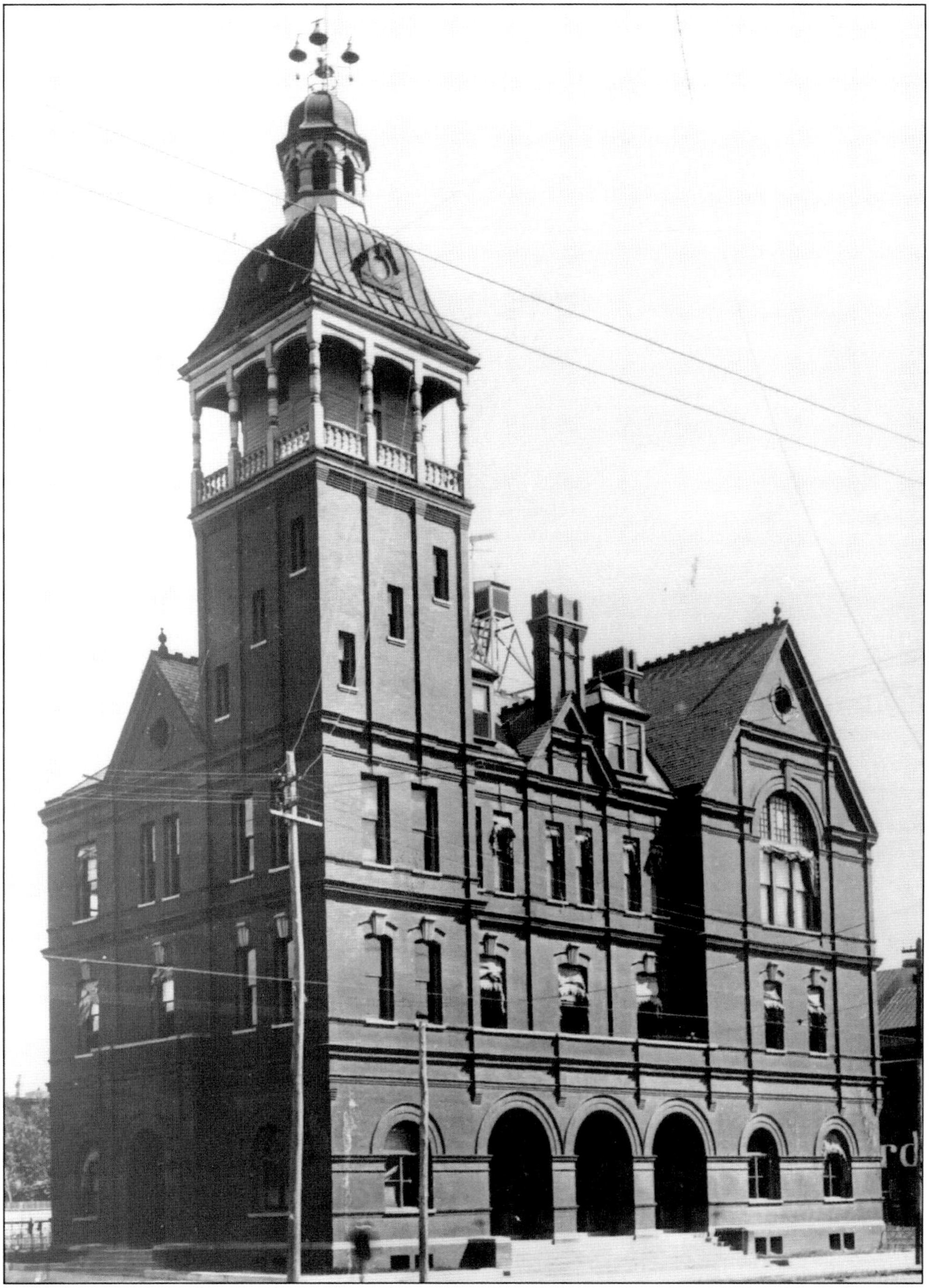

The "Customhouse," the first federal courthouse in Shreveport, was built at 424 Texas Street in 1887. Designed by architect N.S. Allen, its ground floor housed the post office, and its tower, the U.S. Weather Bureau. The large window at right admitted light to the single courtroom. The only judge to preside here was Alec Boarman (1839–1916). At 26, Boarman had been Shreveport's youngest mayor; at 77, when he died, he was the nation's oldest sitting federal district judge.

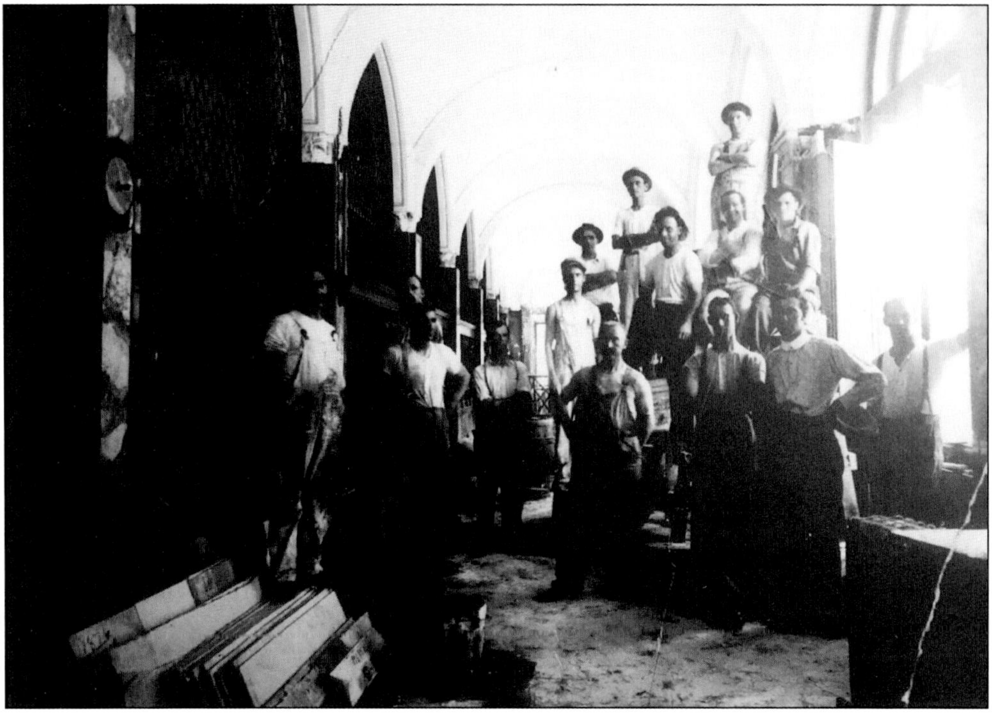

Construction of the second Federal Building was photographed in 1911. Shown above is an interior view of the nearly completed lobby of the post office section of the Federal Building that replaced the old Customhouse in 1911. Designed by architect James K. Taylor, its elegant marble lobby was the work of the craftsmen who posed for this photo. Below is an exterior view.

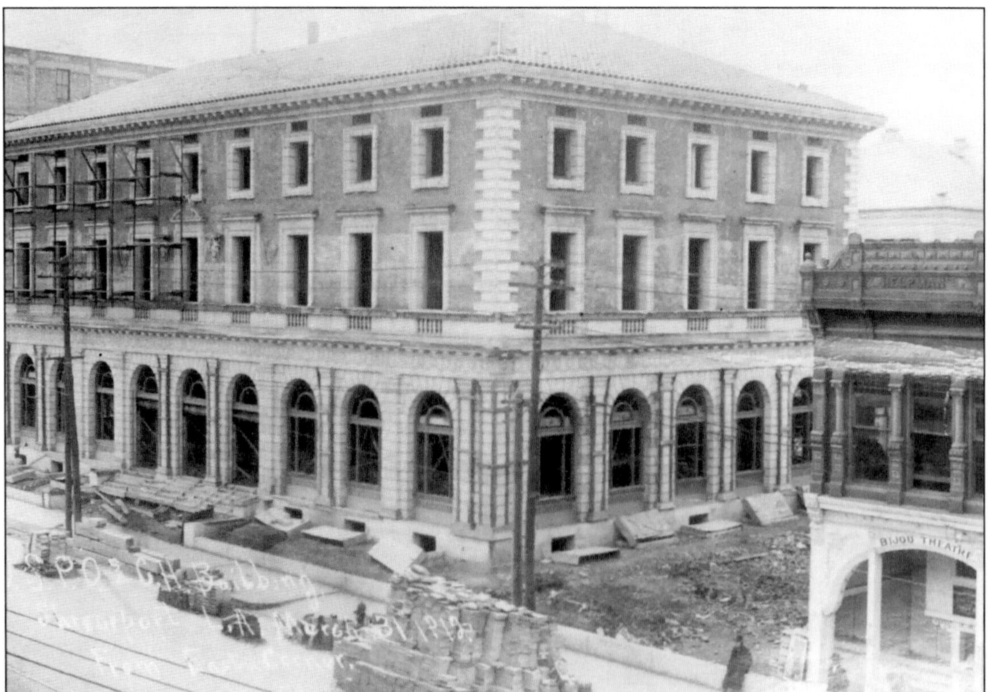

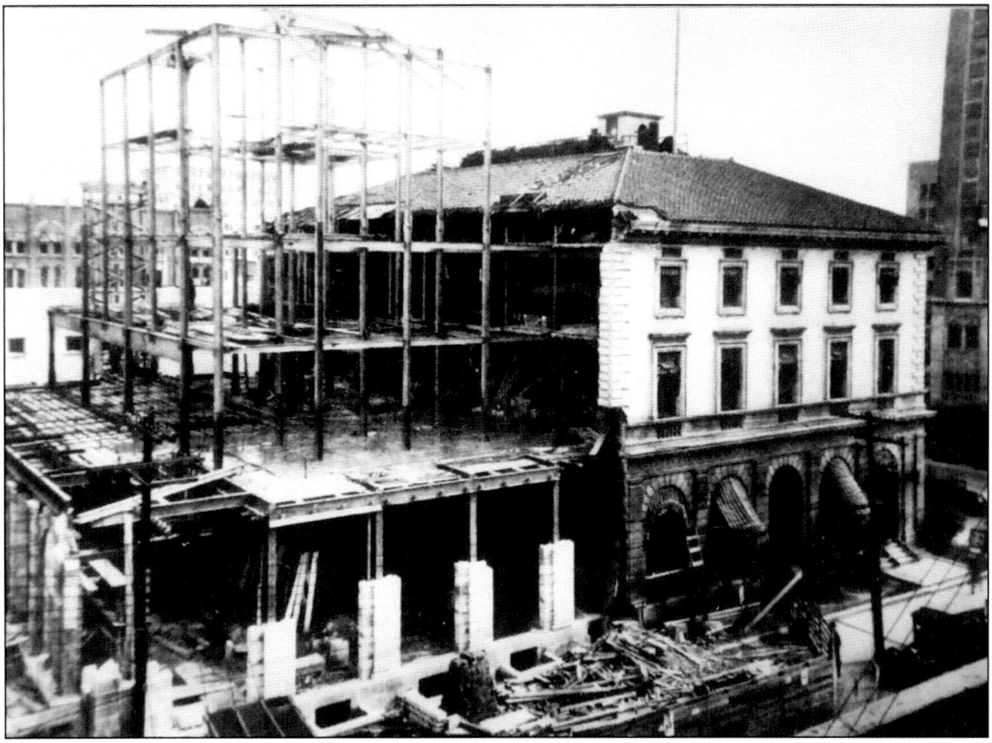

In 1931 the Federal Building was enlarged, as seen in this view by photographer Bill Grabill. In 1974 the court and post office moved to new quarters, leaving the old structure vacant. Since 1980 the building has housed the Shreve Memorial Library, founded in 1923.

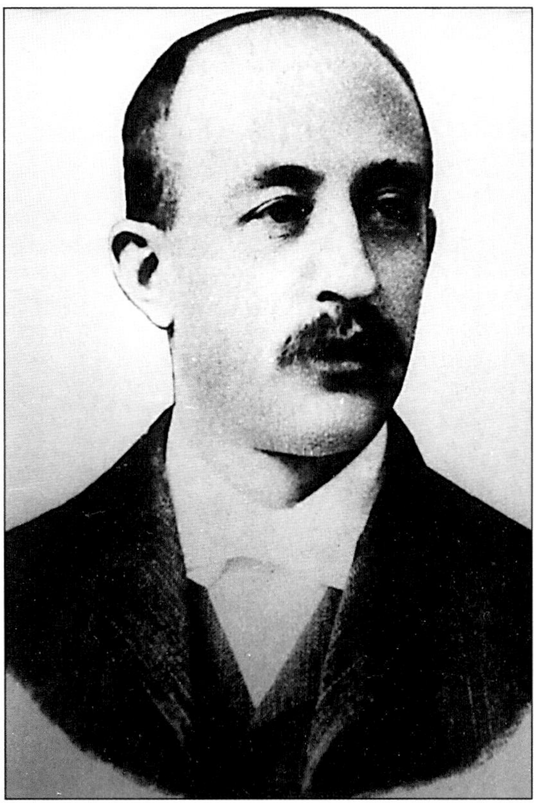

Philanthropist Justin Gras (1868–1959) came to Shreveport in 1891 and entered the grocery business. In time he became one of the city's most influential leaders, though he never held a political office. Through his efforts and philanthropy many civic, social, religious, and educational facilities in the Shreveport area were enriched.

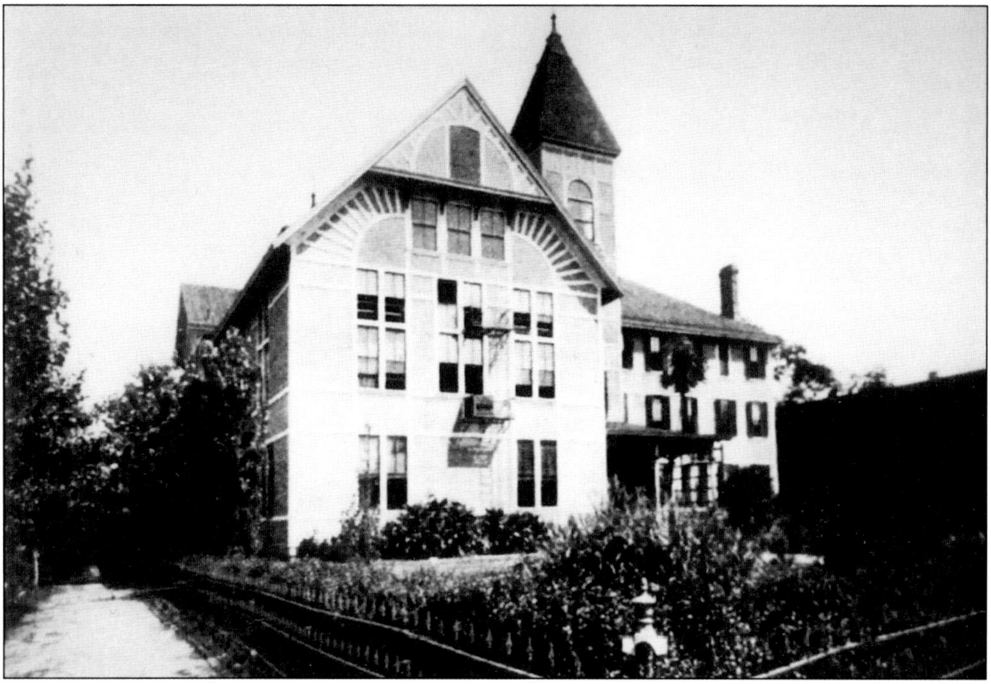

The Schumpert Medical Center was once housed in this building at Texas Street and Grand Avenue. Built as a private girls' school, the building was later acquired by Dr. T.E. Schumpert to house his sanitarium, founded in 1894. The first Louisiana lottery helped fund the purchase.

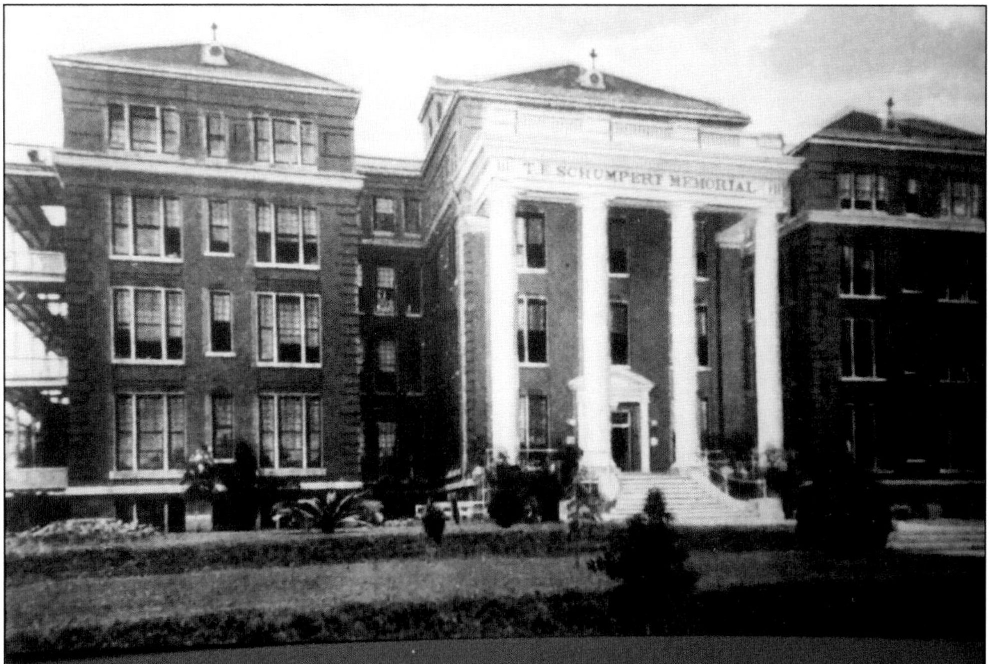

In 1910 the Schumpert Hospital relocated to this building on Margaret Place. Although the large Neo-Classical hospital shown here no longer stands, the Schumpert Memorial Medical Center still occupies the same site.

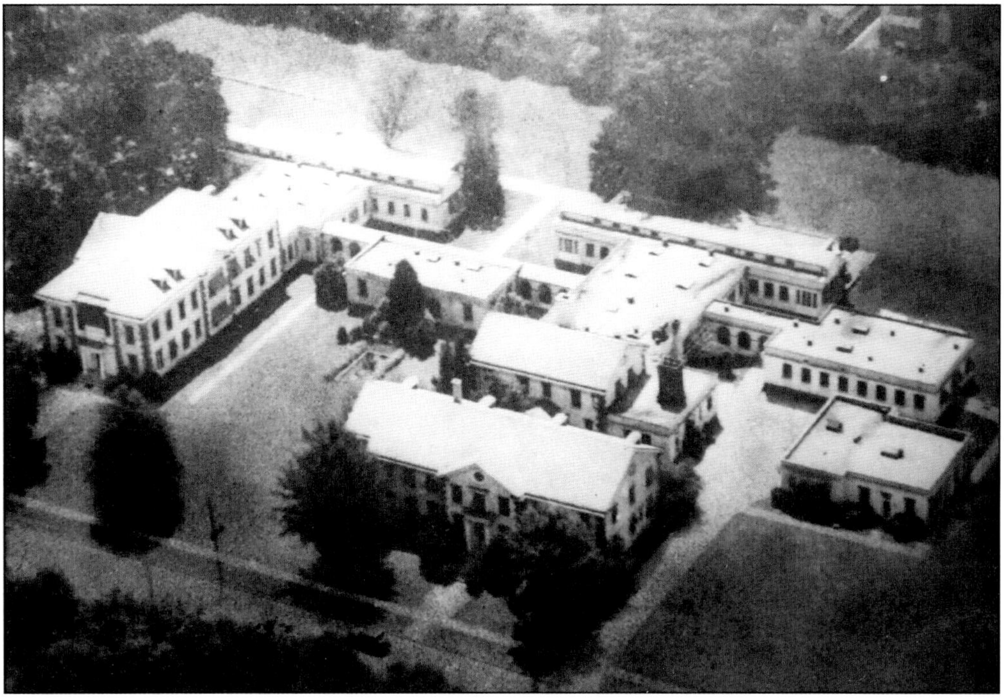

The nation's first Shriners Hospital for Crippled children opened at Samford Avenue and Kings Highway in 1922. Now called the Shriners Hospital for Children, it is still located at the same address, though the original buildings are gone.

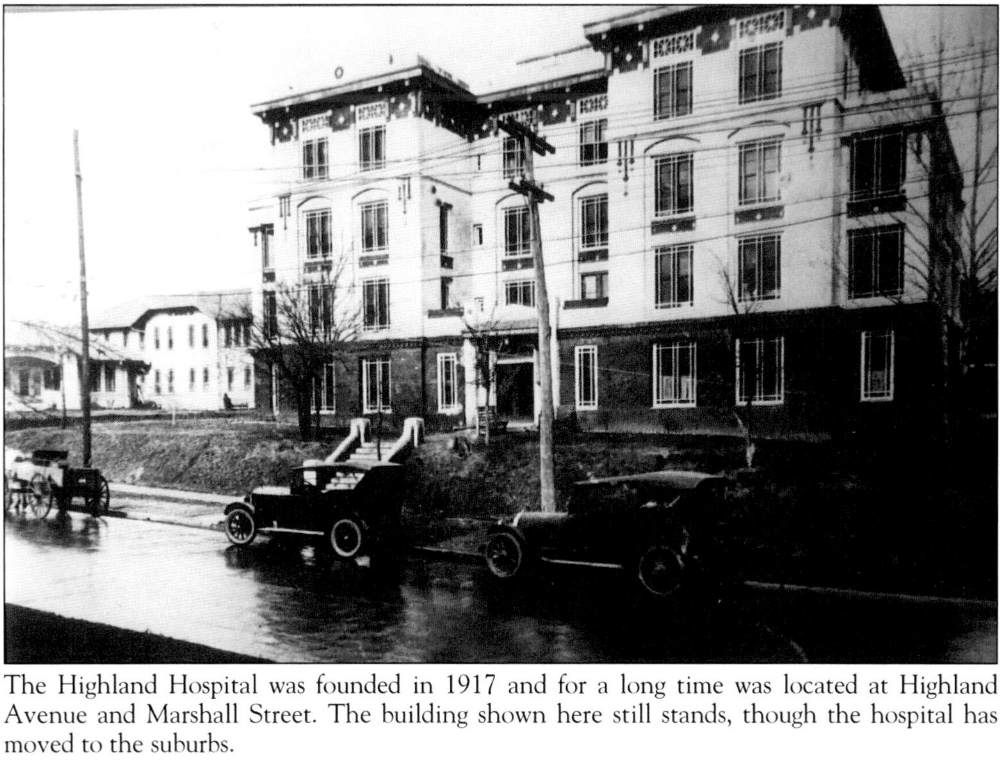

The Highland Hospital was founded in 1917 and for a long time was located at Highland Avenue and Marshall Street. The building shown here still stands, though the hospital has moved to the suburbs.

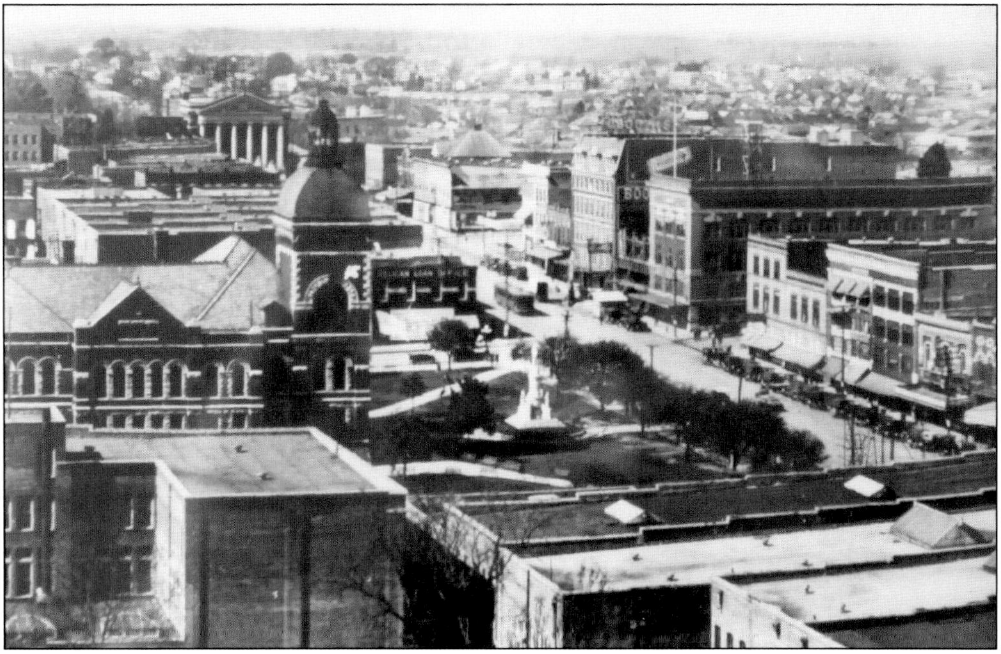

This is downtown Shreveport in 1920 as seen from the roof of the Exchange National Bank Building (now the Johnson Building). The Caddo Courthouse is at left with the Confederate Monument, dedicated in 1906, on the lawn in front.

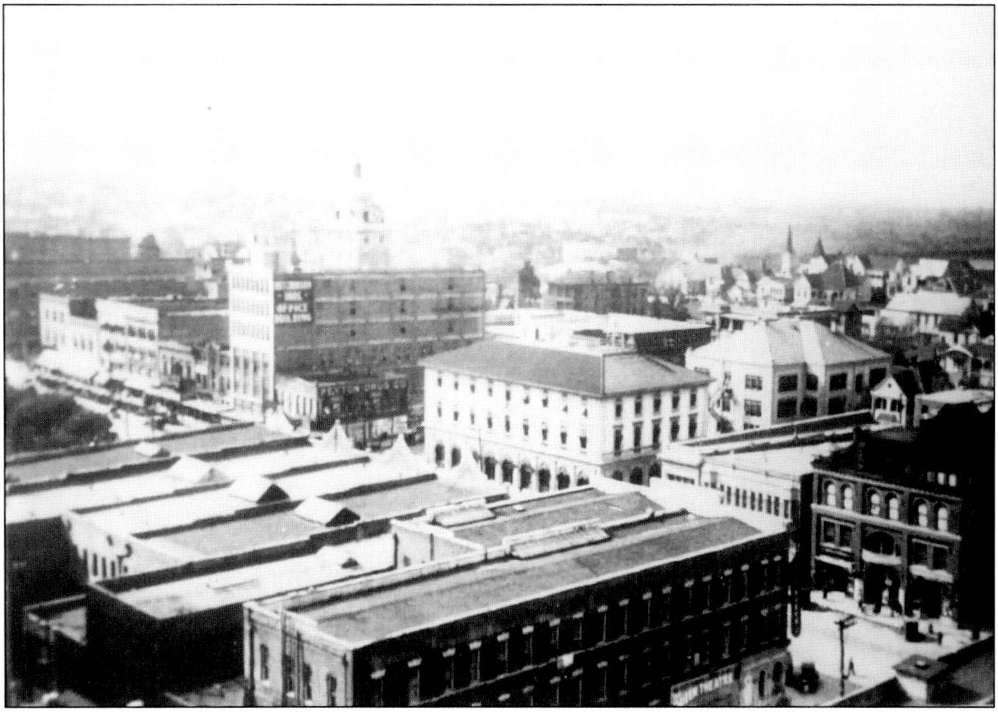

Pictured here is downtown as seen from the Merchants' Bank Building (now demolished) in 1920. The Federal Building is at center, and the Grand Opera House, at far right. The domed tower is atop the First Baptist Church.

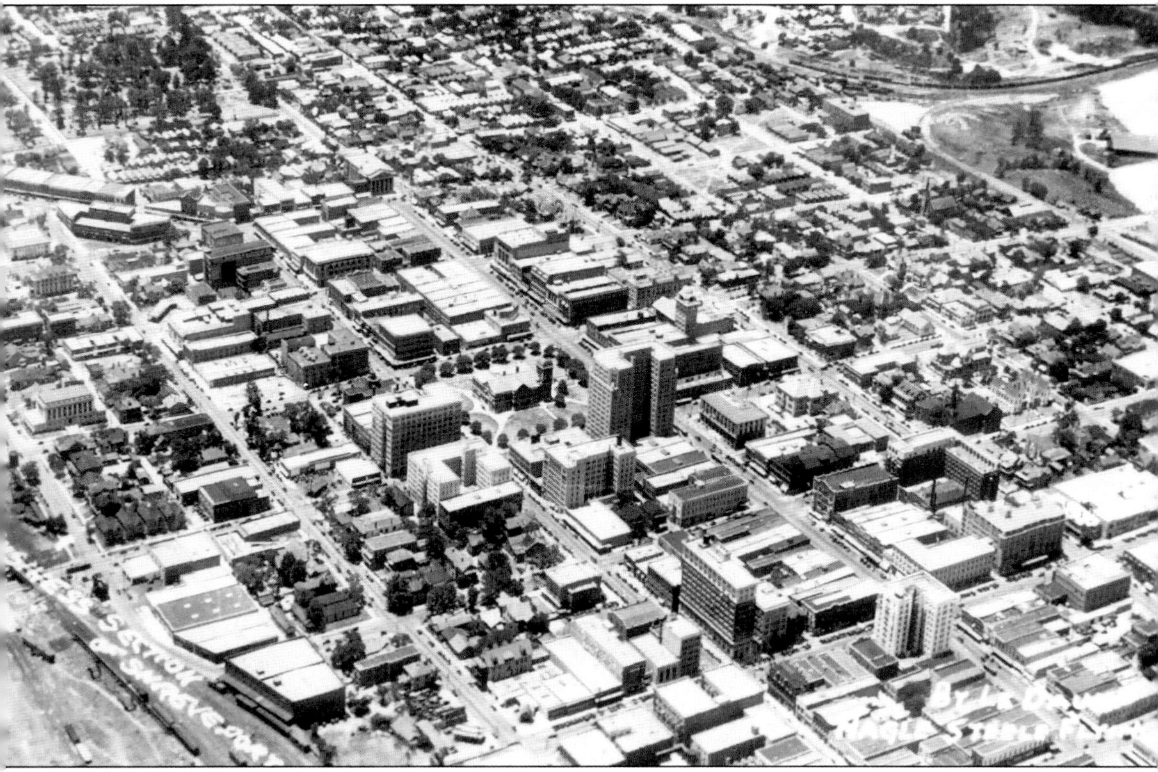

This is an aerial view of Shreveport, taken in 1926, showing the downtown central business district from the southeast. Between 1920 and 1930 the population of Shreveport jumped from 44,000 to 77,000, due in large measure to the oil and gas industry and the establishment of Barksdale Army Air Field. For a time Shreveport was the center of the nation's oil industry, though that distinction was eventually lost to Houston, Texas.

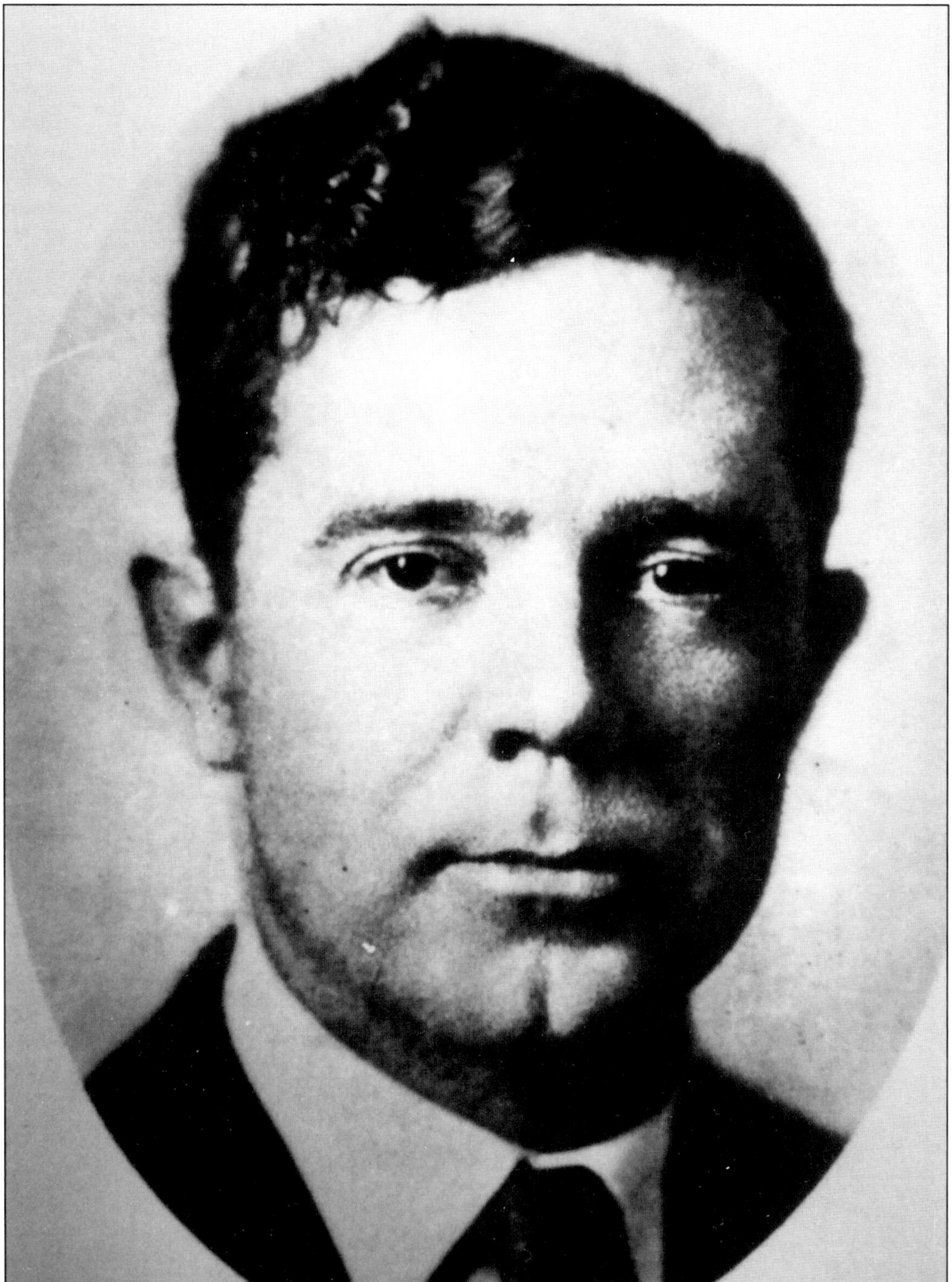

Governor Huey Pierce Long (1893–1935) called Shreveport home from 1918 until his assassination. "The Kingfish," as he was known, was Louisiana's most influential and controversial politician and was a candidate for the White House at his death. Governor Long was buried on the grounds of the capitol building he ordered built in Baton Rouge. His widow, Shreveport native Rose McConnell Long (1892–1970) and their son, Russell, both served in the U.S. Senate as Huey had done.

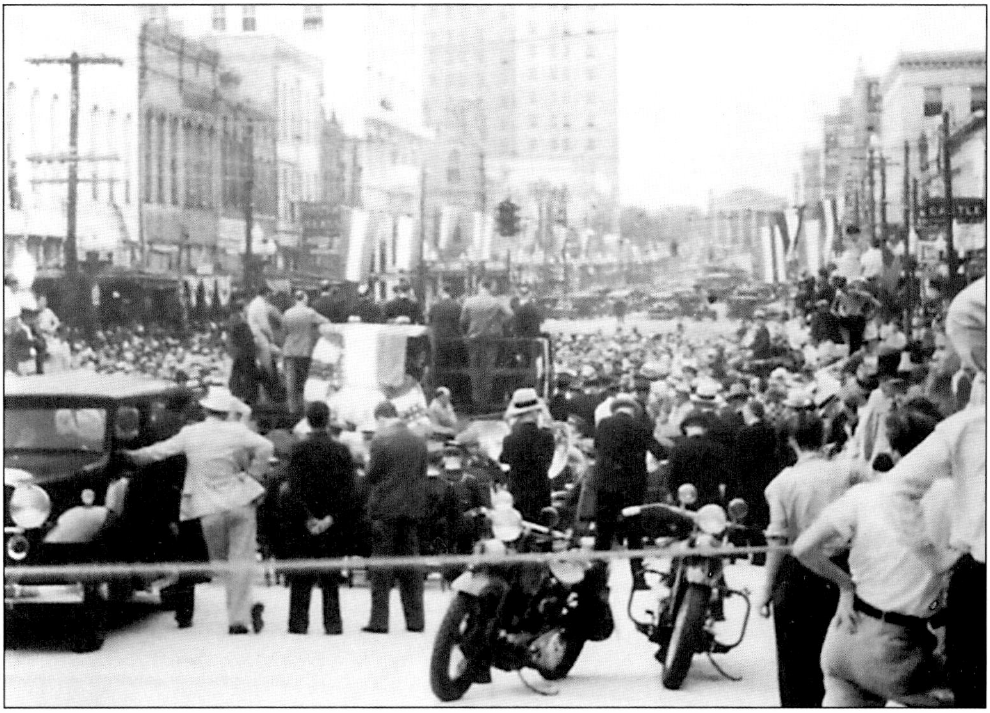

The dedication of the Texas Street Bridge, also known as the Long-Allen Bridge (for Governors Huey Long and Oscar K. Allen) took place in 1933. The scene is at the intersection of Texas and Spring Streets as Huey Long speaks from the dais.

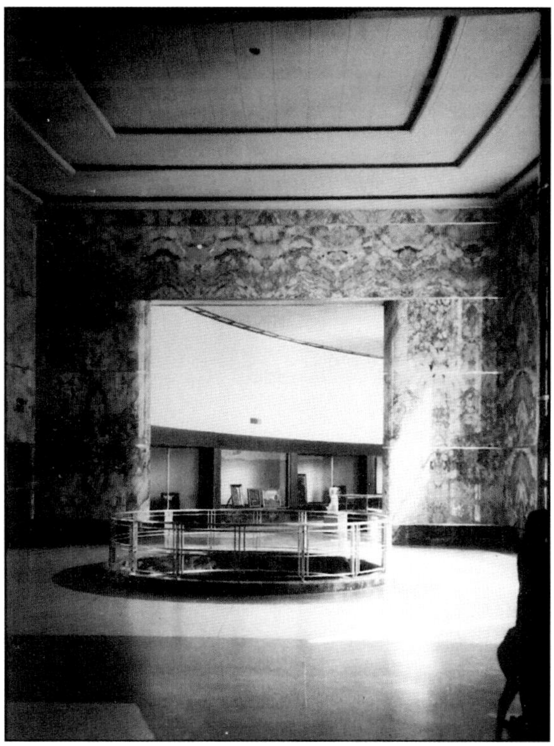

This is the striking lobby of the newly finished Louisiana State Exhibit Building on Greenwood Road. Built in 1937, the monumental round Art Deco edifice is one of Louisiana's most imposing structures even today.

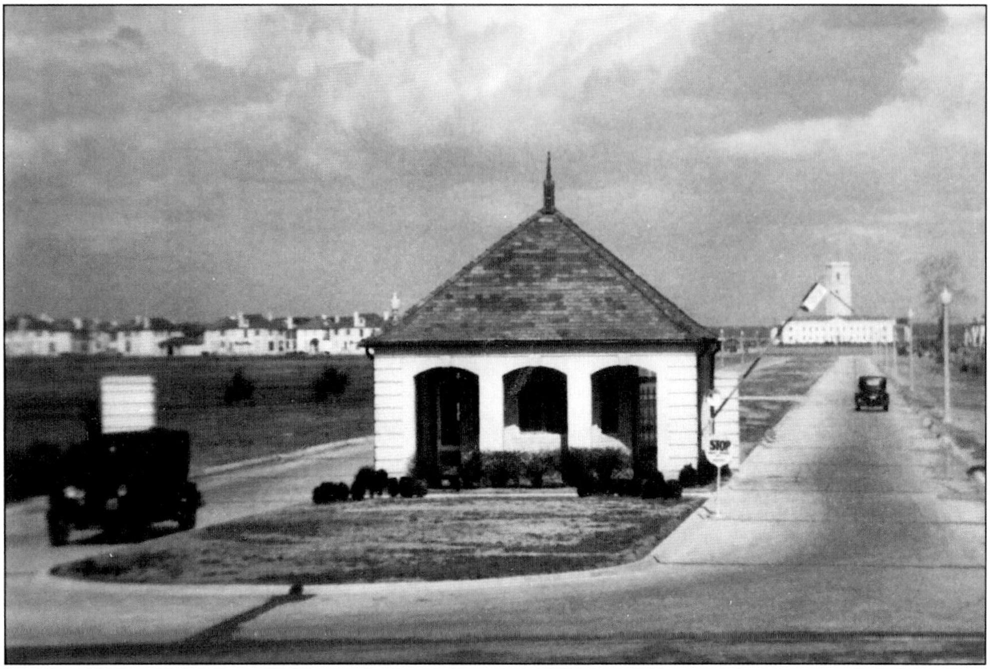

The main gate of Barksdale Army Air Field was photographed in 1933, the year it opened. Named for Lt. Eugene Hoy Barksdale, the facility is now one of the nation's largest Air Force bases and is one of the Shreveport–Bossier City area's principal employers.

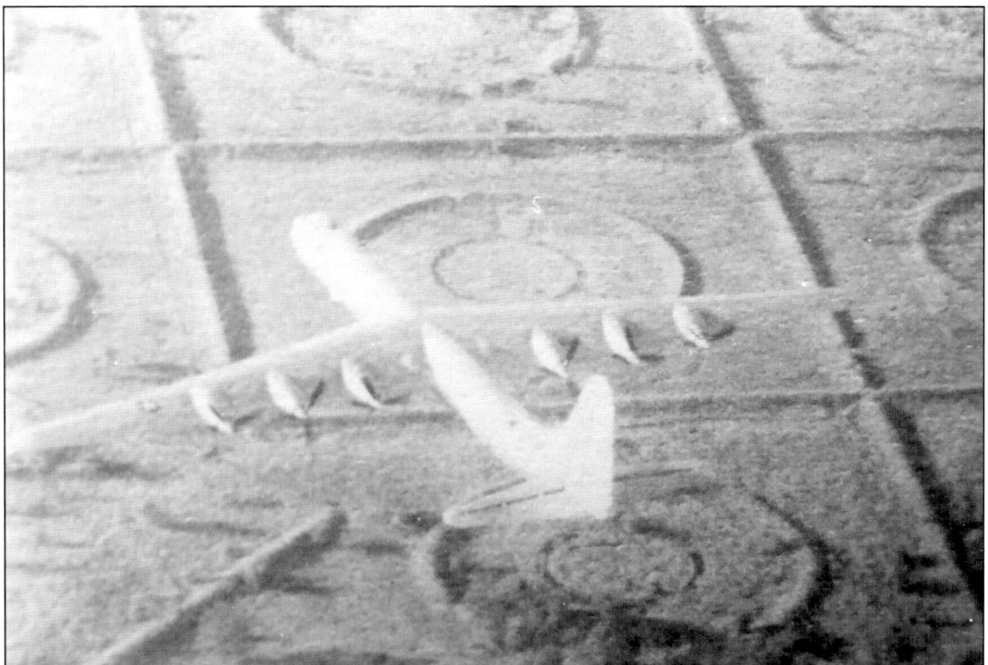

A B-36 from Carswell Air Force Base approaches Barksdale in 1950. Below are the remains of the Texaco Tank Farm, which operated on Shreveport's Anderson Island from 1910 to 1945. A neighborhood occupies the site today.

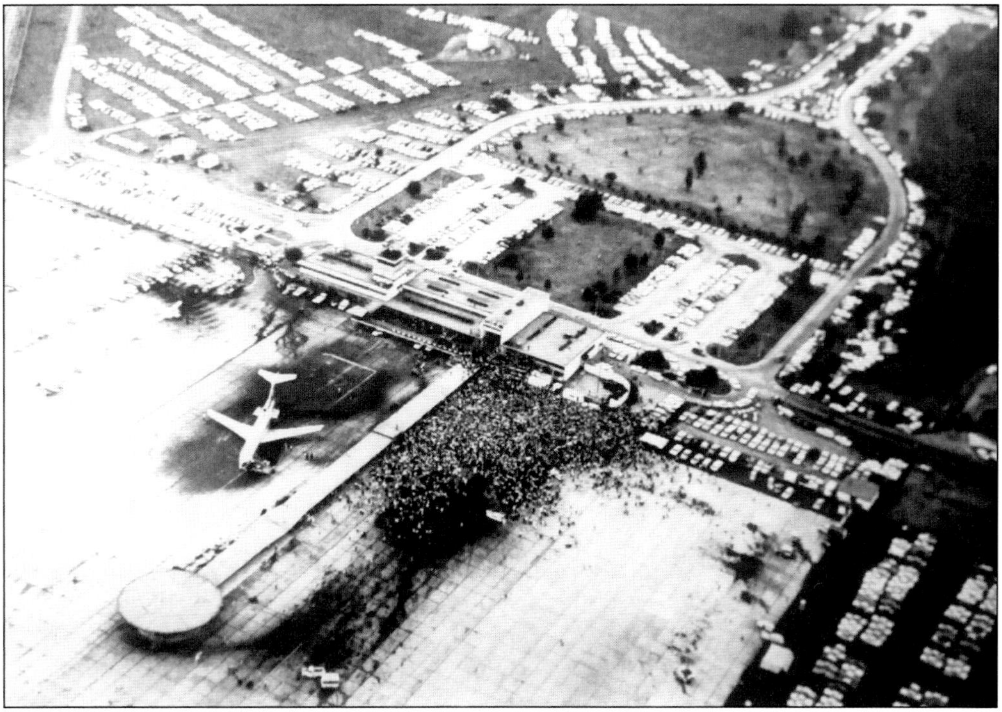

The old Shreveport Municipal Airport opened in 1952 on Hollywood Avenue at Monkhouse Drive. In this aerial view a huge crowd on the tarmac greets Air Force One and President Eisenhower on a visit to Shreveport.

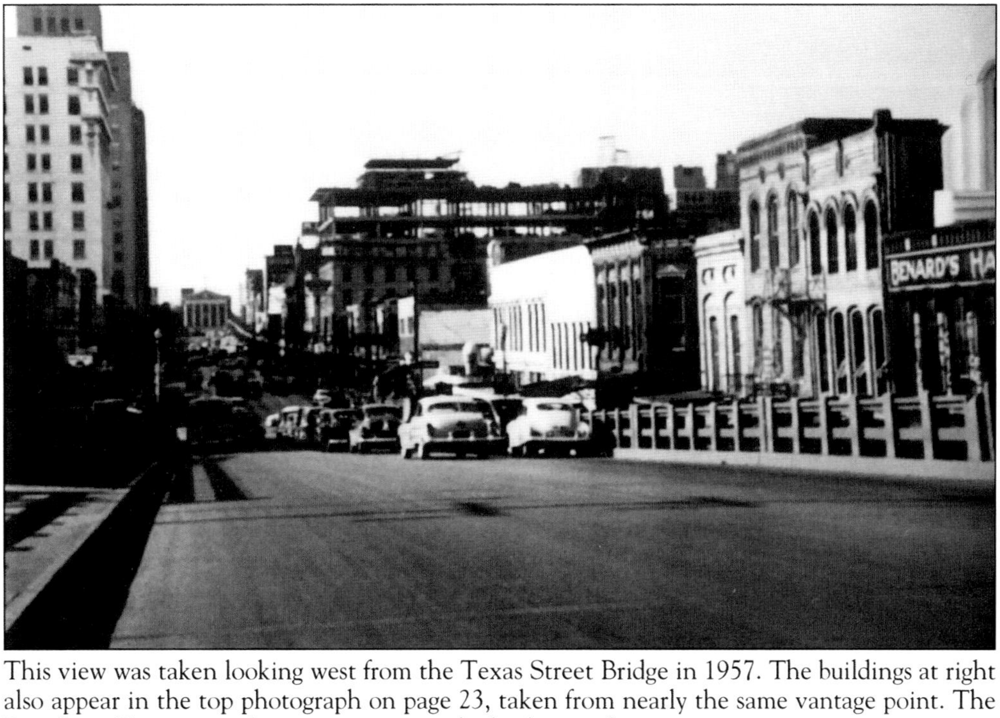

This view was taken looking west from the Texas Street Bridge in 1957. The buildings at right also appear in the top photograph on page 23, taken from nearly the same vantage point. The Petroleum Tower is under construction in the background.

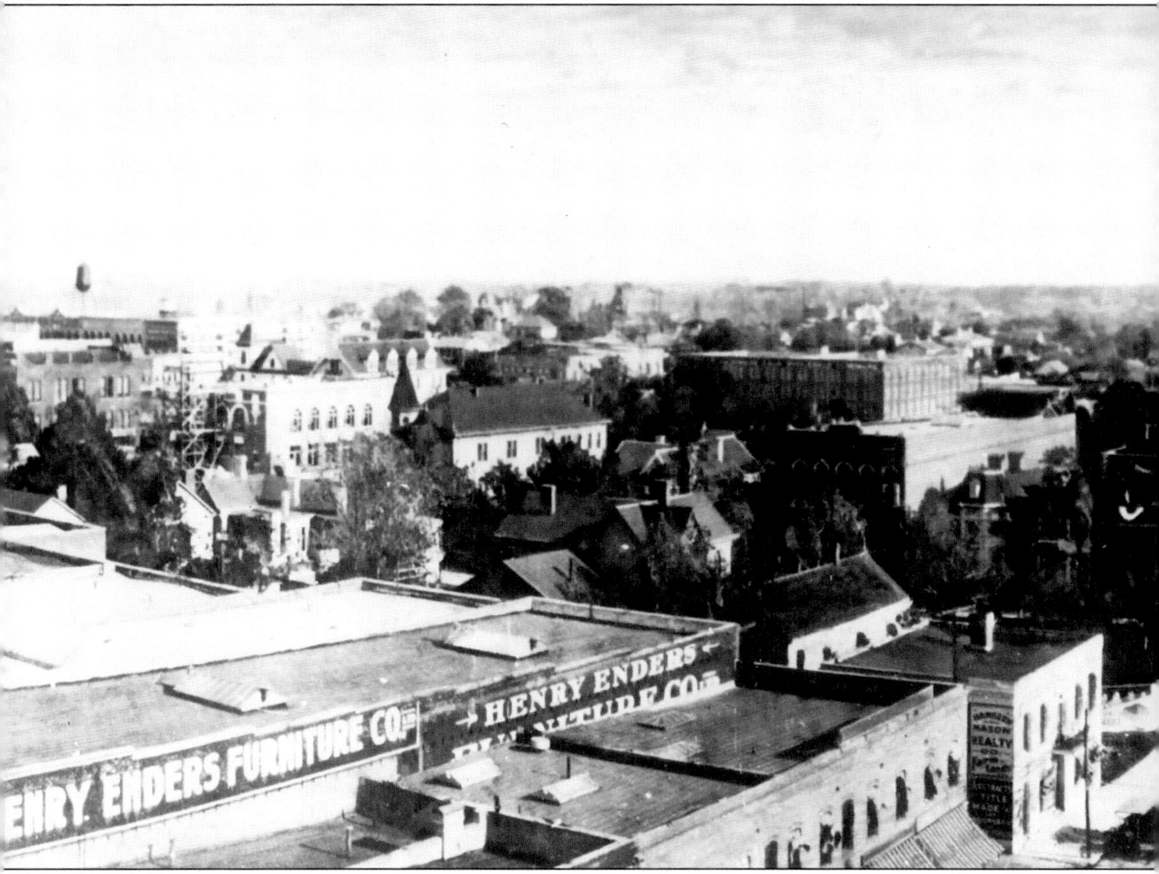

This bird's-eye view to the southeast from the tower of the old Customhouse was taken in 1910. Only the large warehouse just to the right of the center of the photograph still stands. Built as the W.F. Taylor Company in 1898, it later housed the Lee Hardware Company. Note the residences along Milam Street and the Enders Furniture Company where the Slattery Building now stands. Within a decade the entire area had gone commercial, as the oil boom transformed the city.

Three

Commerce

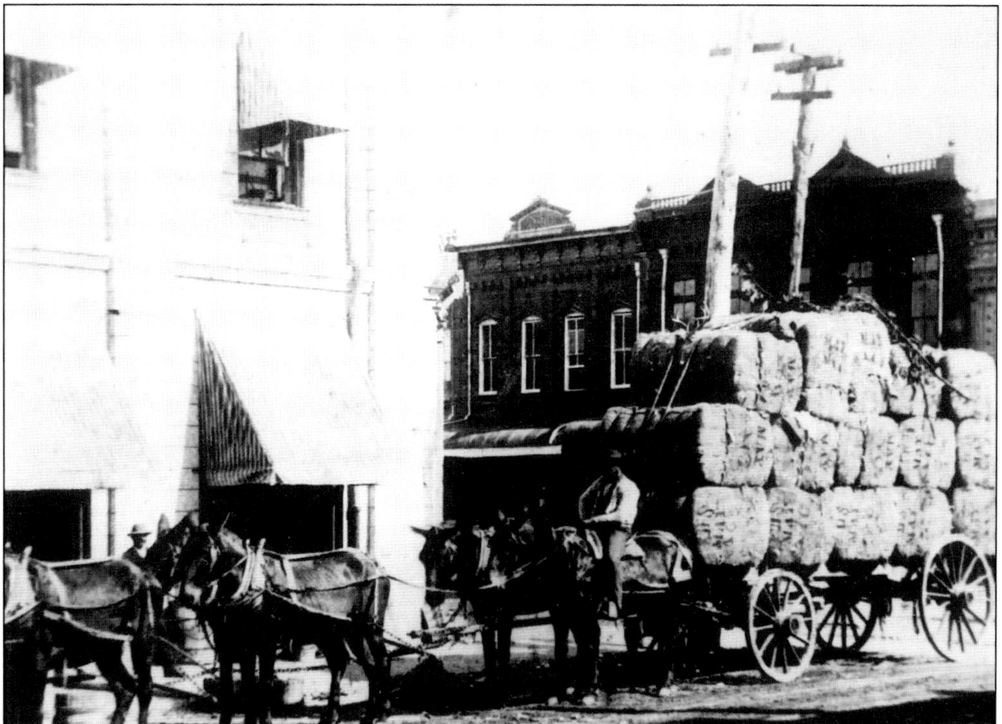

Cotton was the economic lifeblood of Caddo Parish from the 1830s up to World War I. Here bales of cotton are brought to the riverfront for shipment to New Orleans in 1890. The buildings shown all still stand in the 100 block of Texas Street.

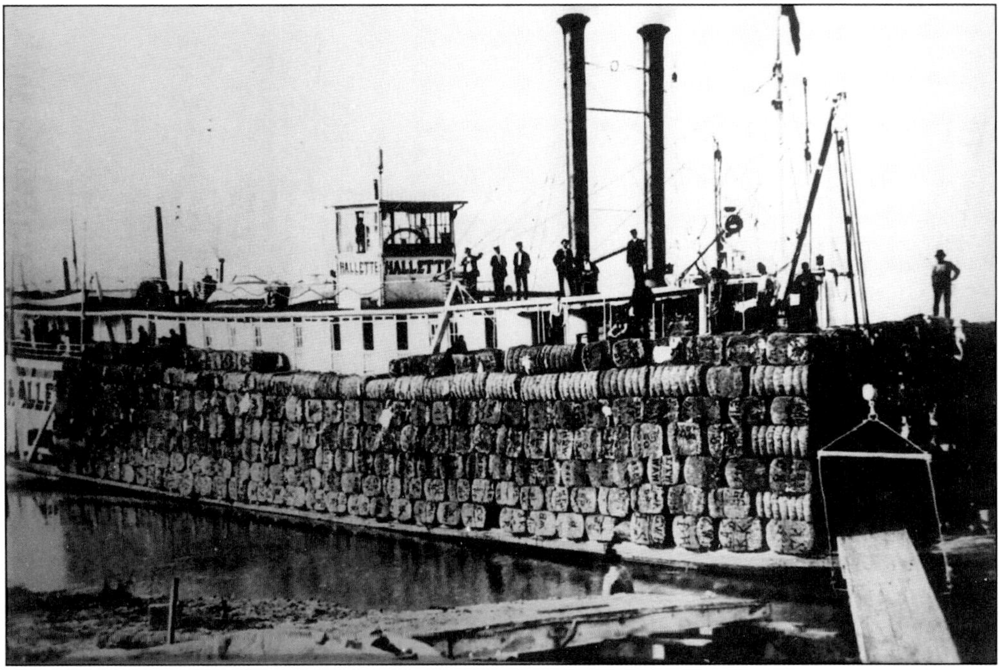

A steamboat loaded with cotton from Caddo and Bossier Parishes prepares to depart from the Commerce Street wharf. The boat is the *Hallette*, built in 1887 and scrapped in 1902.

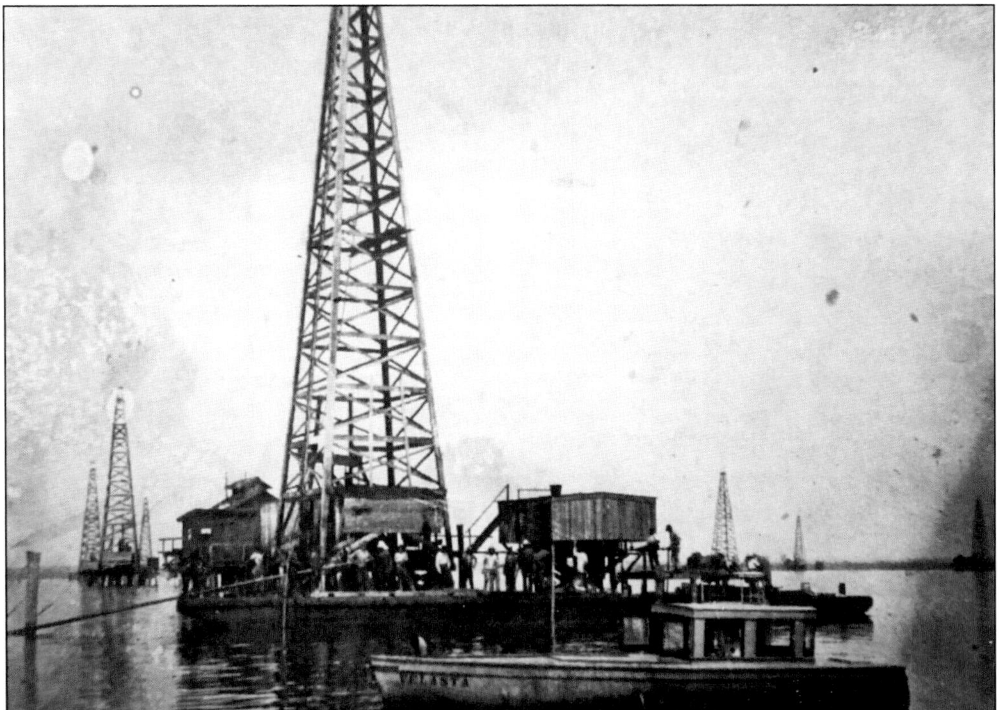

What cotton was to the nineteenth century in Shreveport, oil became to the twentieth century. Here Gulf Oil drills on Caddo Lake north of the city in 1911. Oil was discovered in Caddo Parish in 1905. In 1910 the nation's first offshore wells were drilled on Caddo Lake.

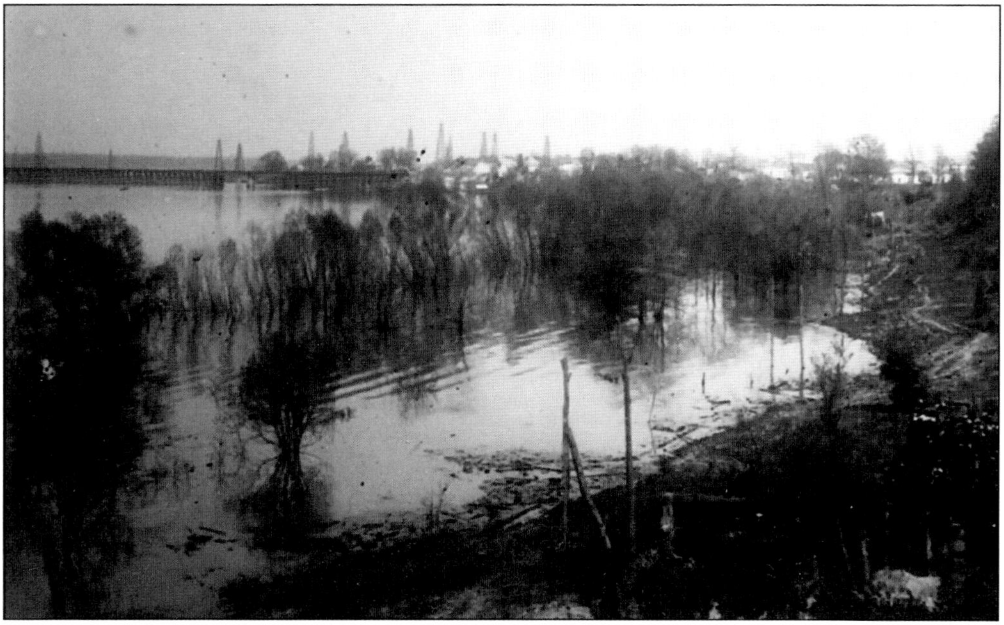

The oilfields of Caddo Parish, in and around Caddo Lake, were among the nation's most productive early in the twentieth century. Many great fortunes had their start here, including those of such noted names as H.L. Hunt and Howard Hughes Sr.

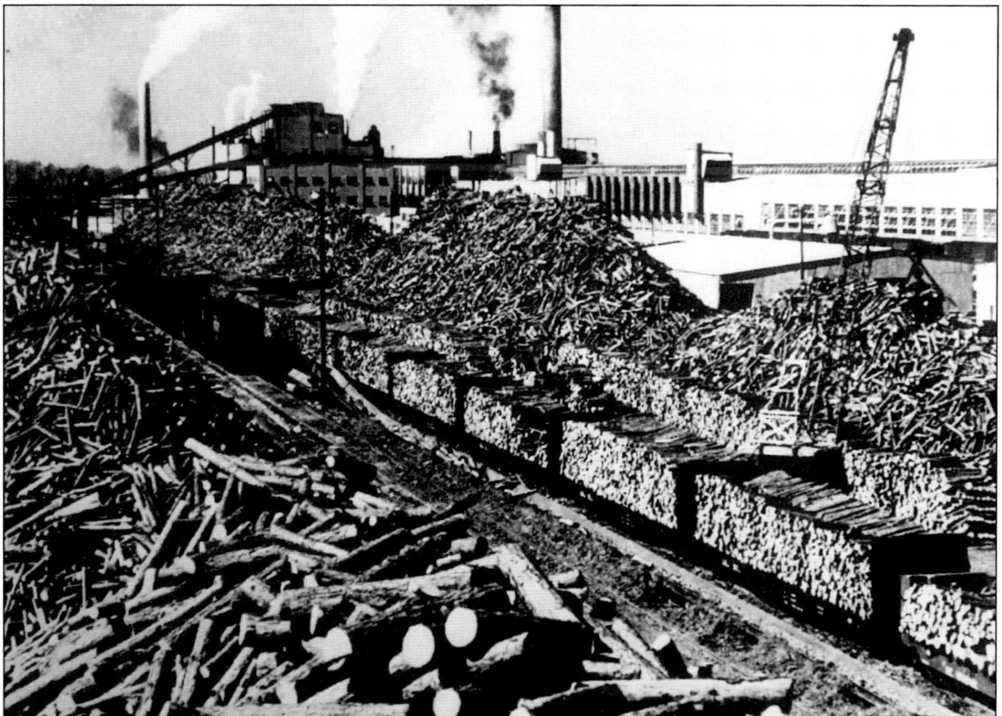

Along with cotton and petroleum, the area's other great commodity is timber. Lumber, pulp, and paper mills in Caddo, Bossier, Webster, DeSoto, and surrounding parishes have immeasurably enriched the economy of greater Shreveport.

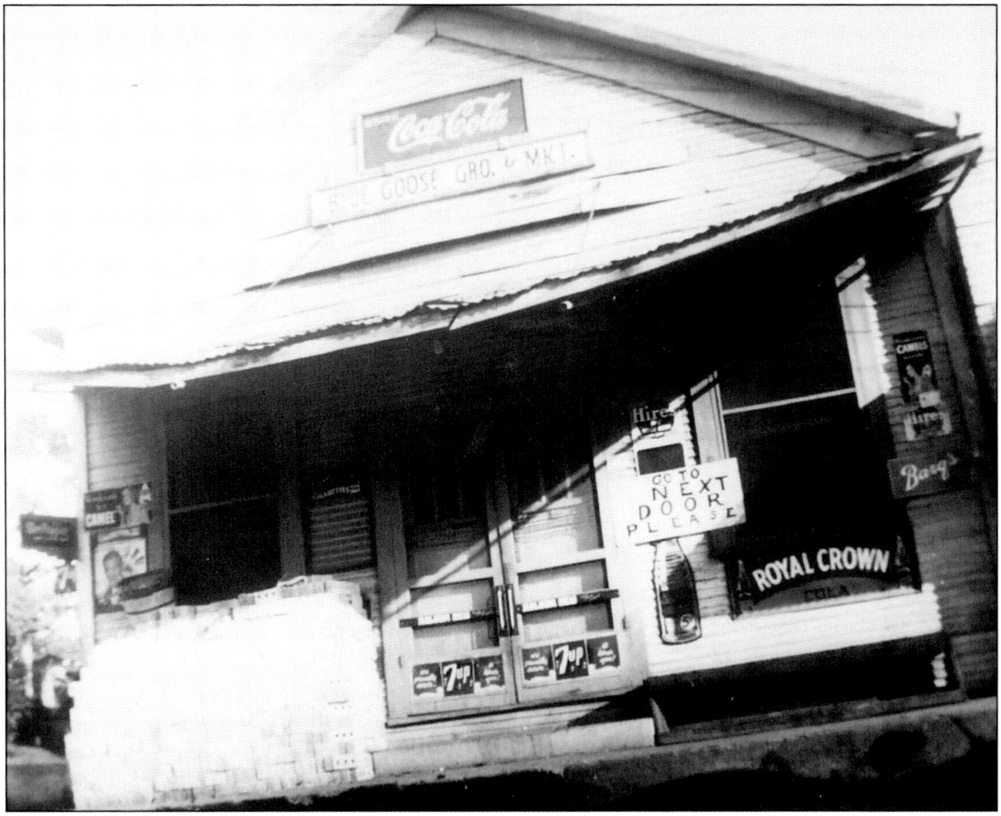

Little groceries such as the Blue Goose (above), which stood at Snow and Pickett Streets in Shreveport prior to 1943, and Webb and Webb (below), which once stood at Harts Island Road and Flournoy-Lucas Road, south of the city, long served their surrounding neighborhoods as meeting places and gathering spots. Webb and Webb is now part of the Pioneer Heritage Center at LSU-Shreveport.

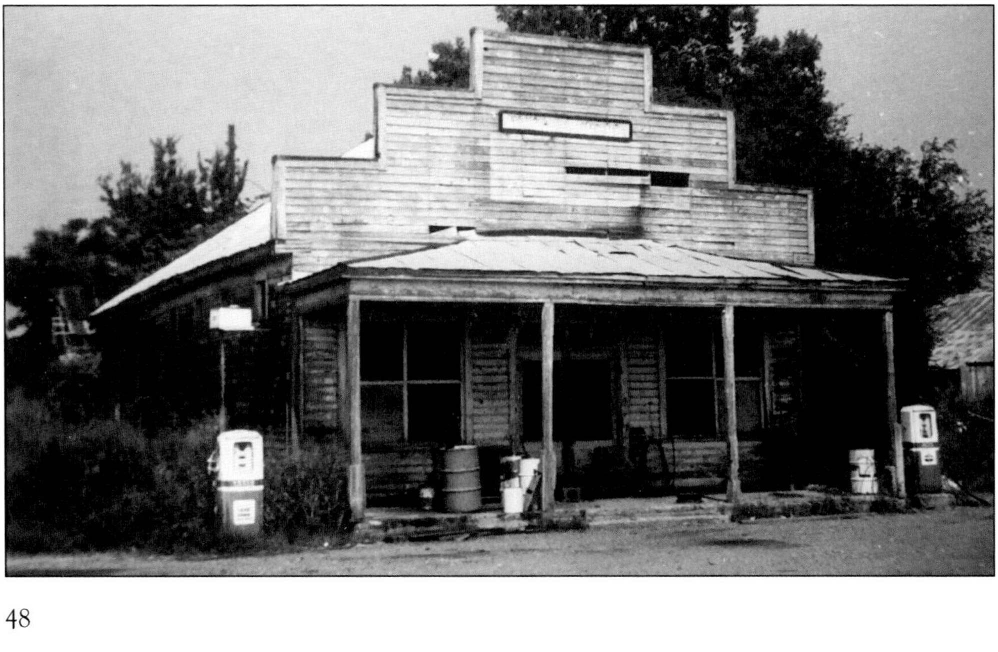

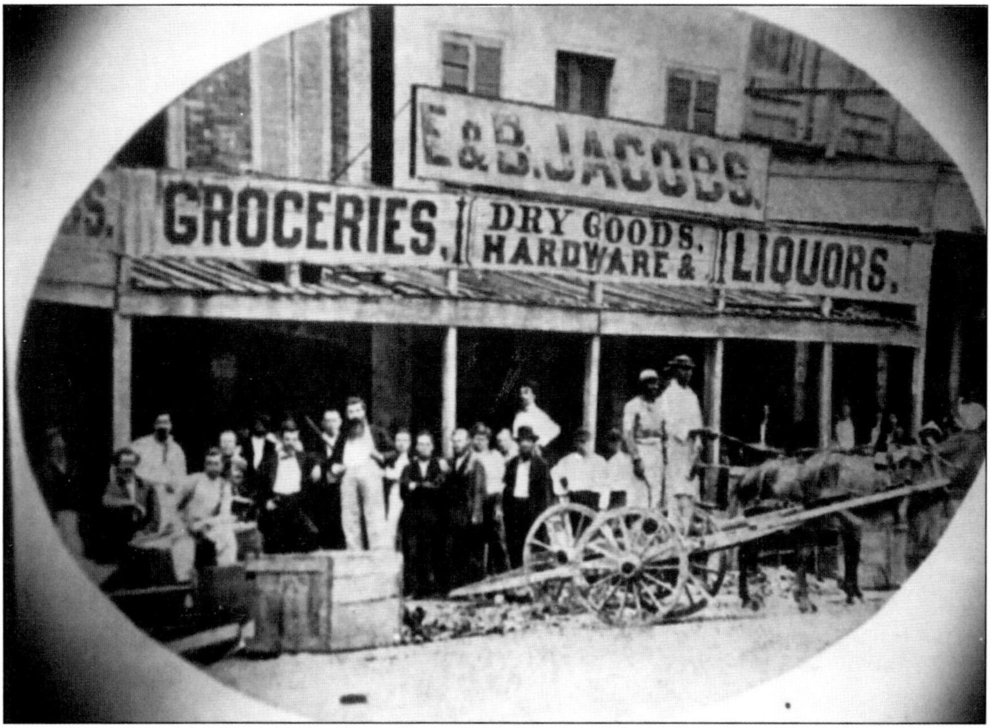

Larger grocery businesses served the wider community and formed an important part of the city's economy from the earliest days forward. Above is E. & B. Jacobs wholesale grocery business, founded on the riverfront in 1844. Below is the Big Chain, Shreveport's first supermarket, located at Fairfield Avenue and Jacob Street, 1929.

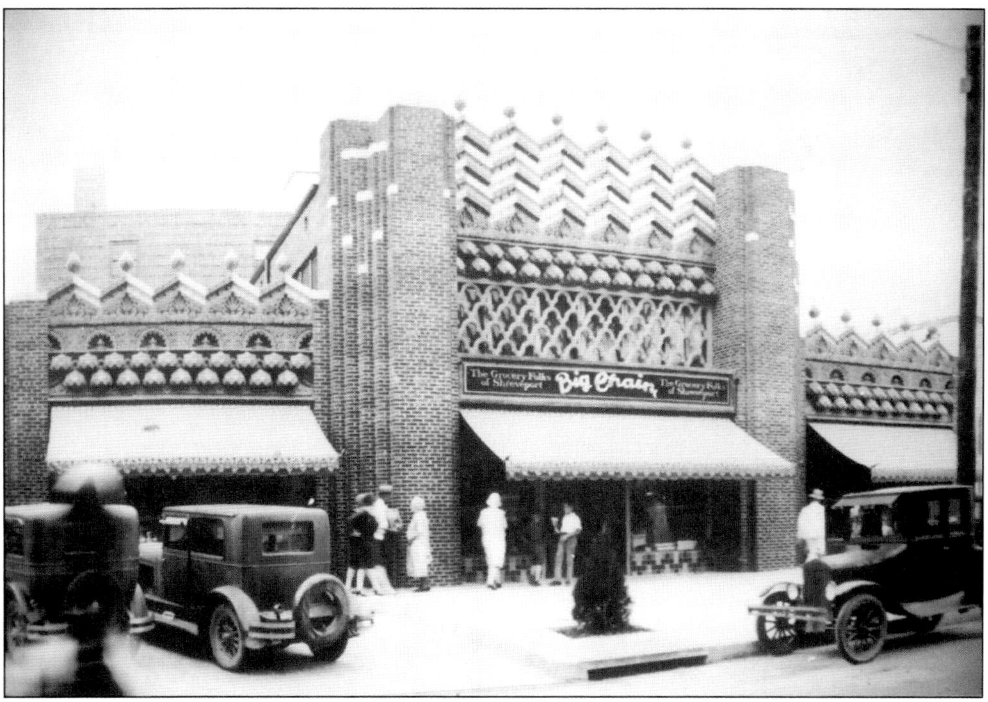

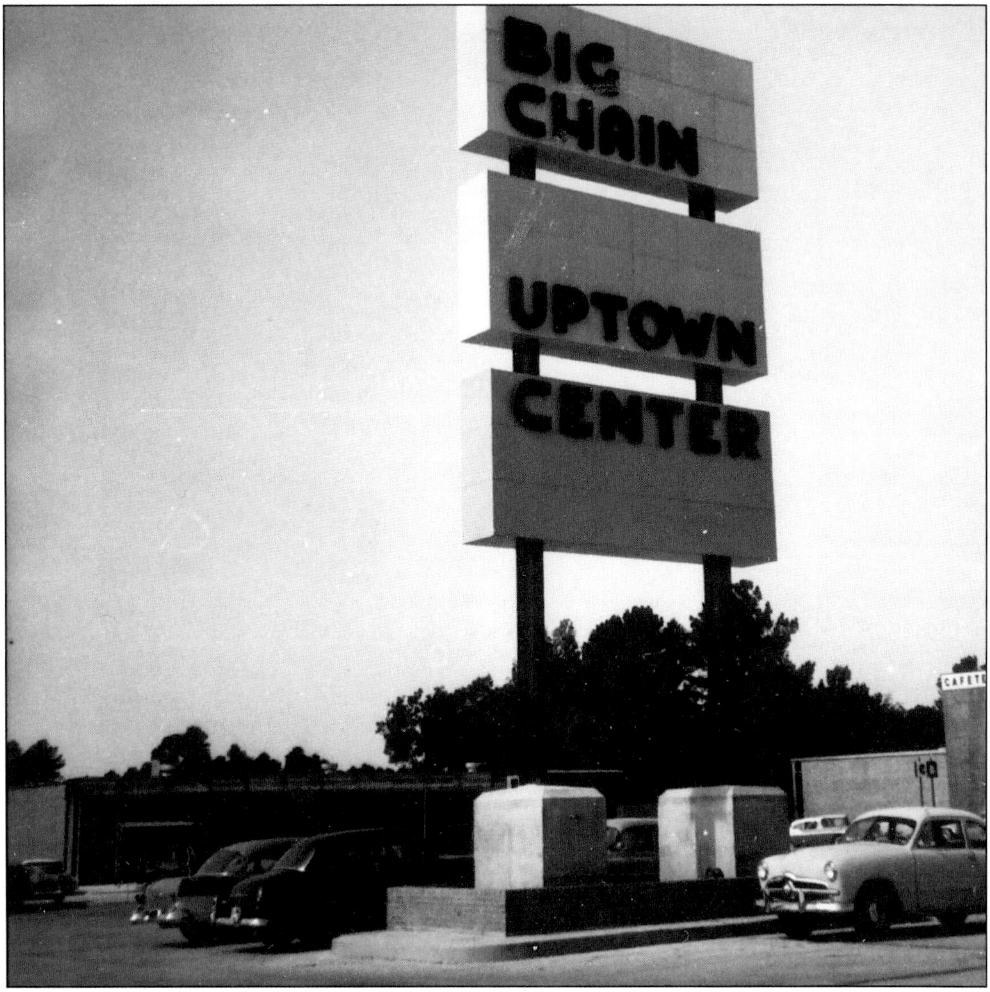

The 1940s and 1950s saw the rise of retail shopping centers, often anchored by a grocery store, a department store, or both. Here is a 1950s view of the new Uptown Shopping Center on Line Avenue, anchored by the Big Chain Grocery and Cafeteria and by Levy's Department Store.

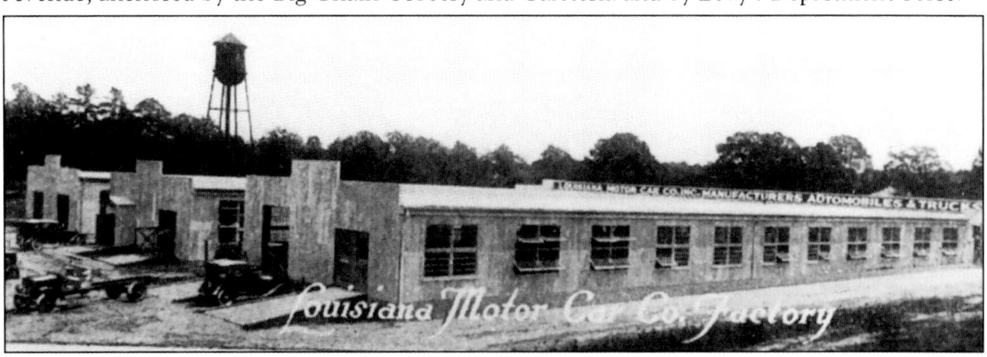

Another major contributor to Shreveport's economy has been the auto industry, both indirectly, due to its demand for gasoline, and directly, as with the Bour-Davis/Louisiana Motor Car Company, located on St. Vincent Avenue at Sixty-Fourth Street in the 1920s (as seen here), and today's huge GM truck facility.

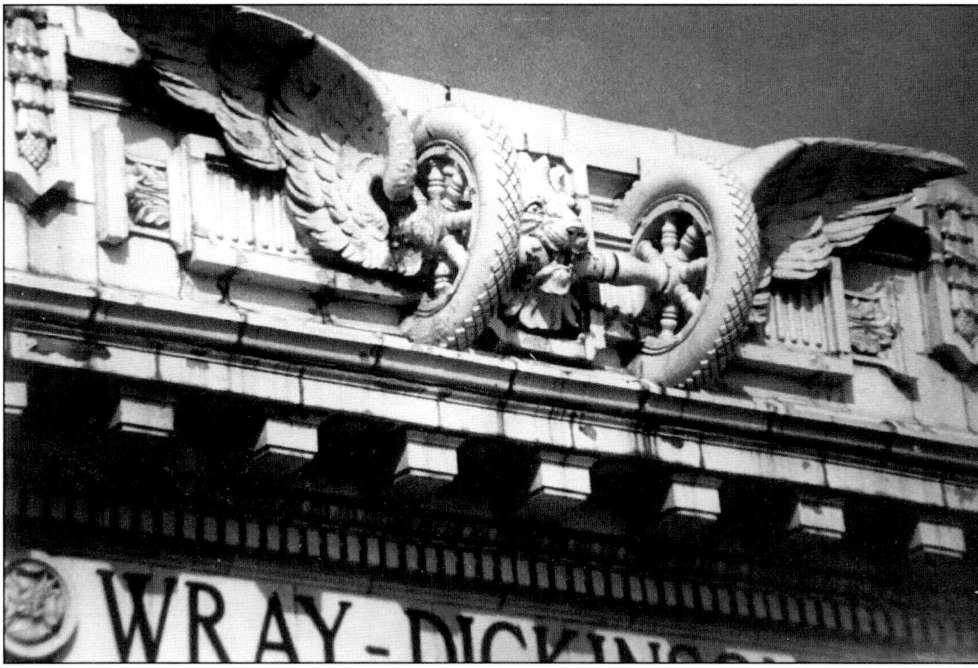

One of the first Ford dealerships in the nation was Wray Ford, founded in 1911 as the Wray-Dickinson Company. In 1913 its new showroom on Market at Fannin Street featured terra cotta winged wheels, symbol of the auto age.

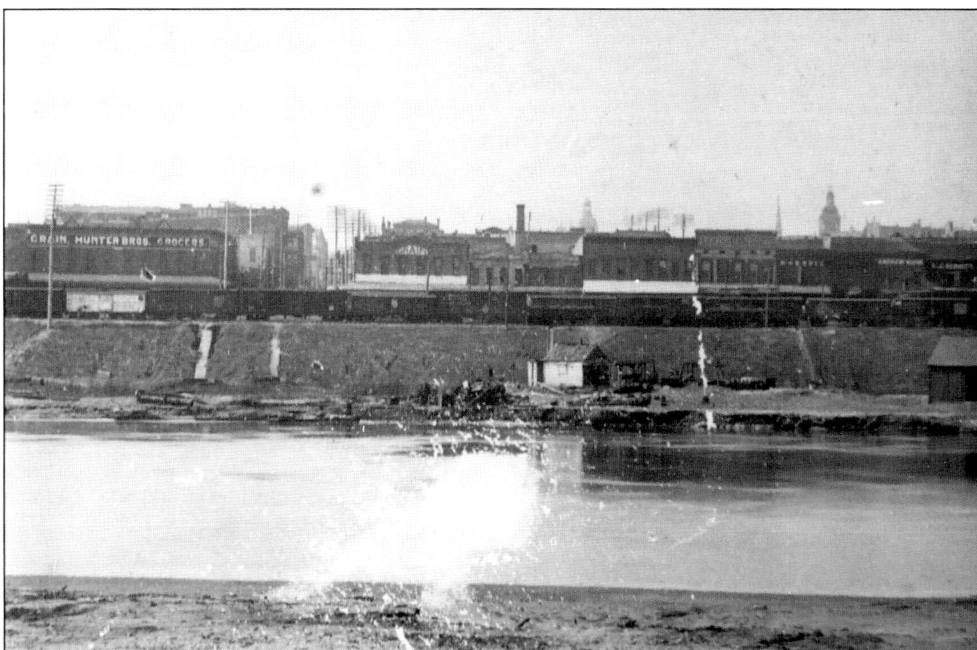

In the first decade of the twentieth century the railroad had begun to supplant the river as the primary artery of commerce to and from Shreveport. Nevertheless, the trains continued to run along the river's edge.

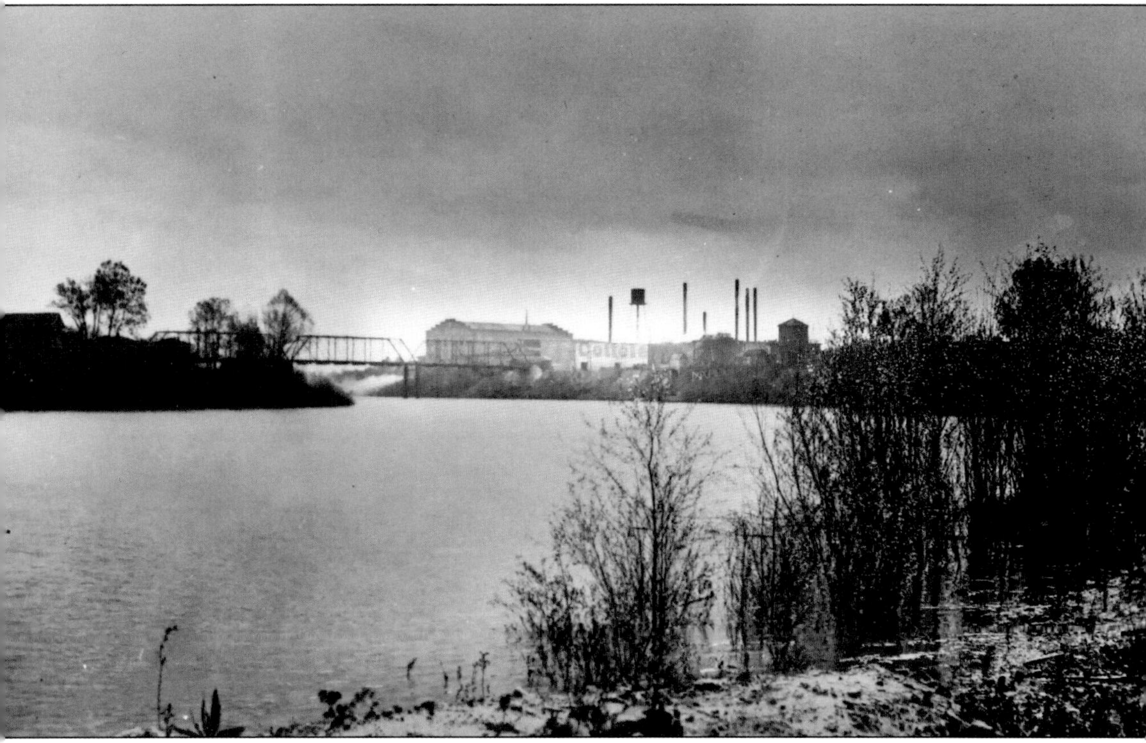

Cross Bayou meets Red River at sunset in this view from around 1900. Industry had begun to replace agriculture as a leading factor in the area's economy, much as the railroad had begun to supplant river traffic. The sun setting above the river and illuminating the railroad bridge connecting downtown with Agurs is particularly poignant.

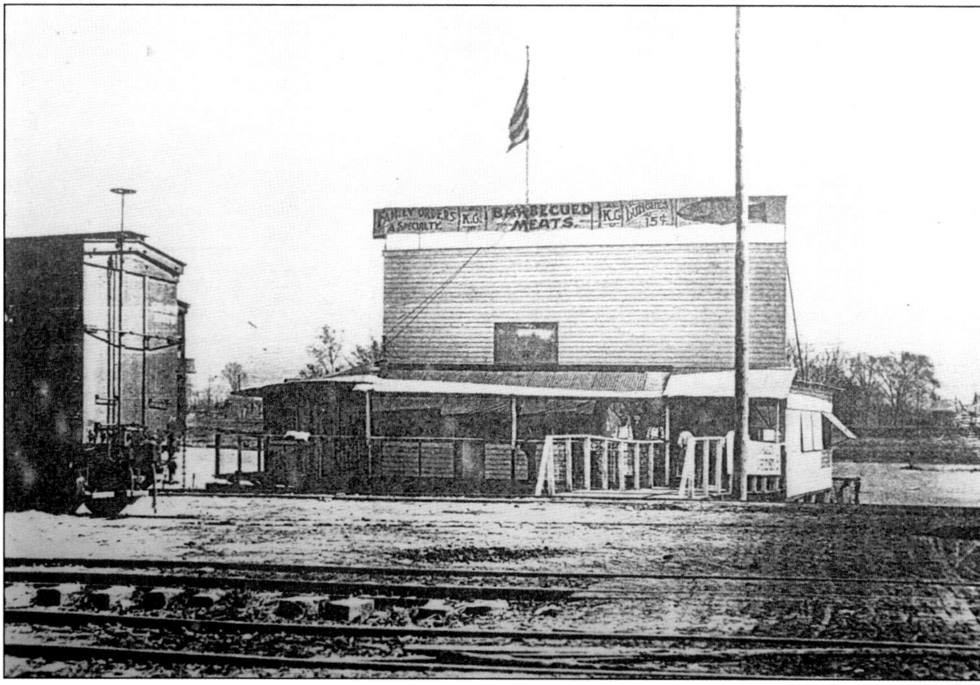

The riverfront where Commerce and Texas Street meet was photographed in 1905. Where today the Texas Street Bridge crosses the Red River stood a lunchroom. The railroad tracks are still there, but the Civic Center and casinos now dominate the area.

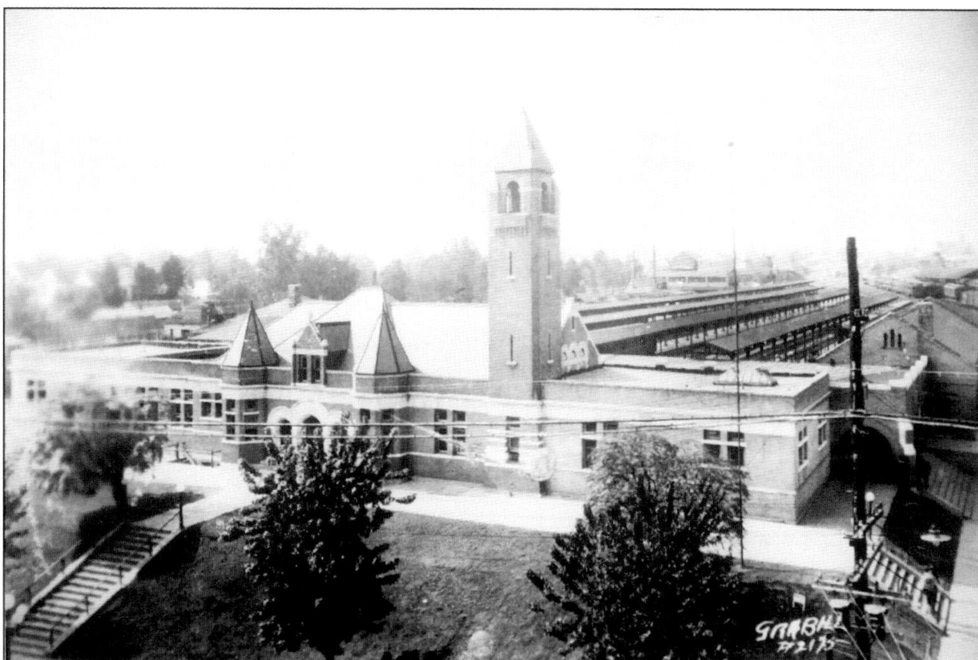

As the railroad attained preeminence early in the twentieth century, large railway terminals for passengers and freight were built. In this photo by Burch Grabill, Union Station on Louisiana and Snow Streets appears as it did in 1915. Only its front steps remain today.

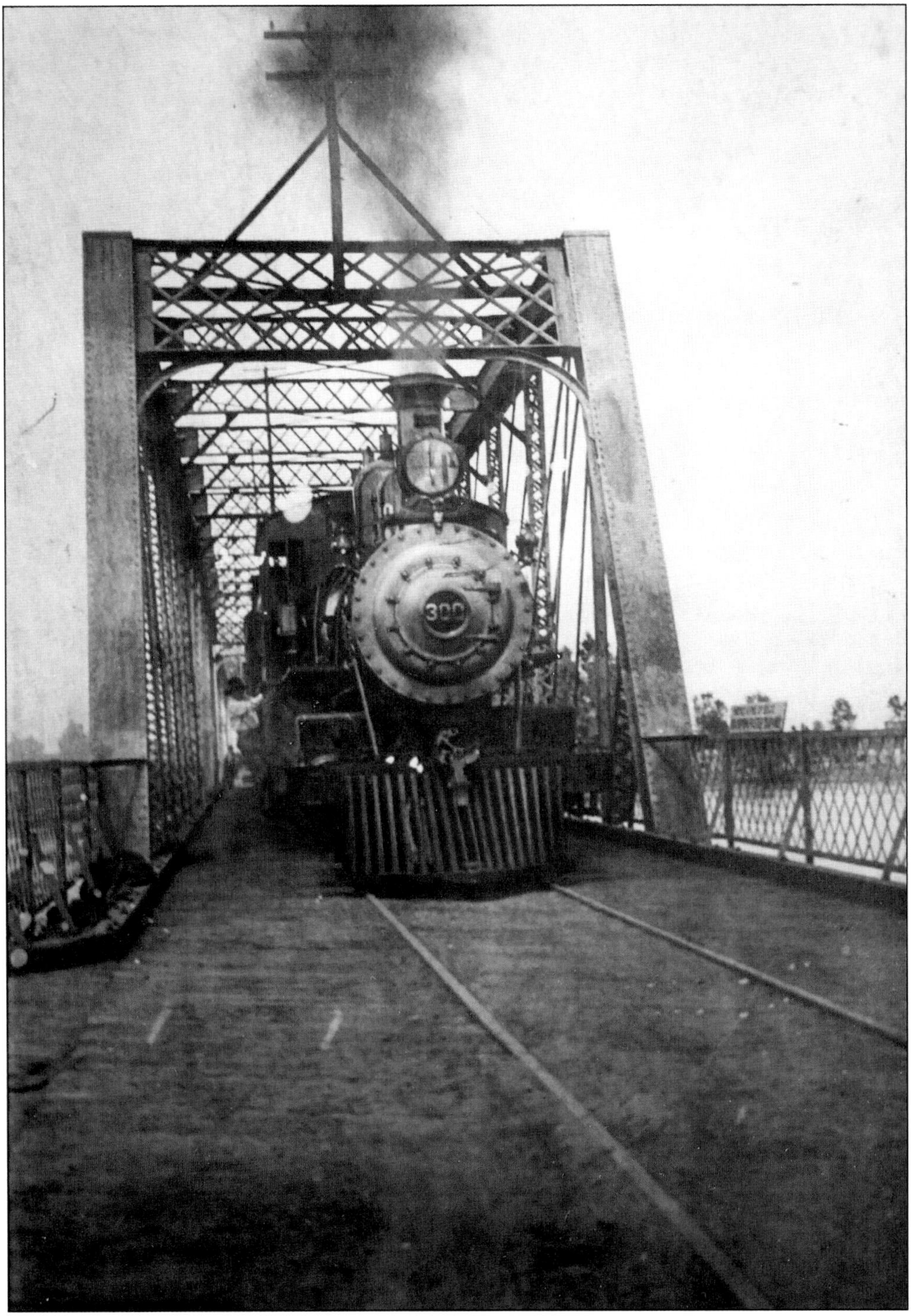

Engine number 300 of the Vicksburg, Shreveport, and Pacific Railroad crosses the V.S. & P. Bridge over Red River from Bossier Parish in 1904. The bridge, built in 1884, was rebuilt in 1916 by Illinois Central after that rail line absorbed the V.S. & P. The newer bridge still stands, supported by stone piers built for its predecessor.

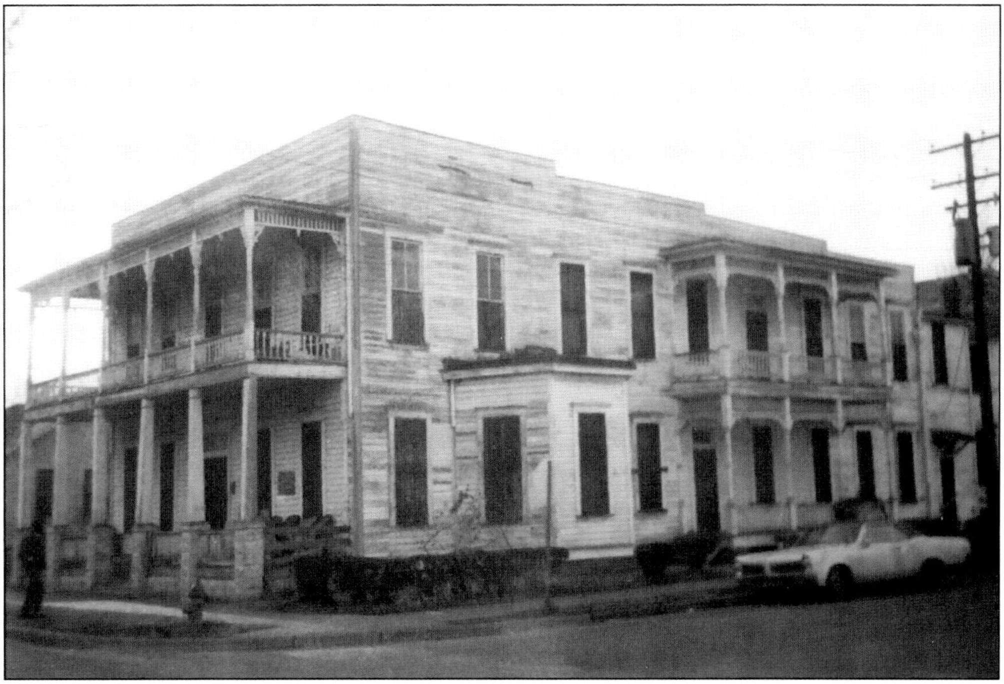

From 1903 to 1917 prostitution was legal in Shreveport, though confined to a designated Red Light District. One of the district's largest brothels was that of Madam Bea Haywood at 900 Fannin Street, shown here as it appeared shortly before fire destroyed it in 1974.

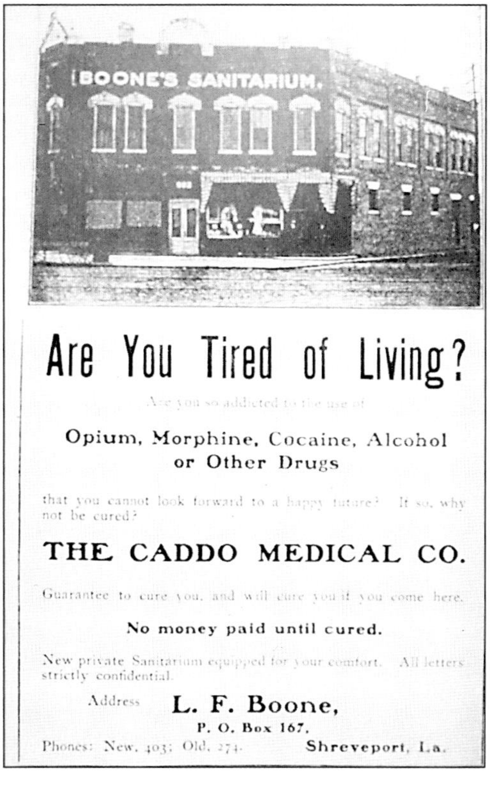

One of the reasons for prostitution then, as now, was drug addiction. This advertisement for a rehabilitation hospital on Texas Avenue in 1905 sounds eerily modern, proving that many social ills are not new at all. The clinic was only blocks from the Red Light District.

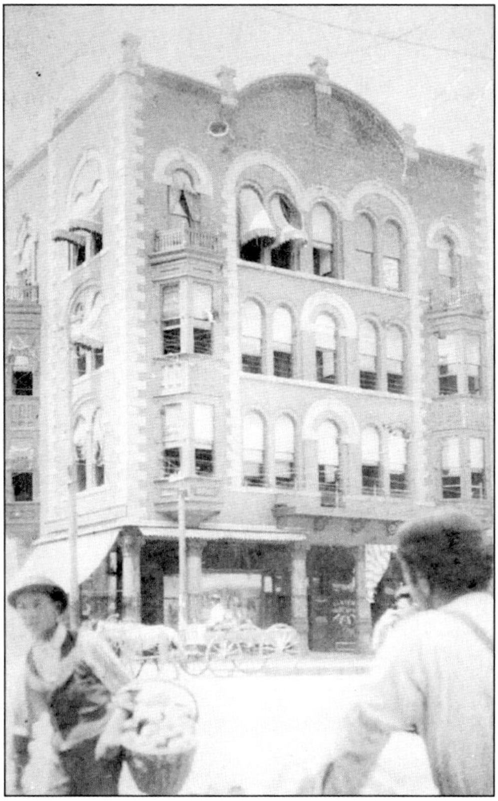

M. Levy's Department Store was long located in the Cooper Building at Texas and Edwards Streets. Built in 1887, the building for a time also housed the Jordan and Booth Haberdashery. It was razed in 1956 to build the Petroleum Tower.

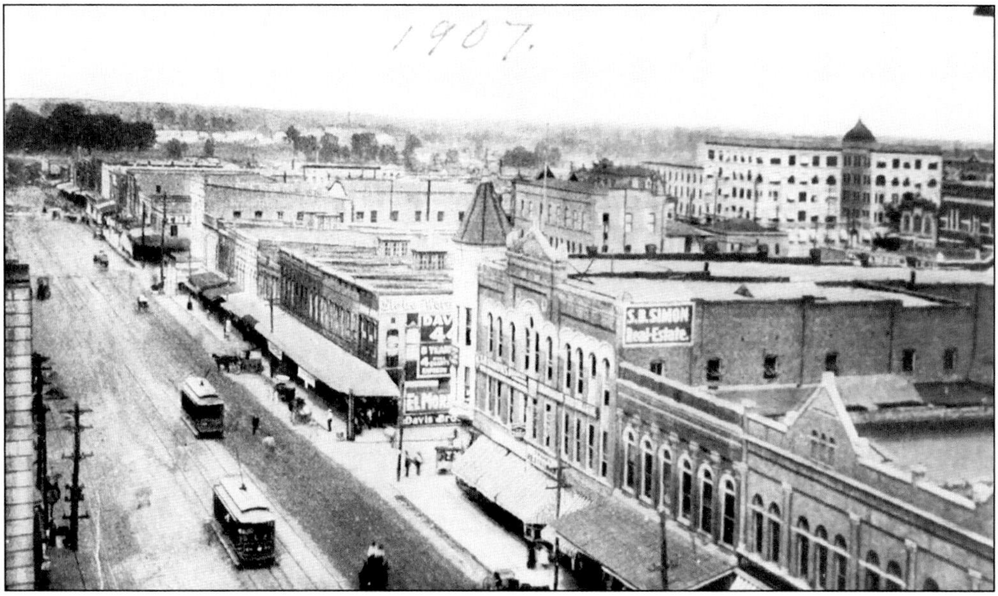

Shown here is a 1907 view of Texas Street looking toward the river. The many businesses along this thoroughfare included the city's most important department stores, banks, and retail shops.

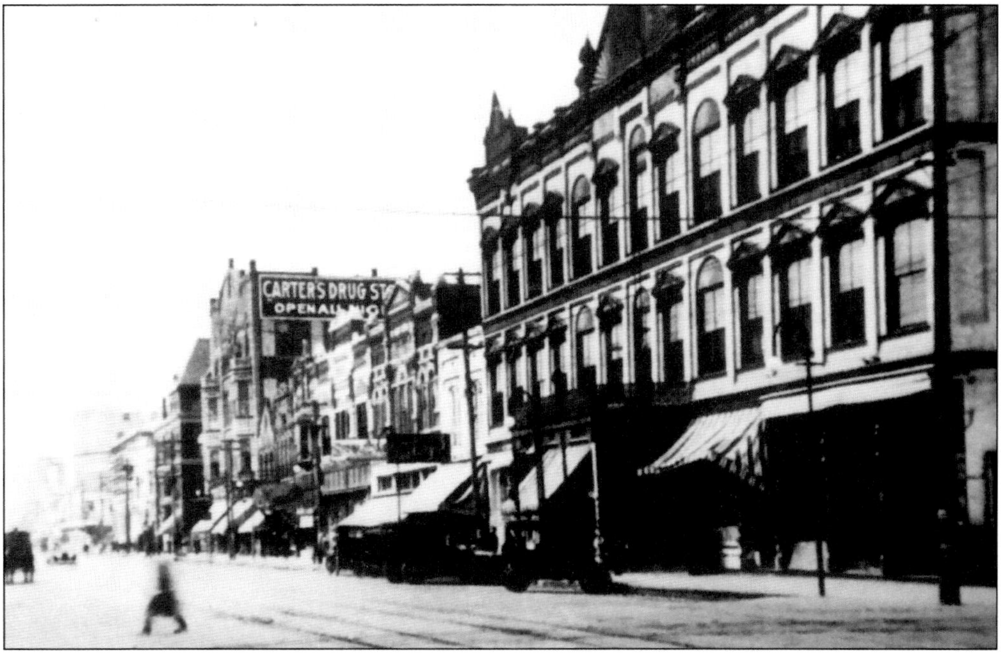

This view of Texas at Market Streets was taken about 1910. The busy commercial district includes the Phoenix Hotel at right and the Levy Building (with the Carter's Drug Store billboard). None of these buildings still stands.

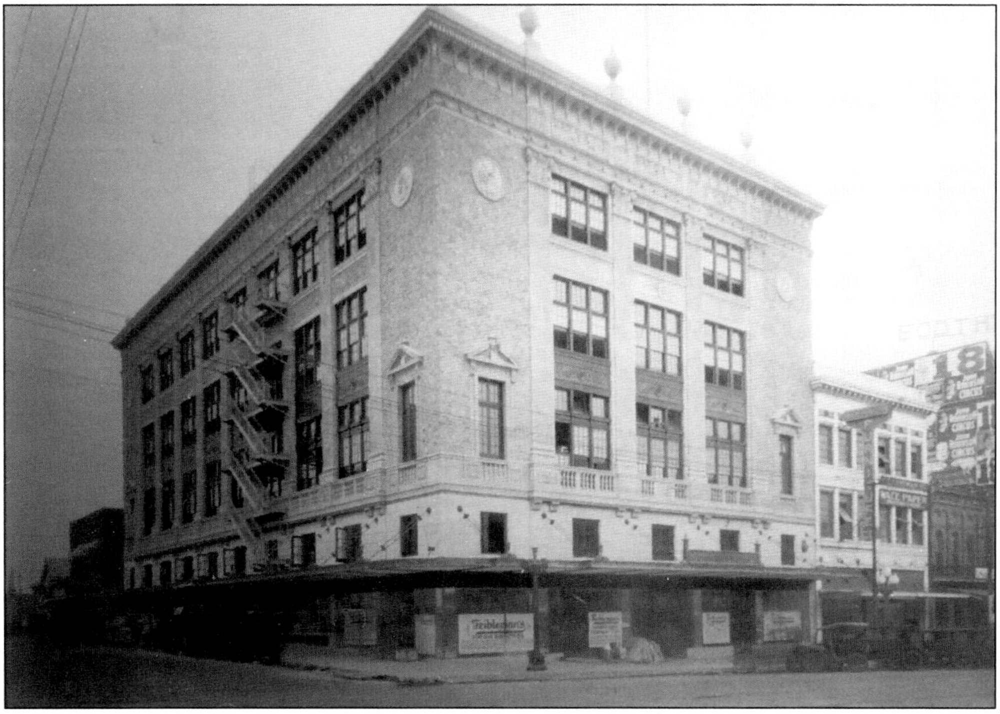

Pictured here is Feibleman's Department Store as it appeared in 1925. Located at Texas and Louisiana Streets, Feibleman's was the first store in Shreveport to offer credit cards and also the first to install an escalator. It later sold to Sears, Roebuck and Co.

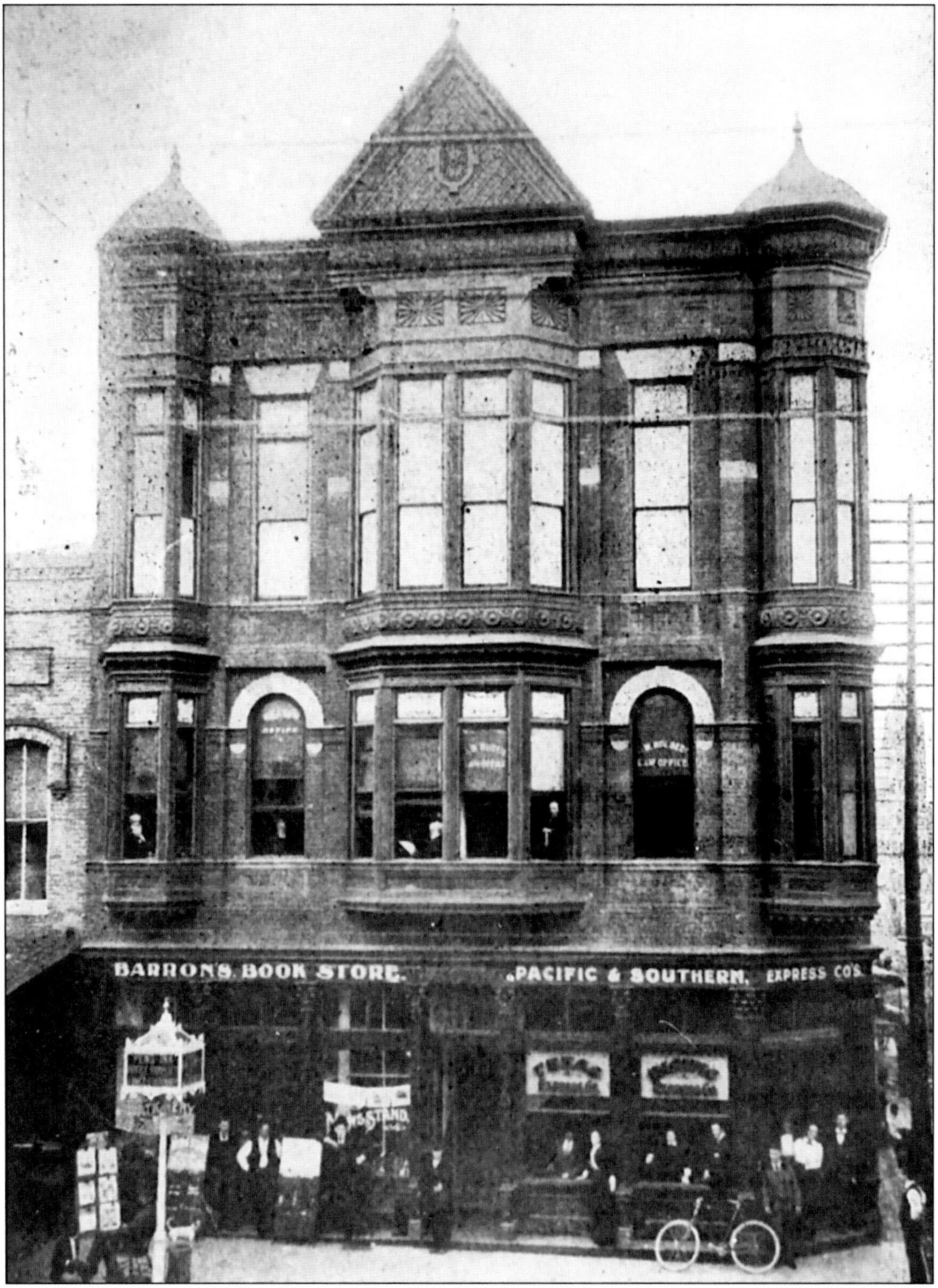

The Randall Building, designed by architect N.S. Allen, was typical of 1880s office structures in Shreveport. Its lower level housed a bookstore and ticket office, and its upper floors housed lawyers and physicians. It was demolished in the 1970s to build a parking garage. The Deposit Guaranty Tower, completed in 1987, today occupies the entire block.

The Marcus Building was built in 1902 and still stands at 711 Milam Street. This 1904 view shows the building as it originally appeared. When completed, this five-story building was the tallest privately owned structure in the city.

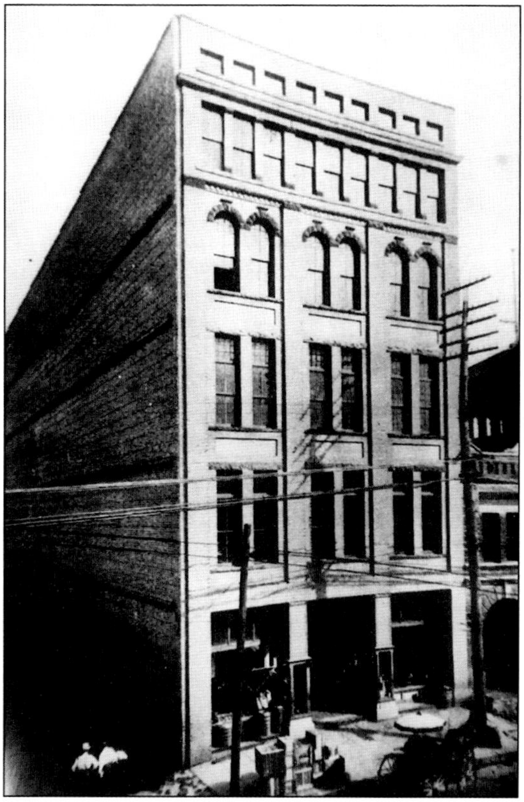

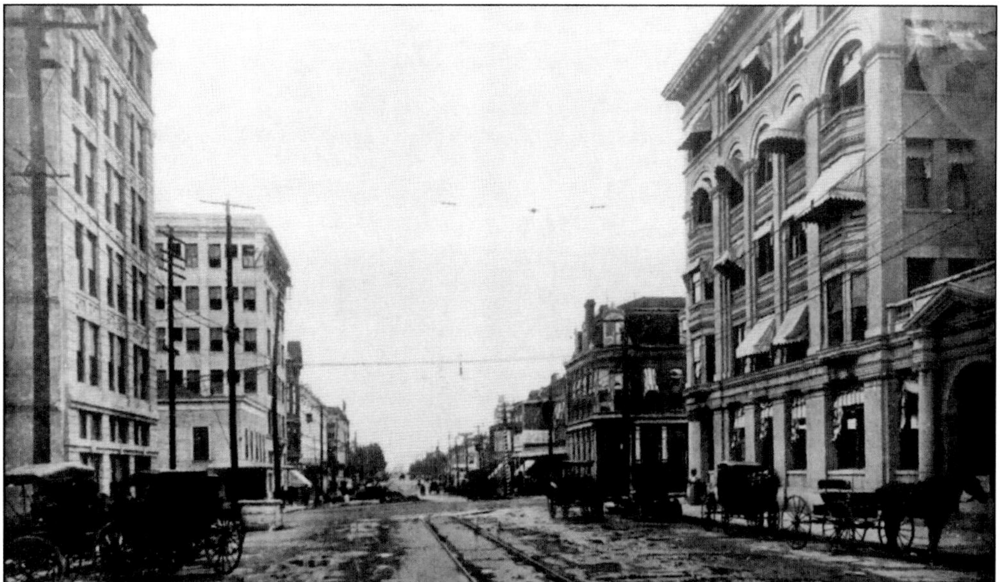

Banks occupied every corner of the Milam and Market Street intersection in 1909. From left to right are the American National Bank, the Continental Bank and Trust, the Commercial National Bank (with mansard roof), and the First National Bank.

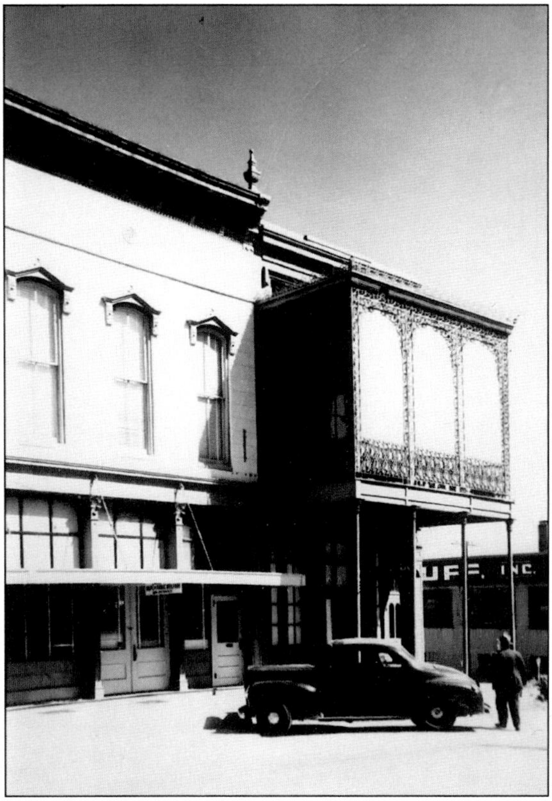

The cast-iron galleries of the building at right are reminiscent of New Orleans. Built as Tally's Bank in 1865, 525 Spring Street became home to the Jacobs Bank in 1877. Jacobs Bank became First National Bank in 1886, and is today Bank One. The Spring Street Historical Museum occupies this building today.

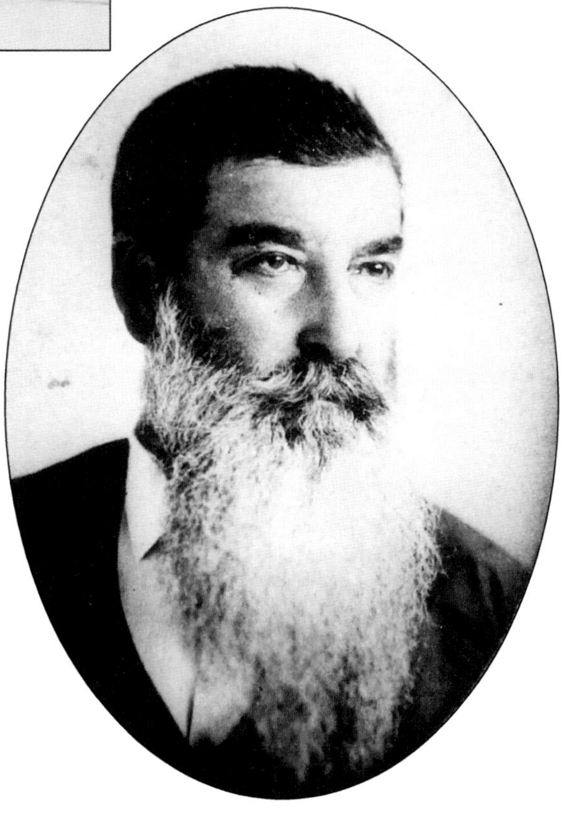

Edward Jacobs (see page 13) founded Jacobs Bank in 1877 after having built a successful grocery and dry goods business with his brother Benjamin. While president of First National Bank from 1886 to 1896, the bank grew to be the city's largest financial institution.

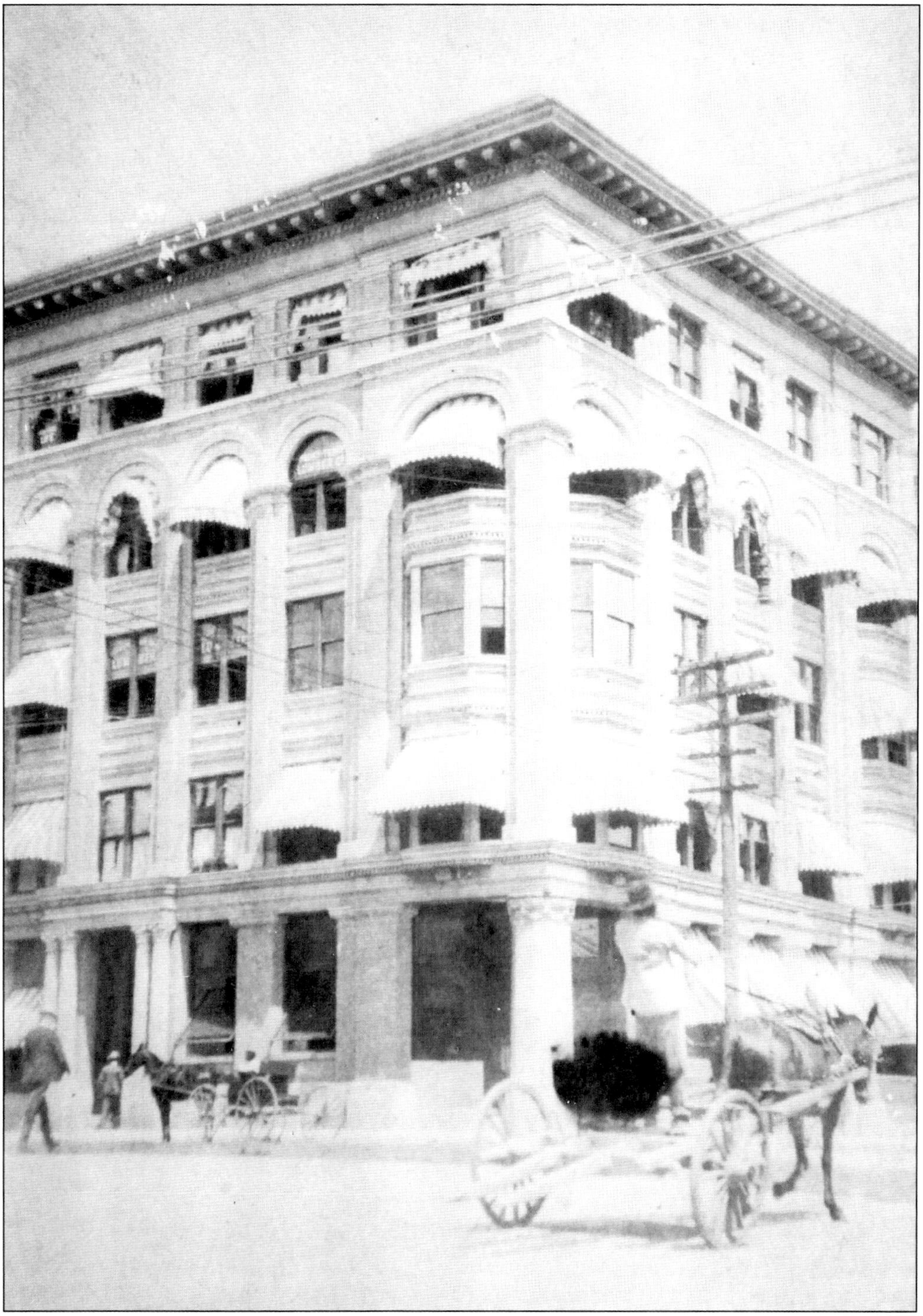

First National Bank's new building at Market and Milam Streets was completed in 1903 under the presidency of Walter Byron Jacobs (1855–1904). Note the traffic in this 1904 photograph by the Kaufman Studios. The structure still stands, though considerably remodeled as the Crystal Oil Company Building.

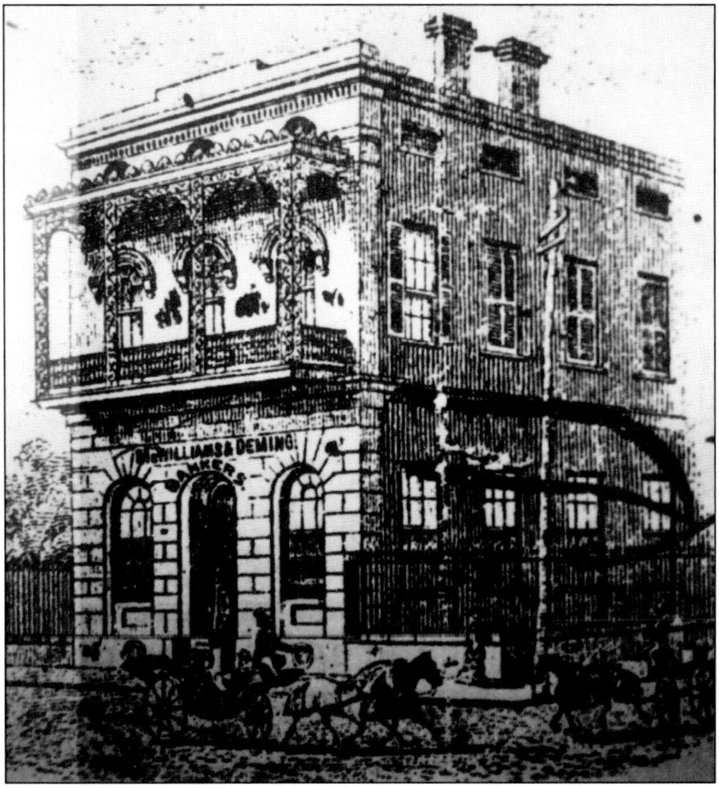

At the same corner of Market and Milam Streets, later occupied by First National Bank, stood the Citizens' Bank of Louisiana, built in 1859. Later the building housed McWilliams & Deming's Banking House.

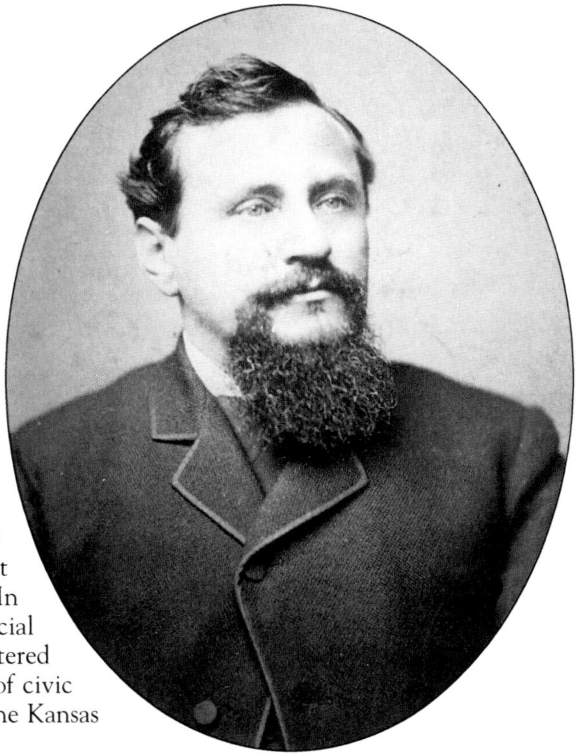

Captain Simon Levy Jr. (1839–1898) founded a private bank in 1887 and built the city's first modern bank building. In 1892 he took control of the Commercial National Bank, which had been chartered in 1886. Levy was a major benefactor of civic institutions and was vice-president of the Kansas City Southern Railroad.

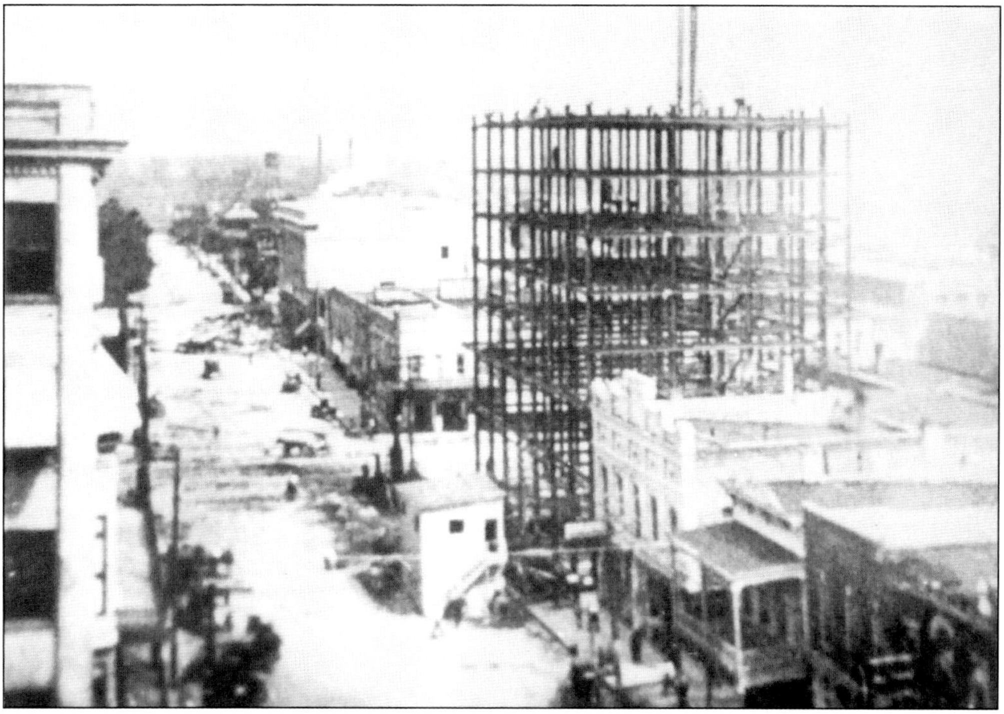

In 1910 Commercial National Bank built Shreveport's tallest building of the era at 509 Market Street. Seen under construction (above), the ten-story building, when completed (right), housed the bank until 1937. The old building still stands, though today it is dwarfed by surrounding structures.

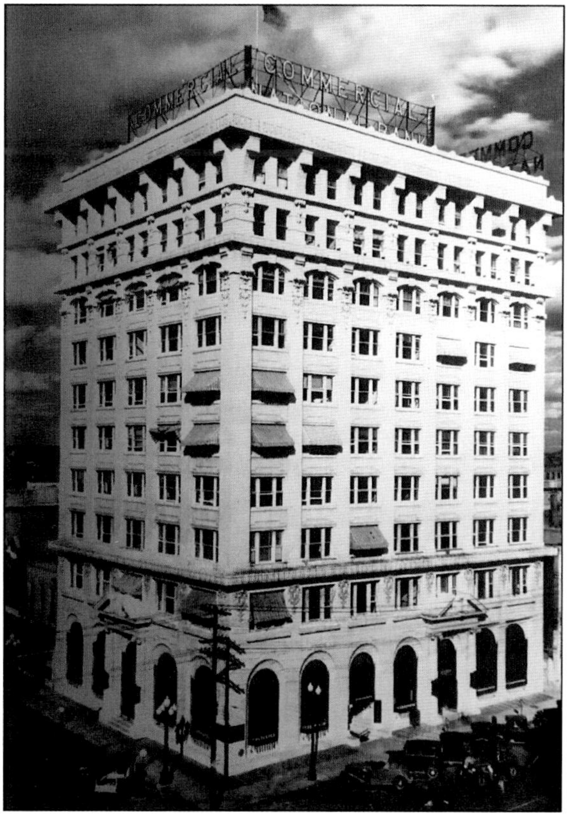

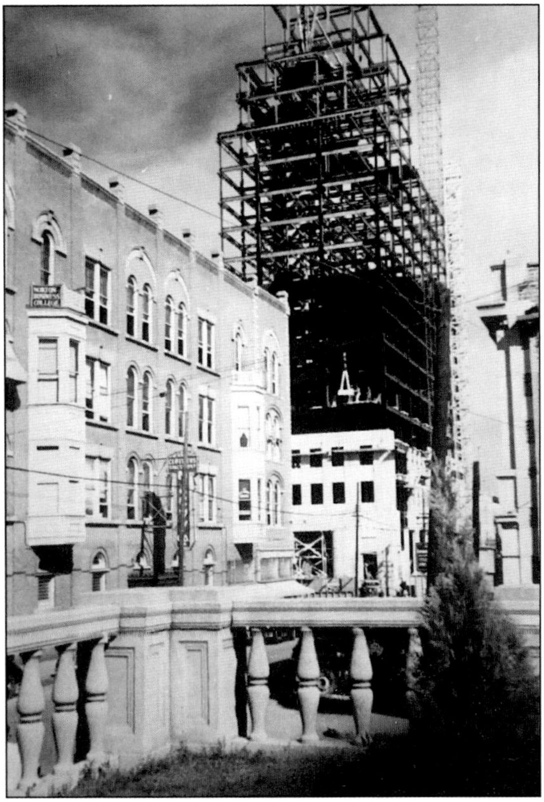

Work progressed on a new headquarters for Commercial National Bank at Texas and Edwards Streets in 1939 (left). Designed by the New York firm of McKim, Mead, and White, it took nearly three years to complete (below). Commercial National became Deposit Guaranty National Bank in 1997.

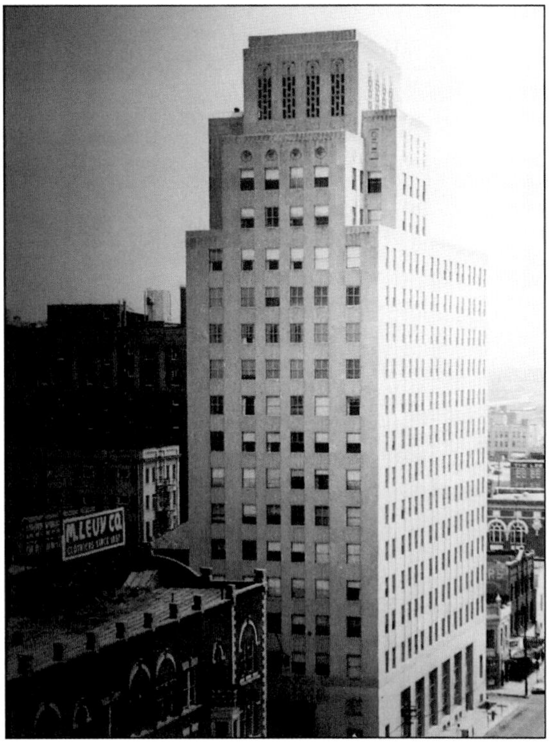

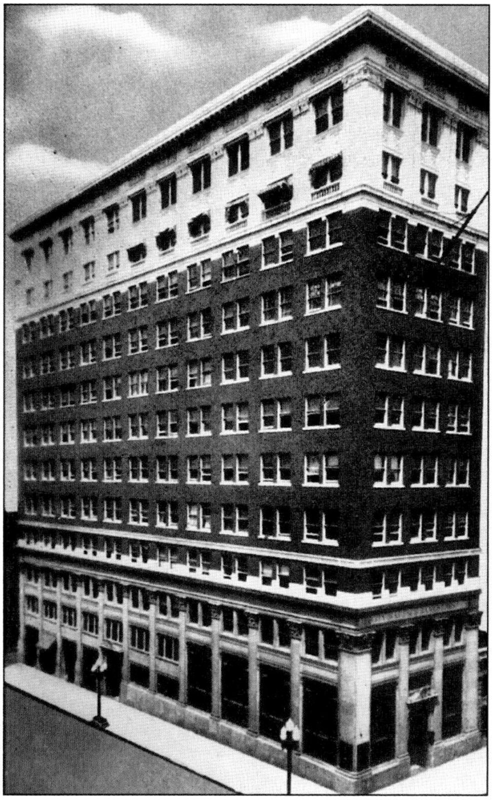

In 1917 the Merchants' Bank Building was erected at Milam and Market Streets, opposite First National Bank (right). It later housed City National Bank, City Savings Bank, and the Texas Eastern Company. In 1984 it was demolished by implosion (below).

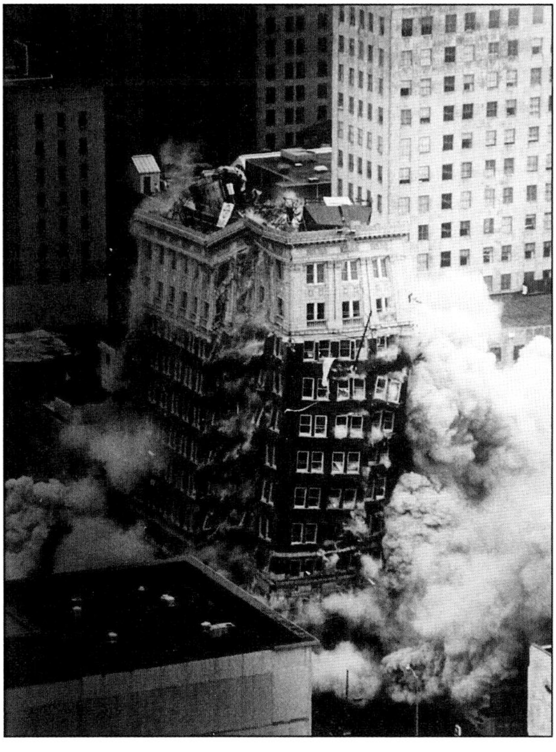

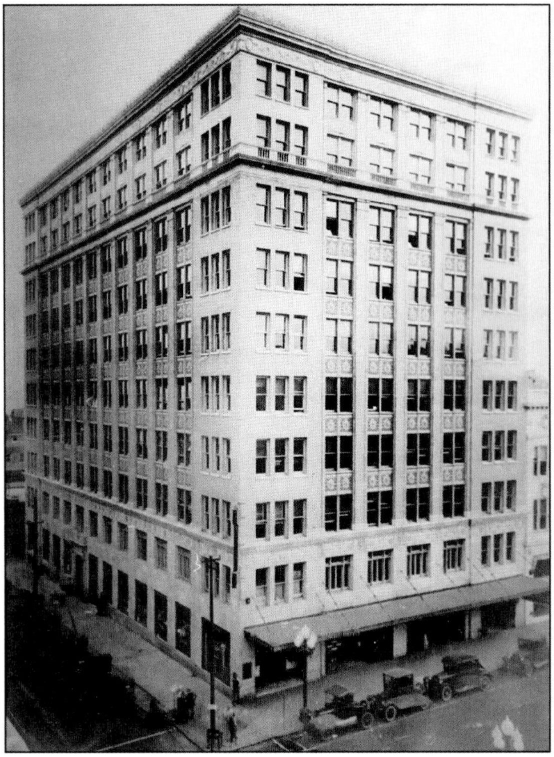

The Giddens-Lane Building was one of Shreveport's oil boom–era skyscrapers. Located opposite the Caddo Courthouse at Milam and Marshall Streets, it still appears much as it did in this 1925 view.

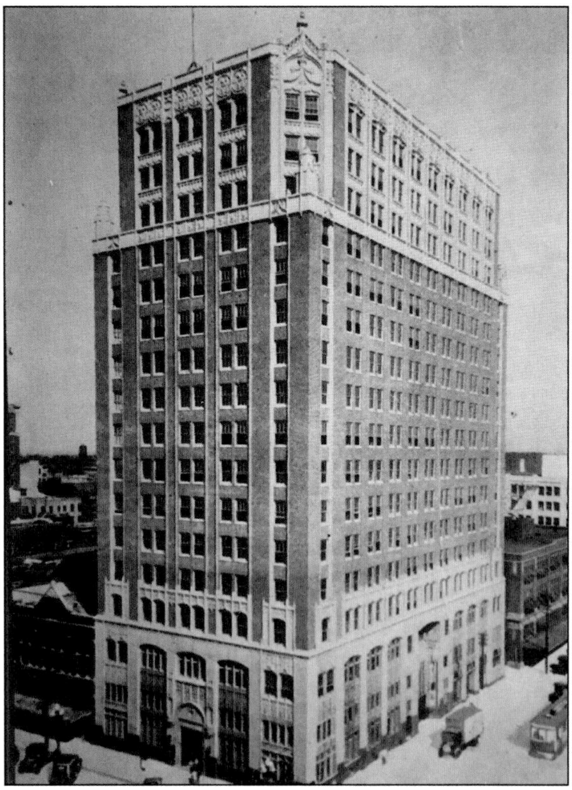

The Slattery Building, at Marshall and Texas Streets, was the tallest privately owned building in Louisiana when built in 1923. It remains a downtown landmark, though it is now dwarfed by surrounding structures.

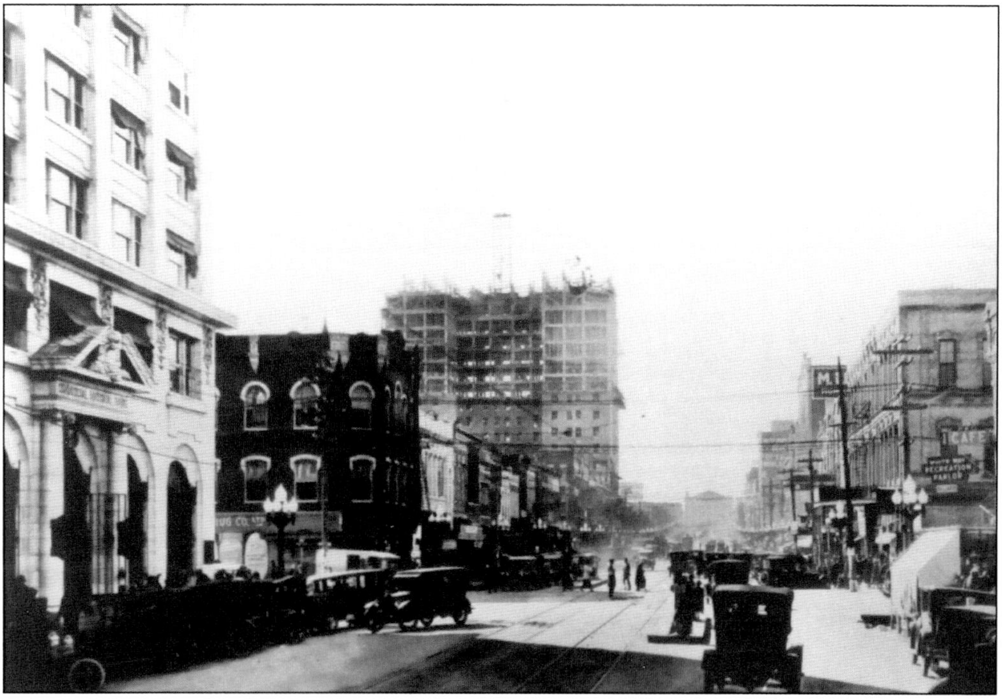

A 1923 photograph of Texas Street shows the Commercial National Bank at left and the Slattery Building under construction at center.

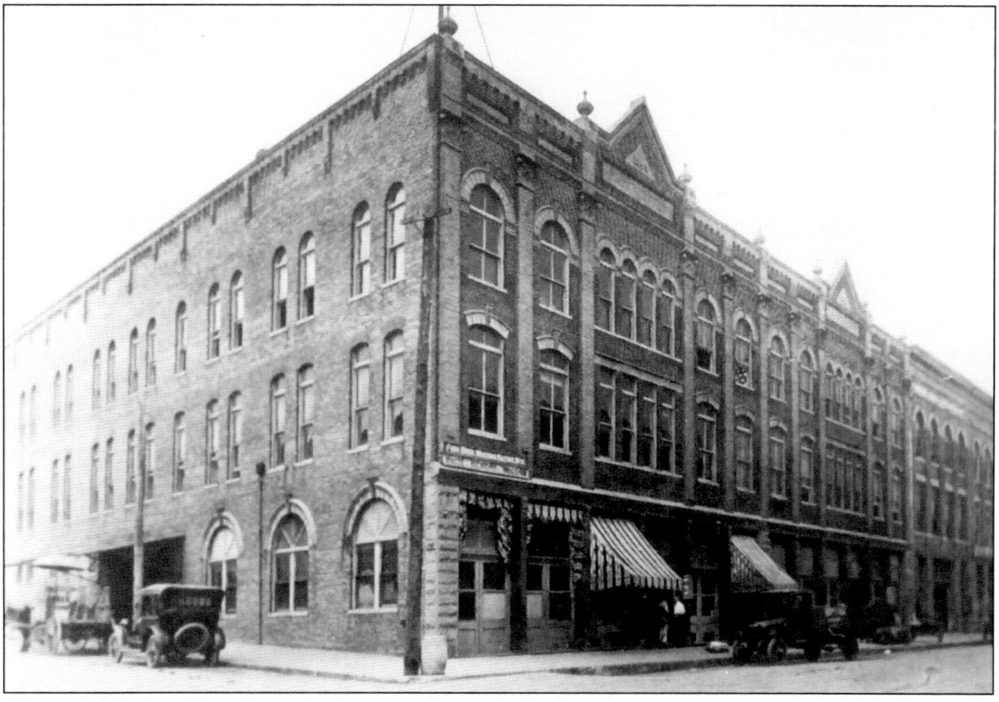

The 200 block of Crockett Street was photographed in the 1920s. Numerous large wholesale supply houses dealing in various commodities from auto parts to hardware to groceries occupied this block. None of the buildings still stands.

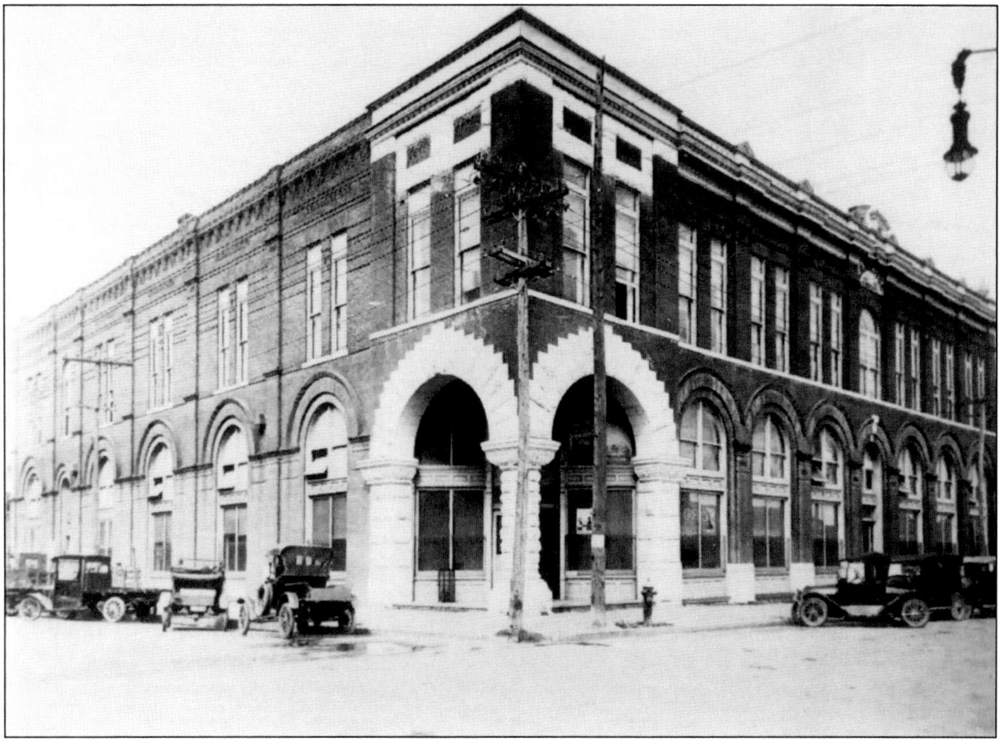

The Interstate Electric Company building at 300 Spring Street was typical of the large office/warehouse structures found near the riverfront early in the twentieth century. Almost none still stand.

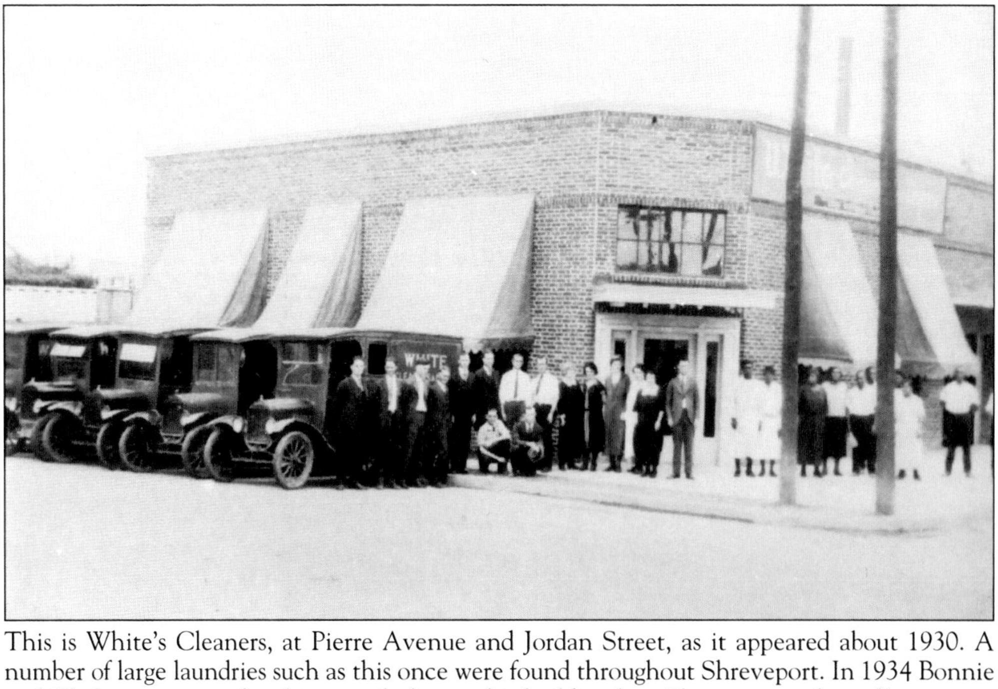

This is White's Cleaners, at Pierre Avenue and Jordan Street, as it appeared about 1930. A number of large laundries such as this once were found throughout Shreveport. In 1934 Bonnie and Clyde were spotted picking up clothes at this building by a Shreveport police officer.

Four

Residential Life

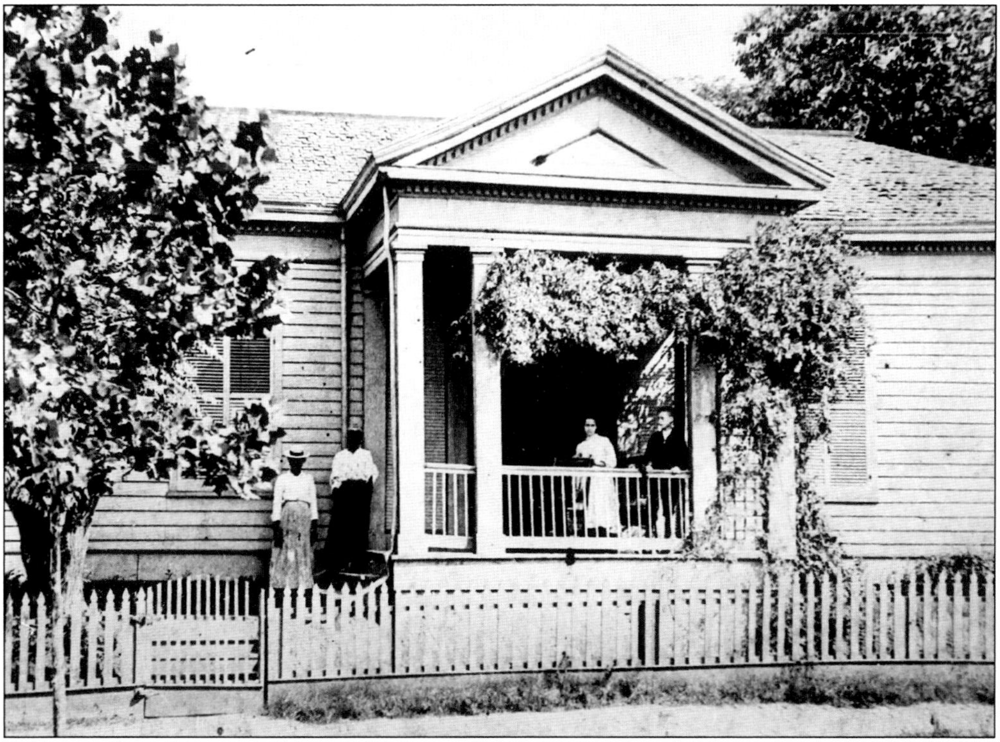

Typical of Shreveport homes of the nineteenth century was this house at the southeast corner of Travis and McNeill Streets. The home was built before the Civil War and was torn down in 1907 to make way for the First Baptist Church, itself now long demolished.

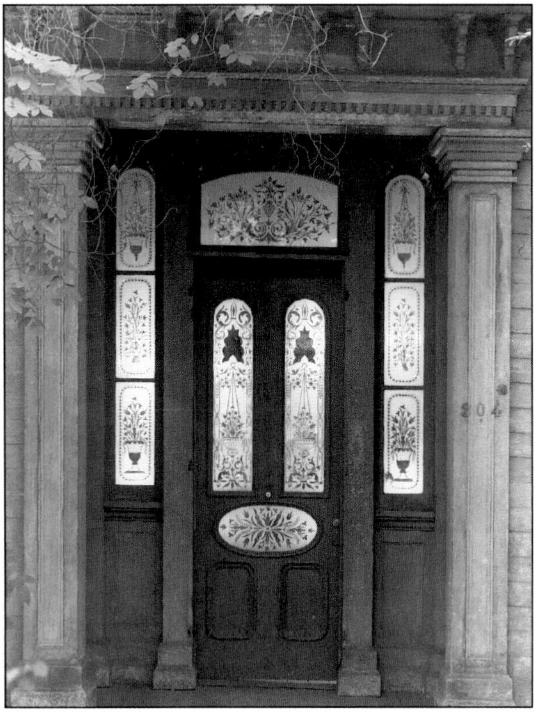

At the southwest corner of McNeill and Fannin Streets once stood the Lindsay-Scofield House, built in 1872. This view of its front door was made in 1949, seven years before the house was moved to its present location on Woodlawn Avenue, where it is known as "The Symphony House."

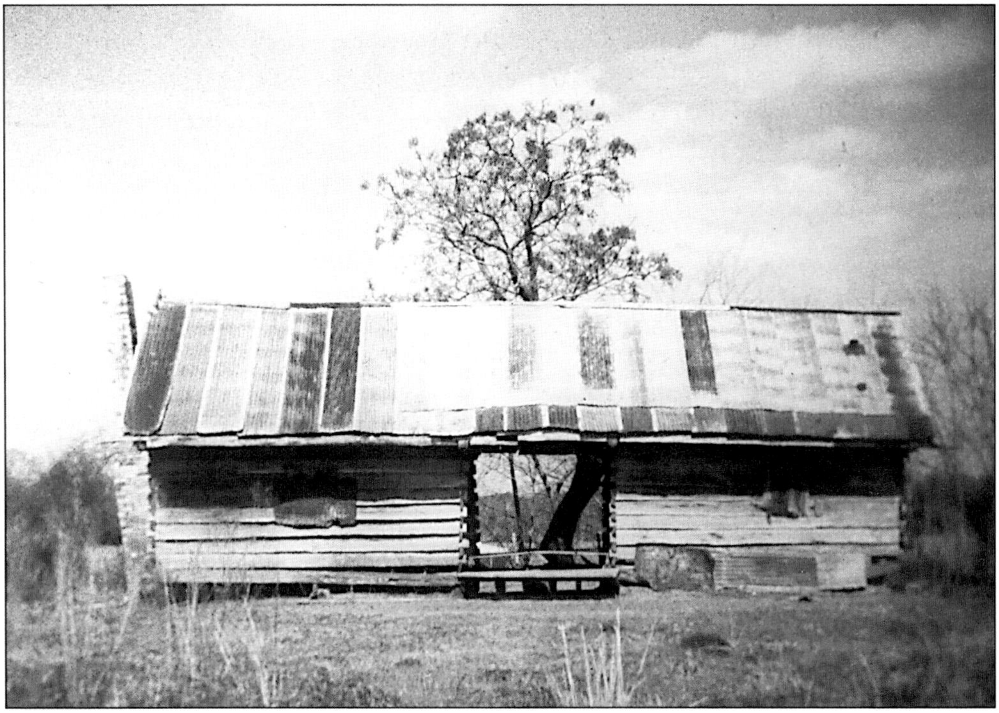

Many early settlers in northwestern Louisiana built two-room log cabins with an open, or "dogtrot" passage down the middle. Many of the first houses in Shreveport looked like this 1830s cabin, originally located at nearby Keithville and now at the LSU-Shreveport Pioneer Heritage Center.

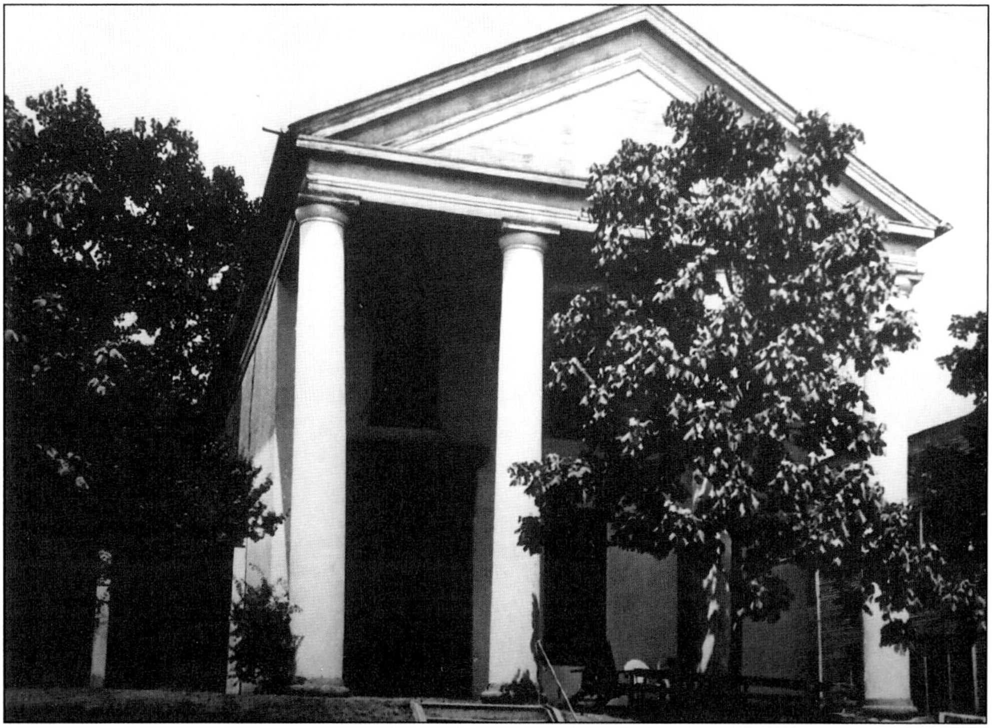

Shown here are two types of antebellum Shreveport houses. At top is the Howell house, built in 1849 at Spring and Lake Streets. It stood until the early 1960s. At bottom is the Henry Levy house at Cotton and Spring Streets, built around 1836 as a dogtrot cabin and subsequently remodeled by the Levys after they acquired it in 1852. The home burned in 1933.

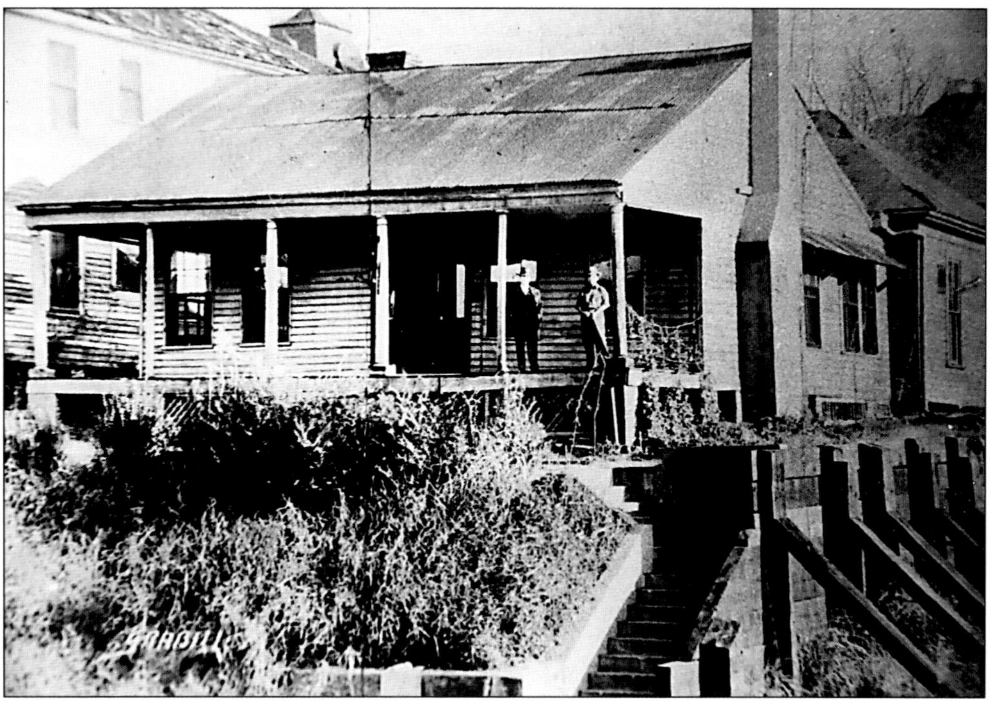

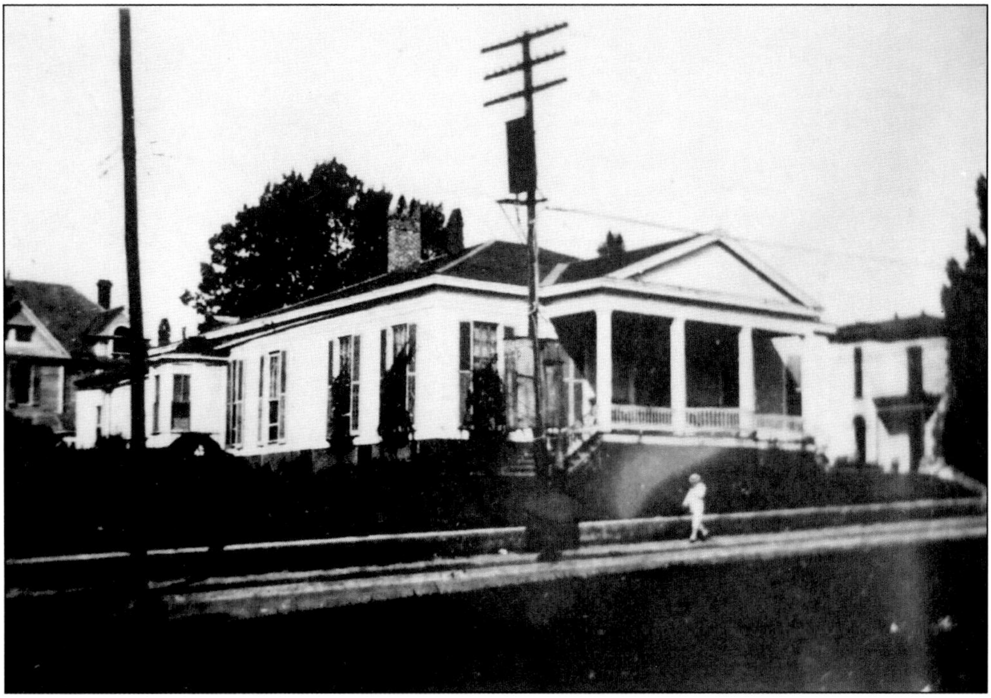

This Neo-Classical home at 400 Edwards Street (above) was built about 1848 by Thomas T. Williamson, a co-founder of Shreveport. It was later bought by merchant Henry Dreyfuss, whose family lived there until 1922, when the house was demolished to build the old Shreve Memorial Library (below). Above the library's roof can be seen the antebellum Hicks mansion and Holy Trinity Catholic Church, built in 1896.

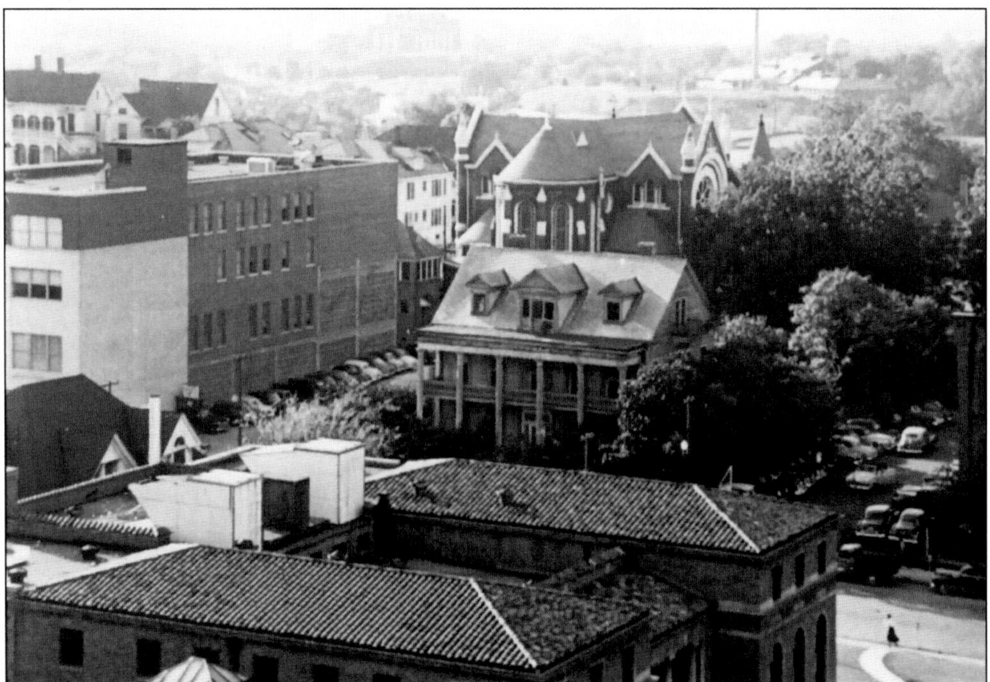

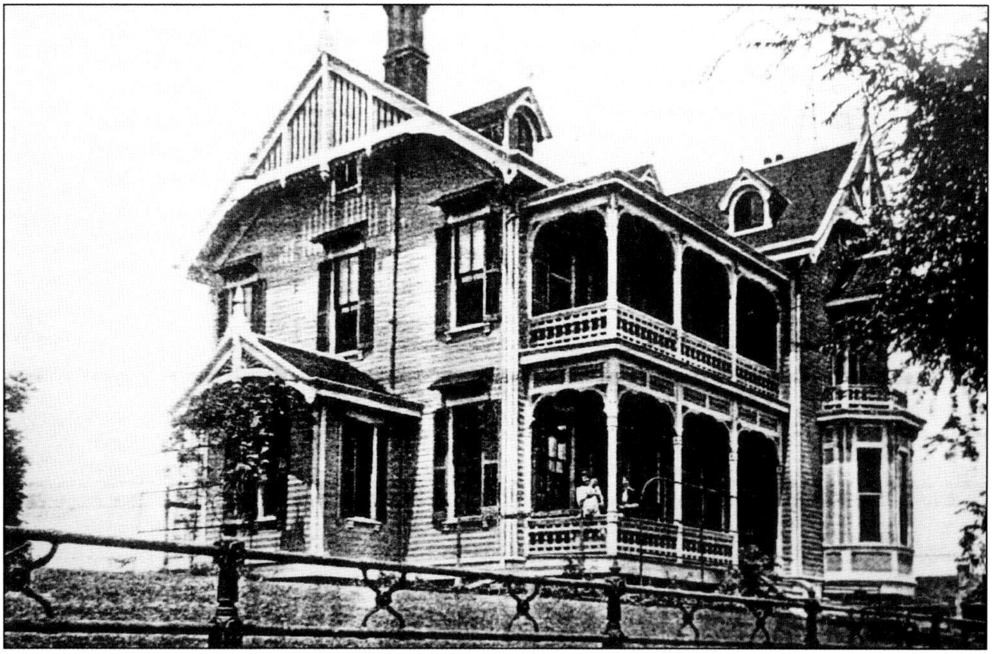

At top is the home of Mayor Samuel A. Dickson at Caddo and Edwards Streets, 1885. At bottom is the George S. Dickson house at Stoner Avenue and Coty Street, 1886. The Samuel Dickson house is gone, but the George Dickson house still stands, though much remodeled and twice moved since 1939. It is now off Leonard Road in south Shreveport.

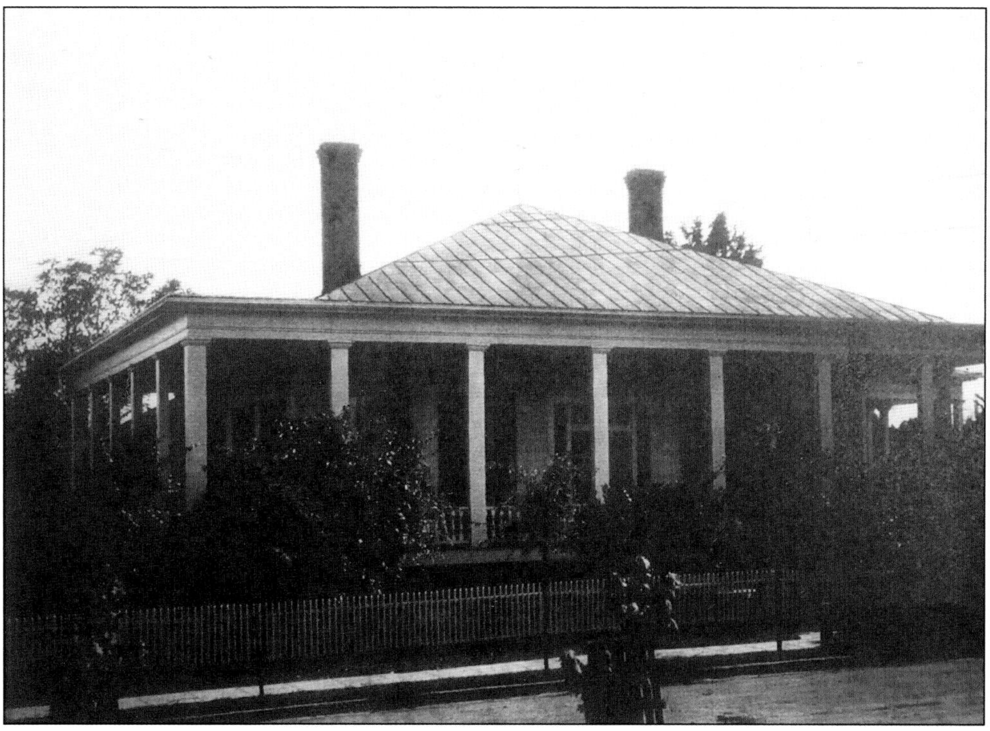

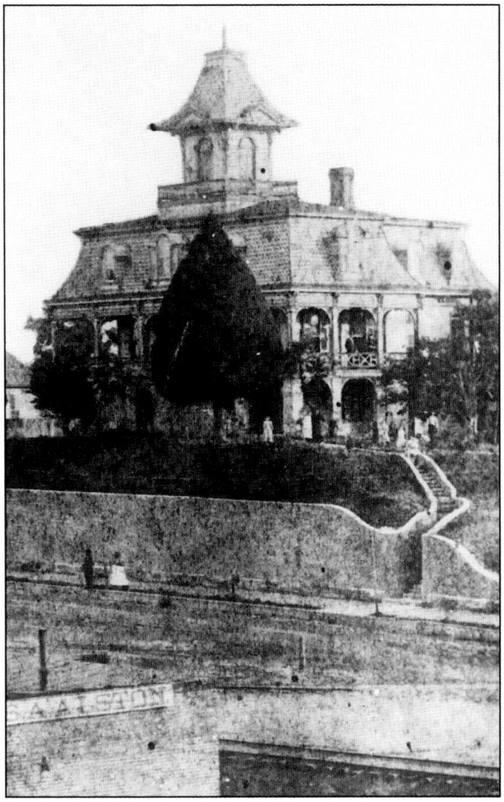

The S.J. Ziegler house (left), built in 1870 at Commerce and Lake Streets, sat high atop the bluff overlooking Red River. From its widow's walk was a commanding view of the river and the city. The T.H. Morris house (below) stood nearby at Spring and Lake Streets. Built in 1886, it burned in 1935, though the shell of the house was salvaged and rebuilt on Lake Bistineau.

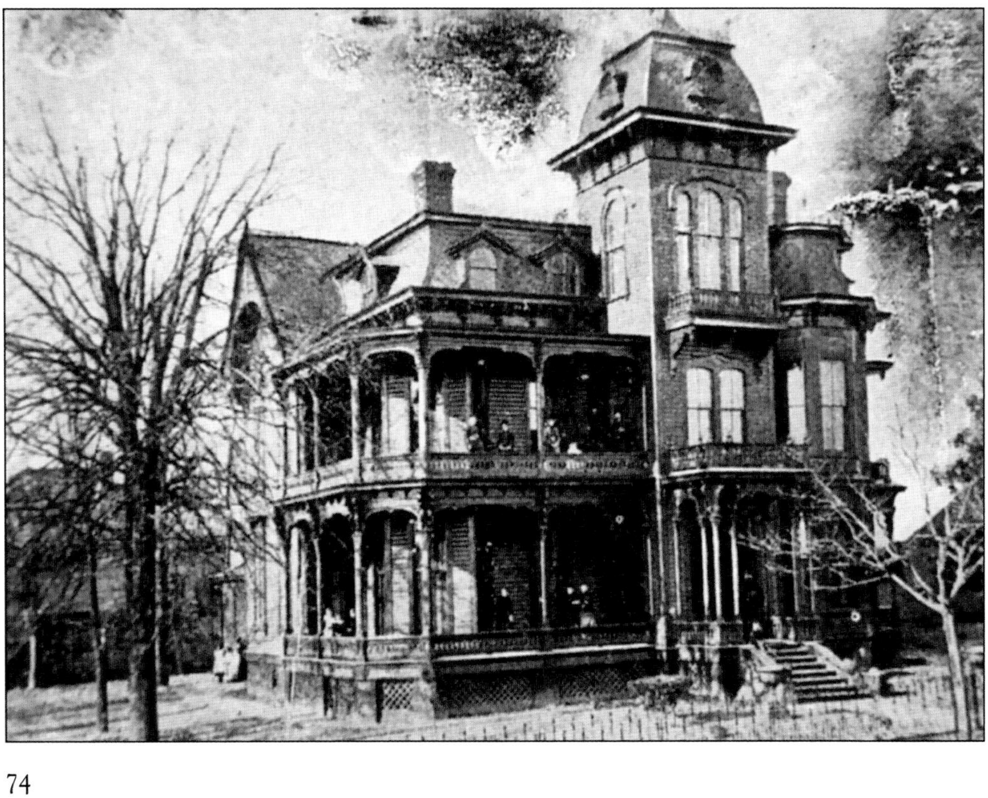

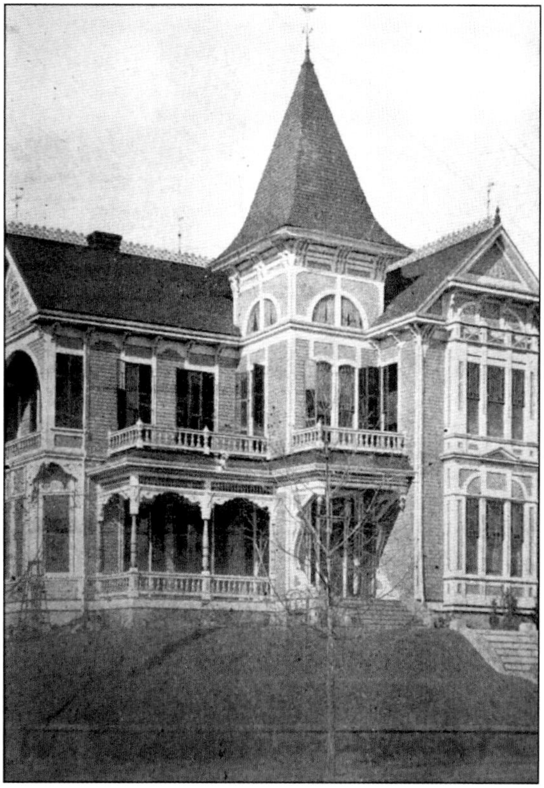

The Howard F. Doll residence (right), known as "The Doll House," stood at Fannin and McNeill Streets from 1888 to 1971. Designed by N.S. Allen, its porch was later remodeled into a curving gallery. Another Allen design was the L.R. Logan mansion (below) at 725 Austin Place, built in 1887. It still stands, though minus its corner gazebo.

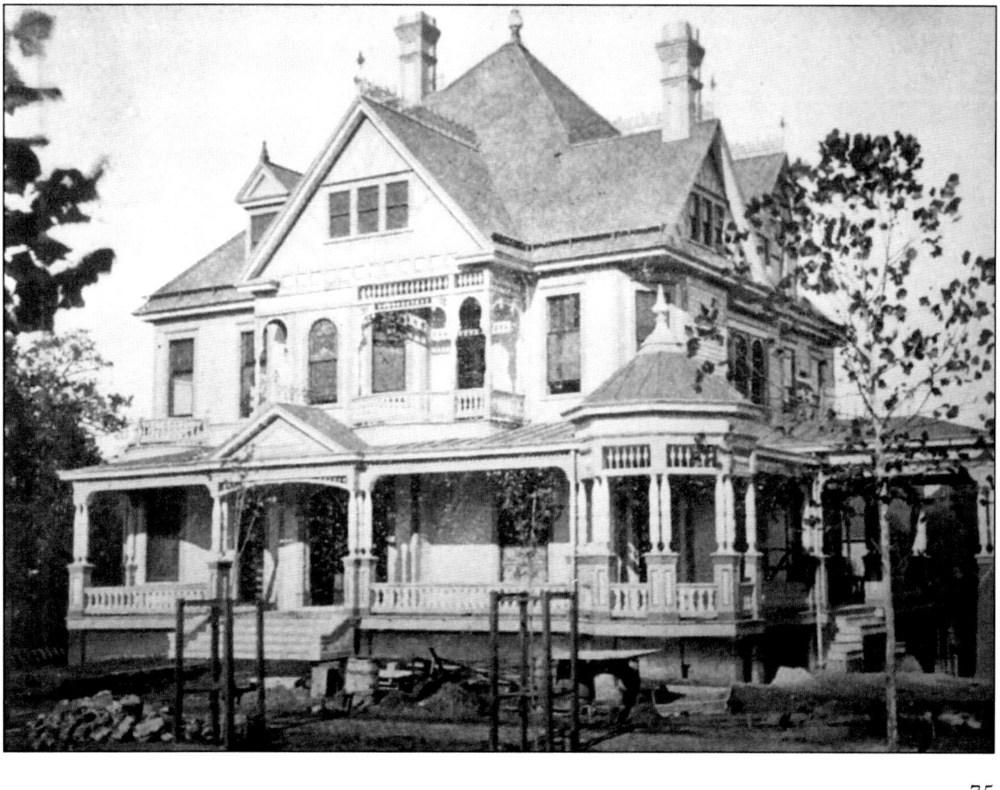

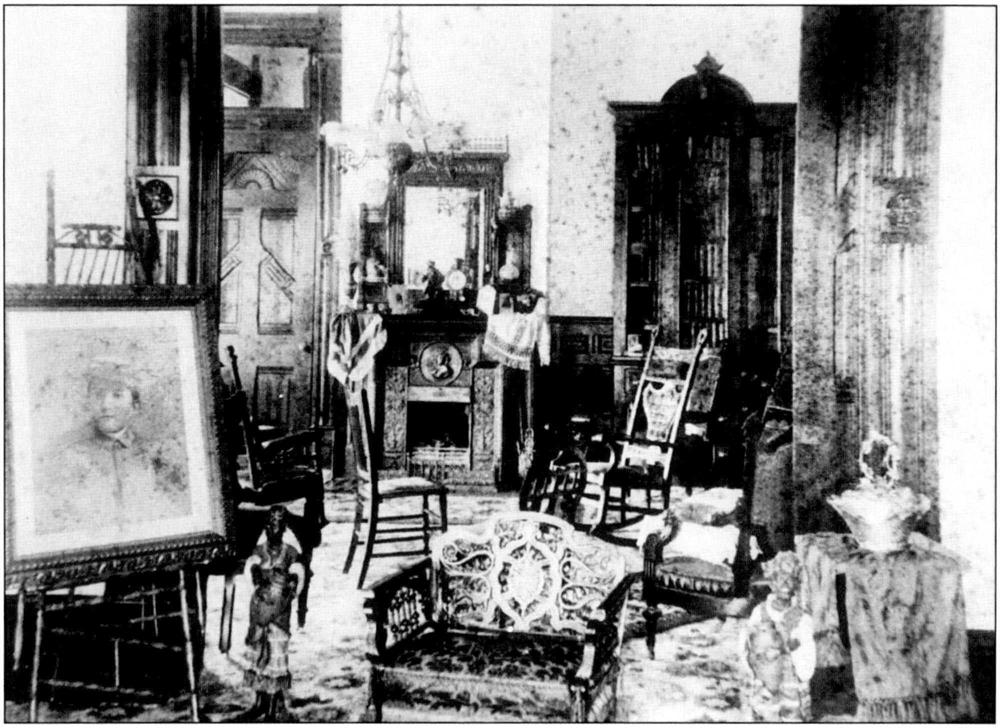

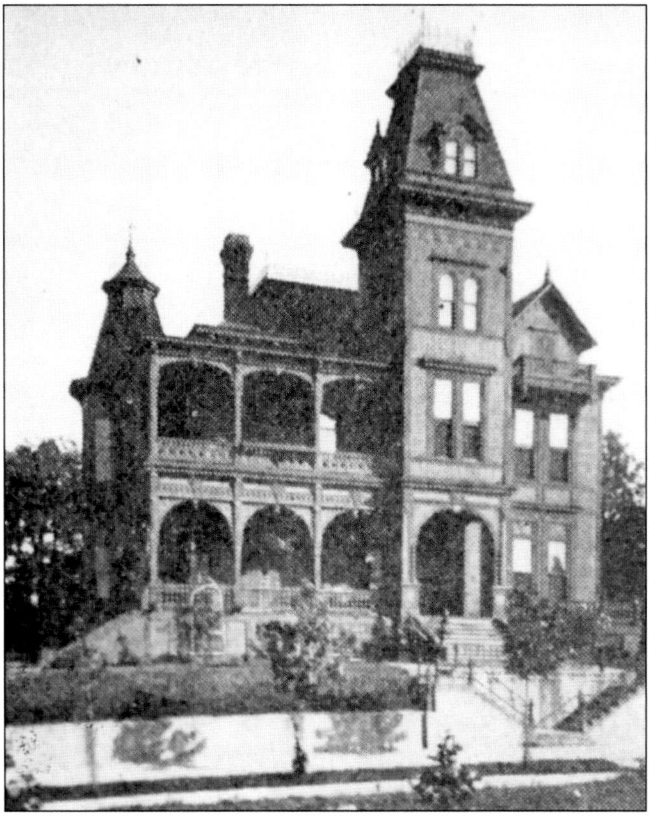

Victorian interiors tended to be just as elaborate as exteriors. At top is a parlor in the home of banker W.B. Jacobs at 939 Jordan Street in 1897. The Cathedral of St. John Berchmans replaced it in 1928. To the left is the home of grocer and cotton factor W.F. Taylor at 218 Lake Street. Taylor's home was demolished in the late 1930s.

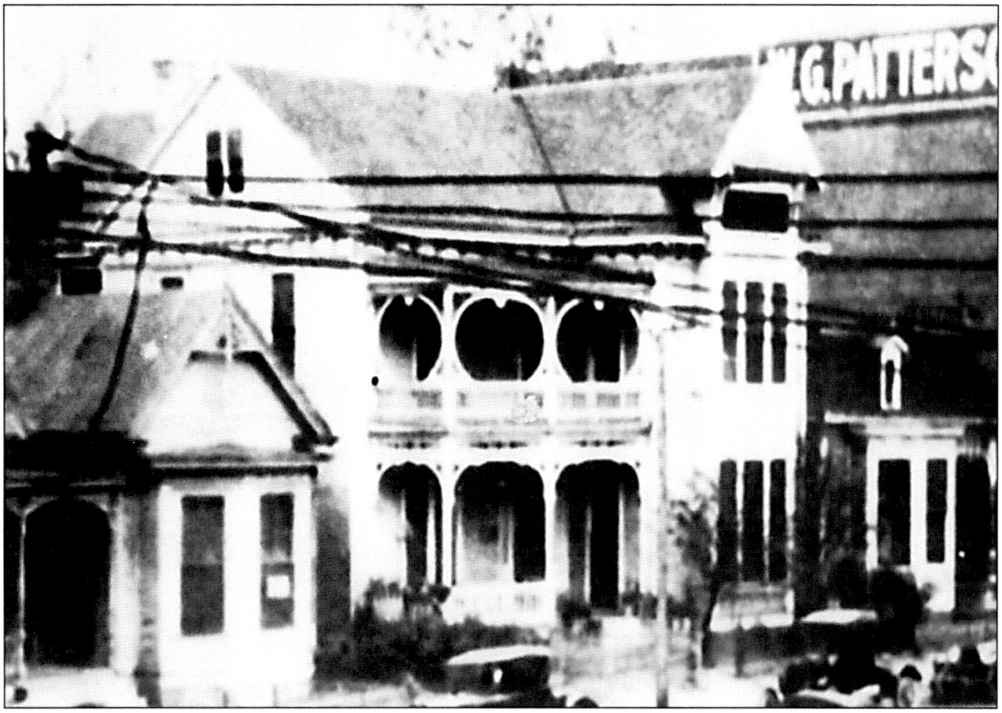

Above is a detail from a 1920s view of the 400 block of Milam Street, showing the home of former mayor Andrew Querbes shortly before its demolition. Below is the Slattery House at Fairfield Avenue and Dalzell Street, built in 1903 and designed by architect N.S. Allen. It is one of only two known remaining Allen-designed homes in the city.

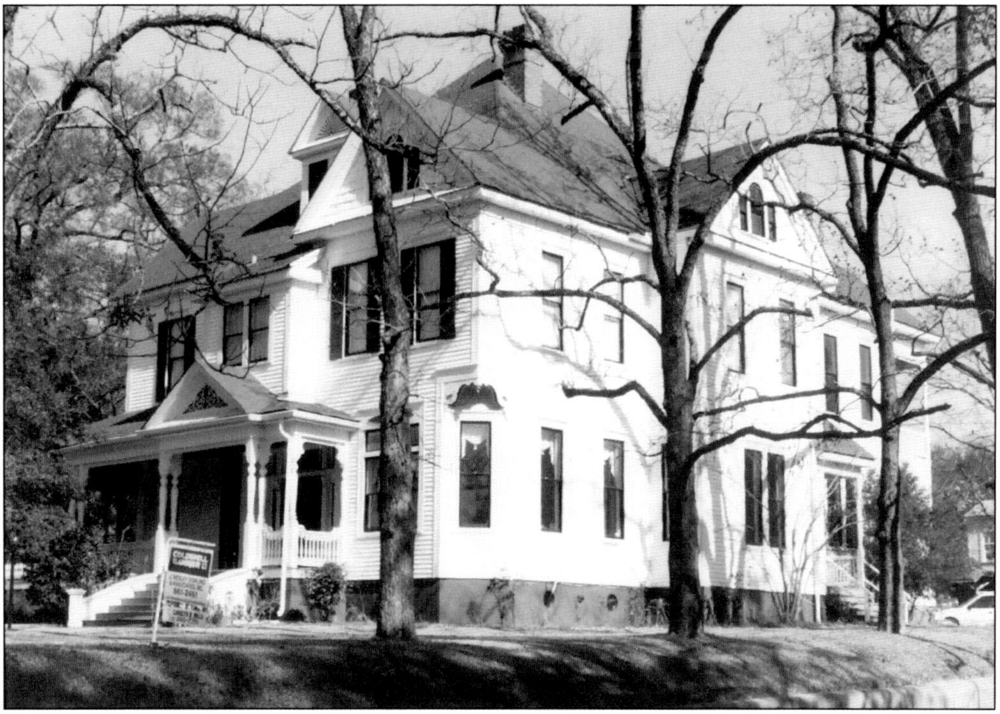

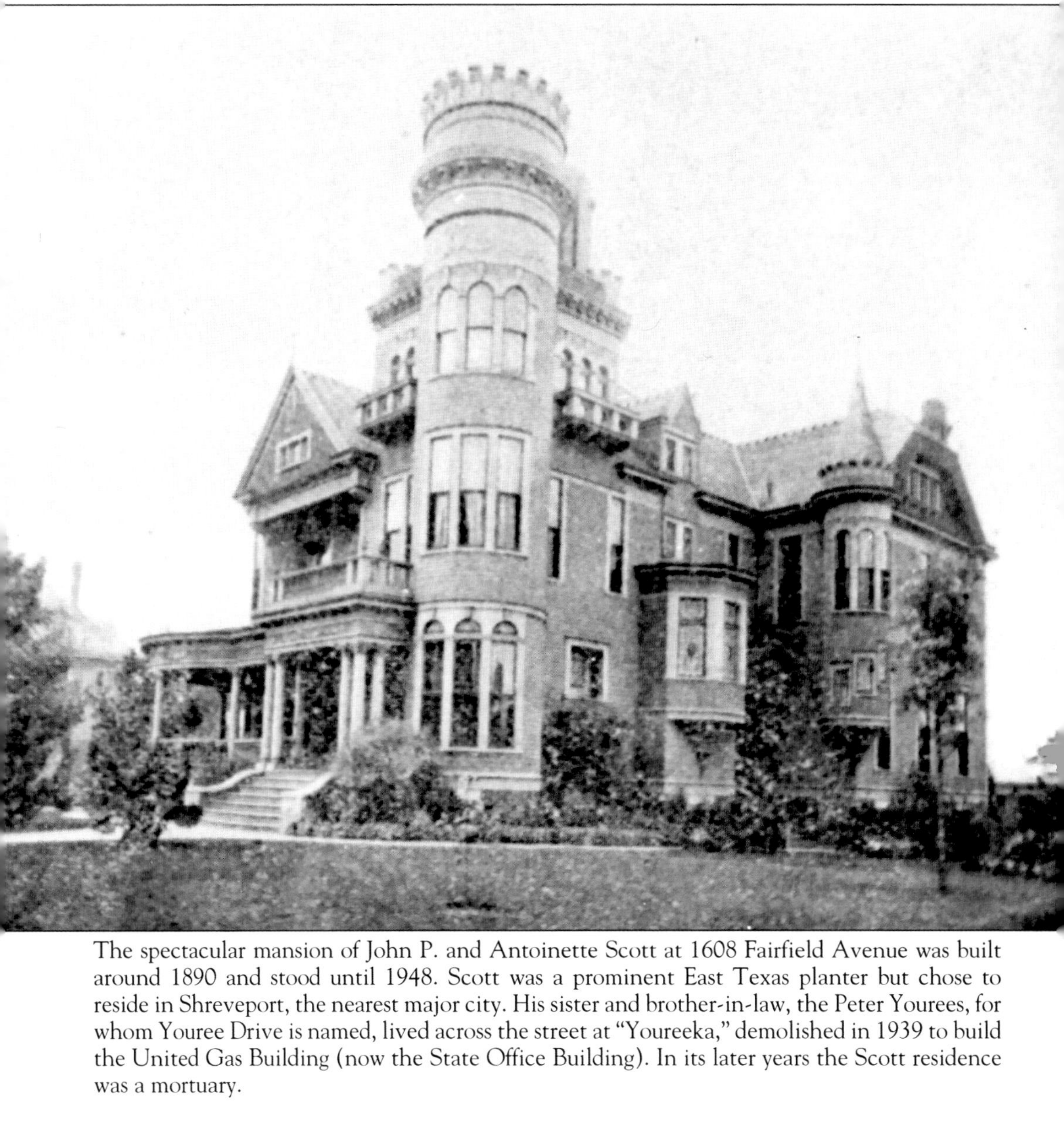

The spectacular mansion of John P. and Antoinette Scott at 1608 Fairfield Avenue was built around 1890 and stood until 1948. Scott was a prominent East Texas planter but chose to reside in Shreveport, the nearest major city. His sister and brother-in-law, the Peter Yourees, for whom Youree Drive is named, lived across the street at "Youreeka," demolished in 1939 to build the United Gas Building (now the State Office Building). In its later years the Scott residence was a mortuary.

"Curraghmuir," the James Martin Foster house, was built in the 1870s, though the estate itself predated the Civil War. Part of the grounds became home to the Confederate Memorial Medical Center in 1953. A short time later the house was removed to build the adjoining nursing school.

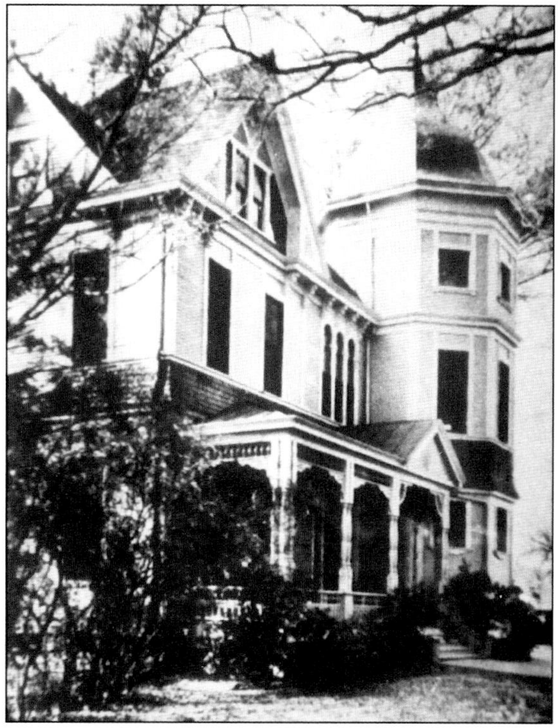

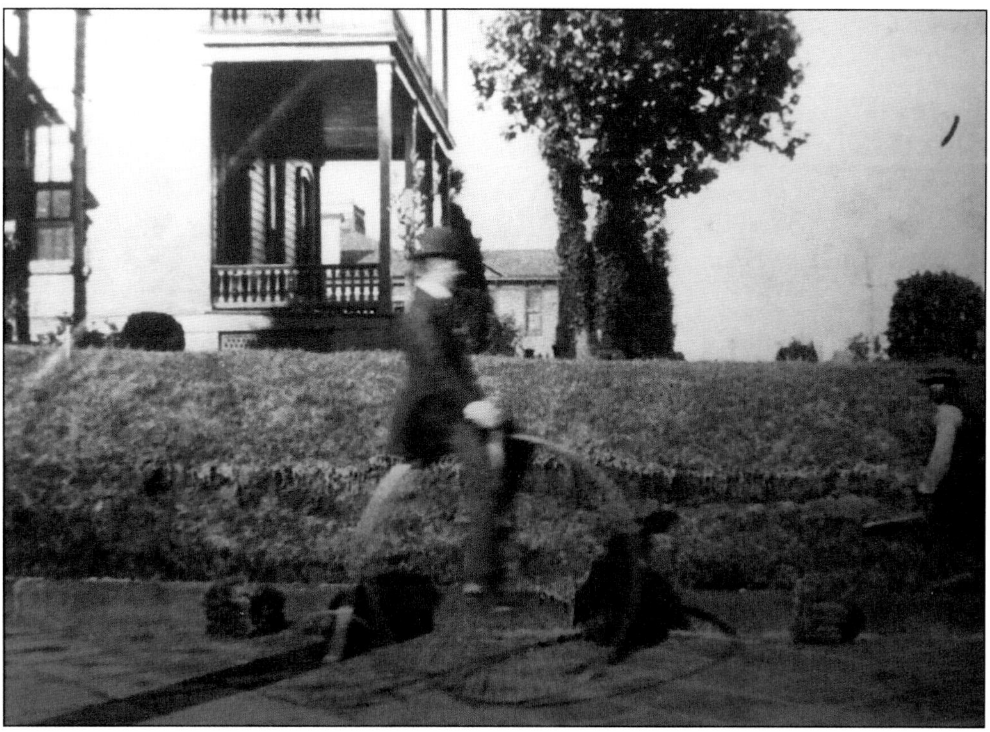

A cyclist whizzes down the 300 block of McNeill Street in the 1890s. In the background is the Kahn home, an antebellum residence long ago demolished. It stood at the southeast corner of the 300 block, where McNeill intersects with Travis Street.

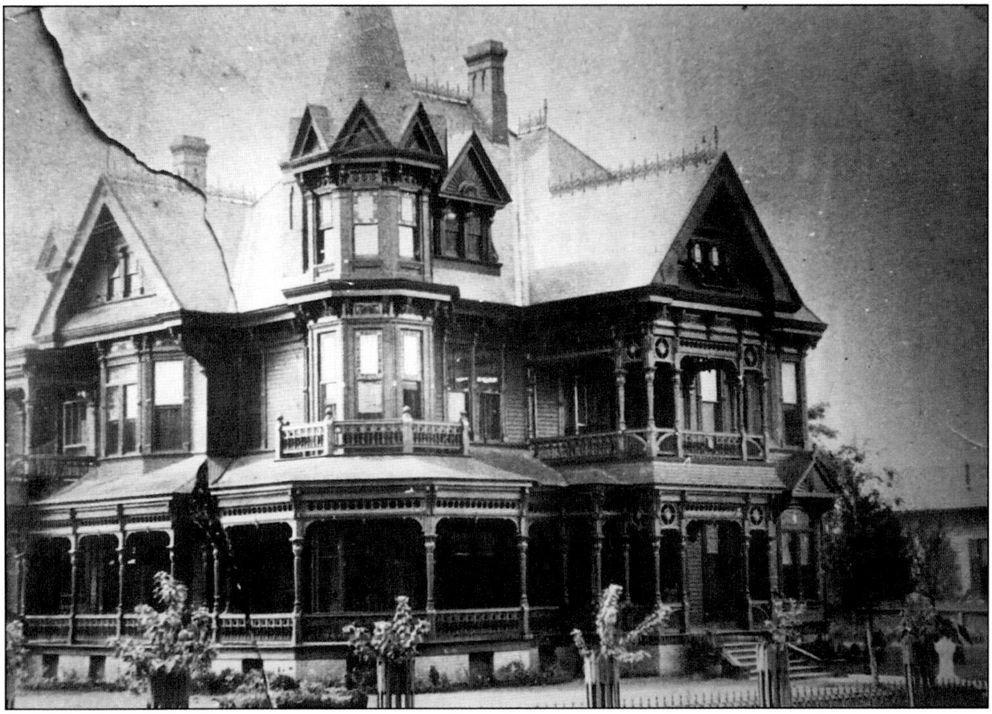

This is the imposing mansion of Edward and Palestine Jacobs at Travis and McNeill Streets. Built in 1886 on the site of the family's earlier home, it stood until 1923, when it was removed to build the Central YMCA.

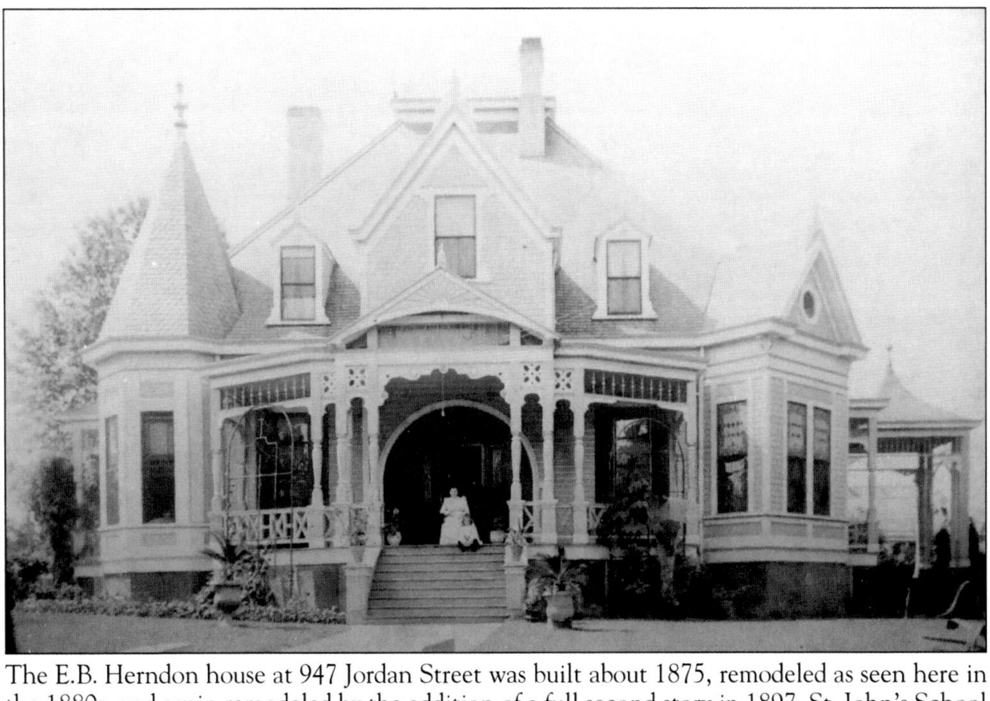

The E.B. Herndon house at 947 Jordan Street was built about 1875, remodeled as seen here in the 1880s, and again remodeled by the addition of a full second story in 1897. St. John's School occupies the site today.

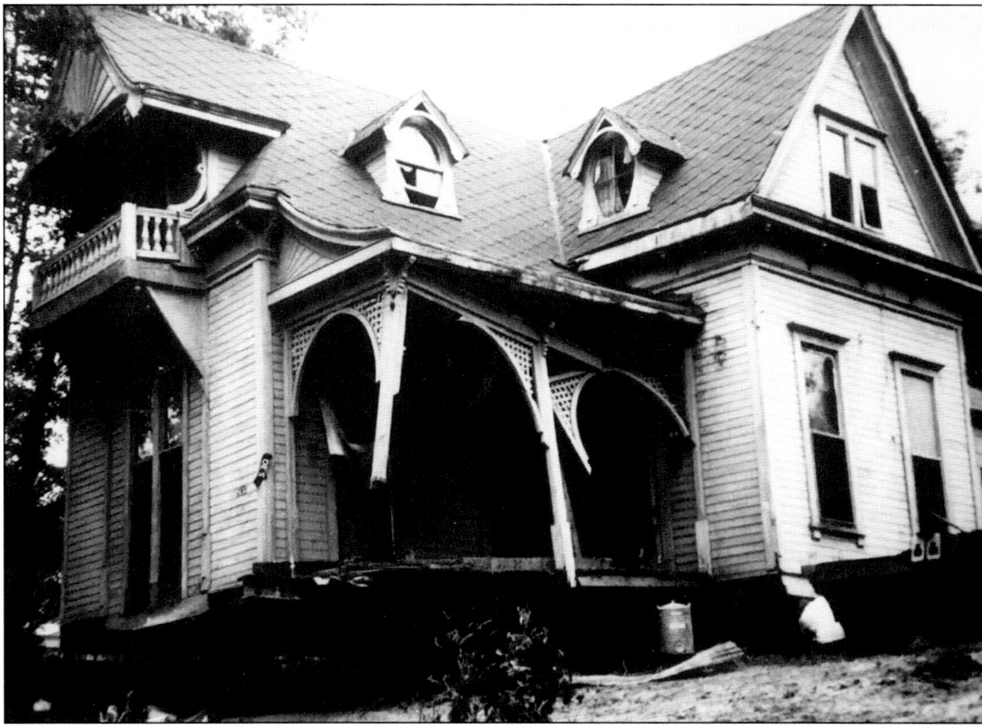

Here are two views of the Christian house, which was built in 1883 at Christian and Jewell Streets. Later moved to Oakland Street and again to Austin Place at Oakland, where it stands today, the house is seen above in an advanced state of deterioration in 1976 and below as it appears now. It has been used by nationally noted graphic artist and Shreveport native J.K. Potter as a model for his Neo-Gothic illustrations.

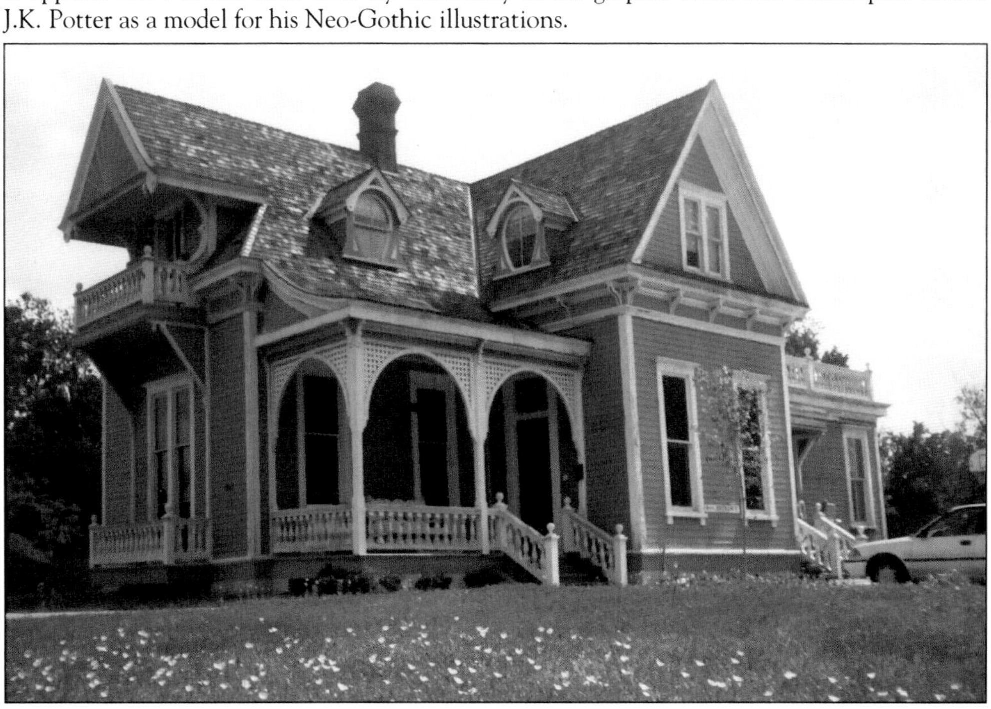

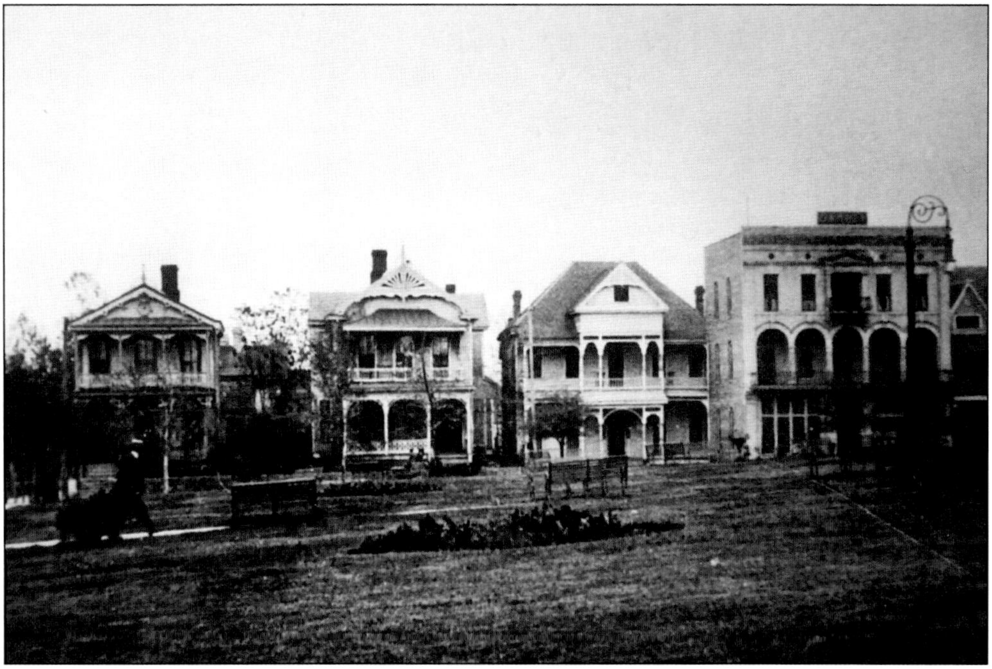

This is a view of the 500 block of Milam Street as seen from across the Courthouse Square around 1900. Today the Lane, Giddens, and Rubenstein buildings occupy the sites of the houses and lone commercial building seen in this photograph.

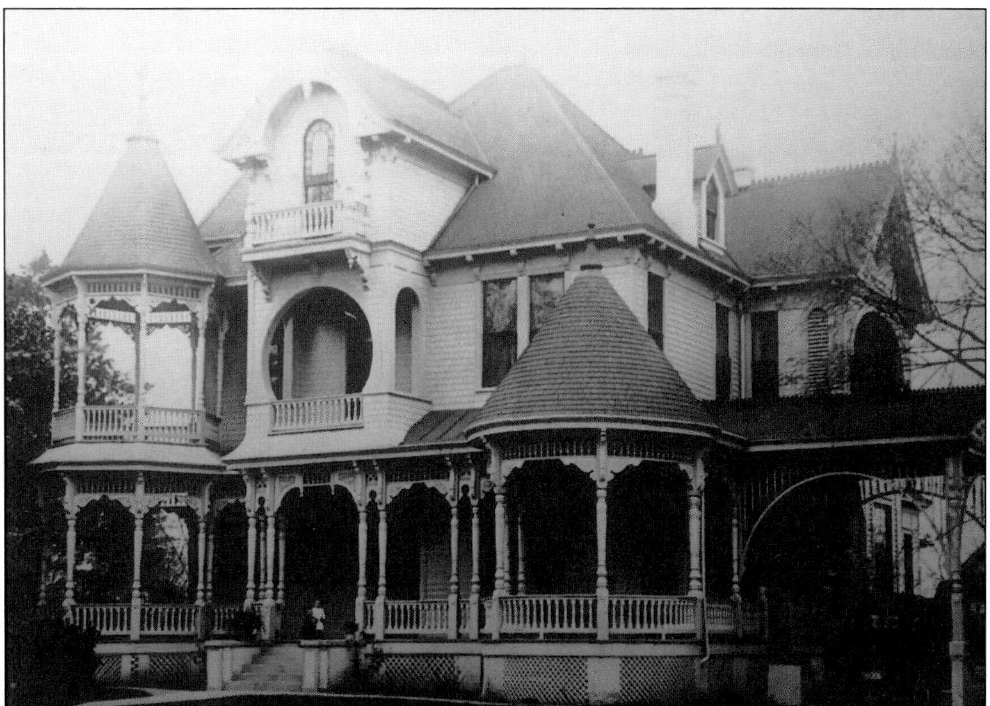

Shown here is the A.J. Peavy house in the 900 block of Jordan Street about 1920. Built in the 1890s, it was removed in 1925 to make way for the First Presbyterian Church.

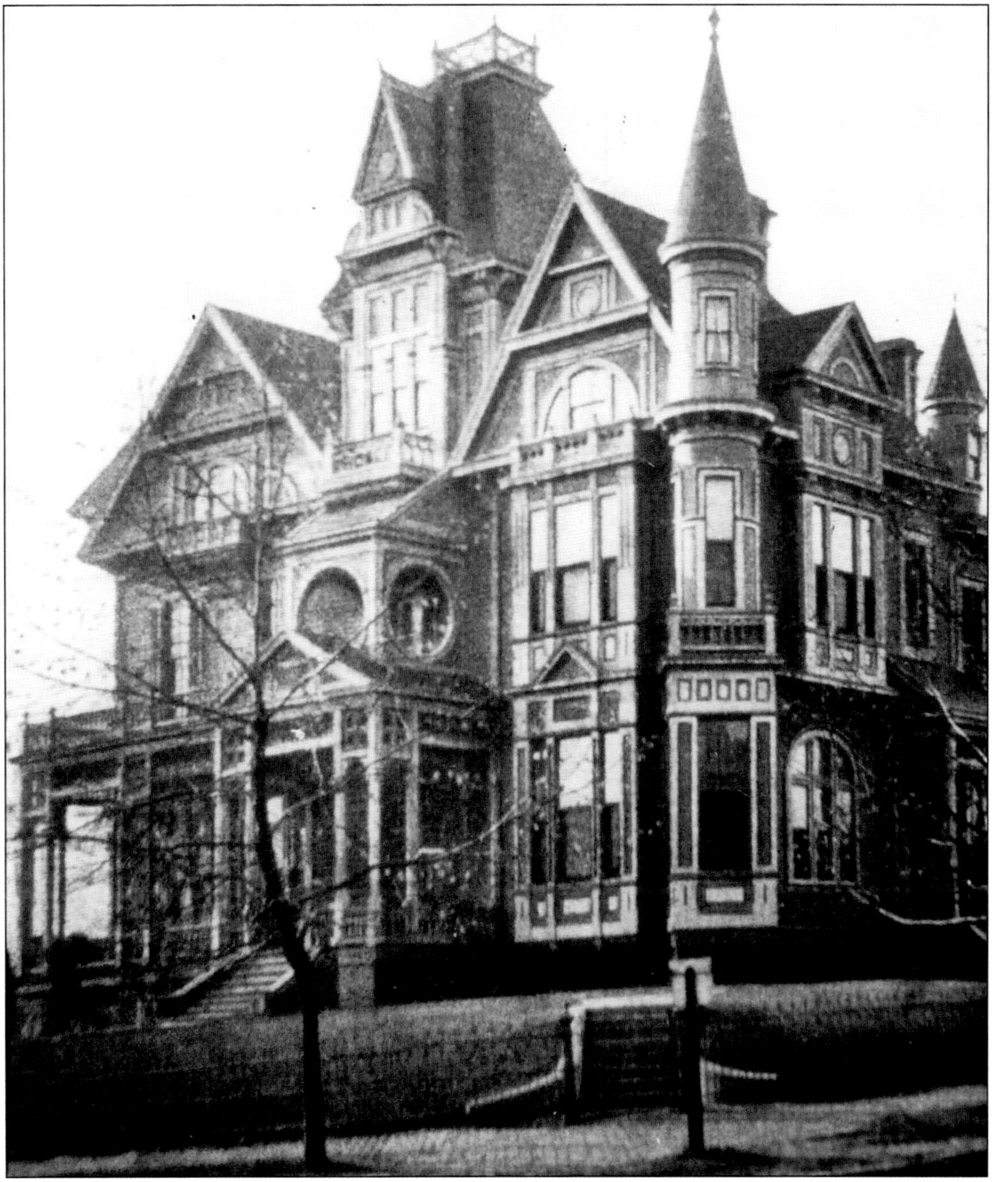

The residence of Governor Newton Crain Blanchard, designed by N.S. Allen, was a wedding-cake mix of the Eastlake, Queen Anne, and Stick styles of Victorian architecture. Built *c.* 1890 at the southwest corner of Common and Cotton Streets, it was also home for a time to newspaper publisher Albert Harris Leonard, founder of the *Shreveport Times*. It was demolished in 1935.

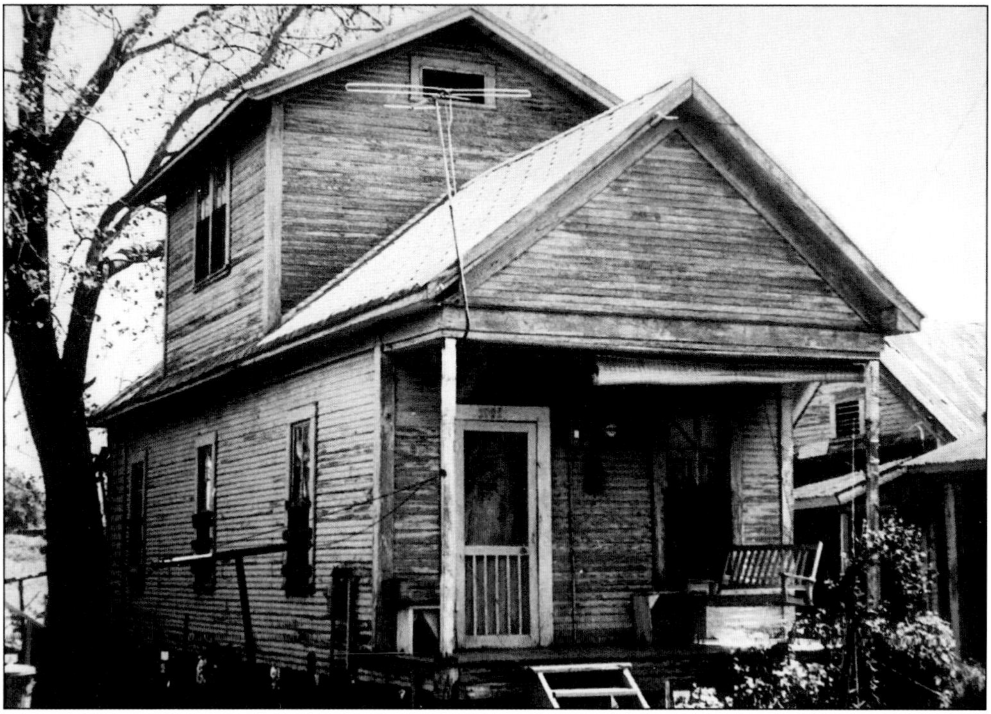

Shotgun houses were once very common in Shreveport, though few survive today. This example formerly stood in the Allendale neighborhood and would have been simply one of many if not for its "camelback" second-story room.

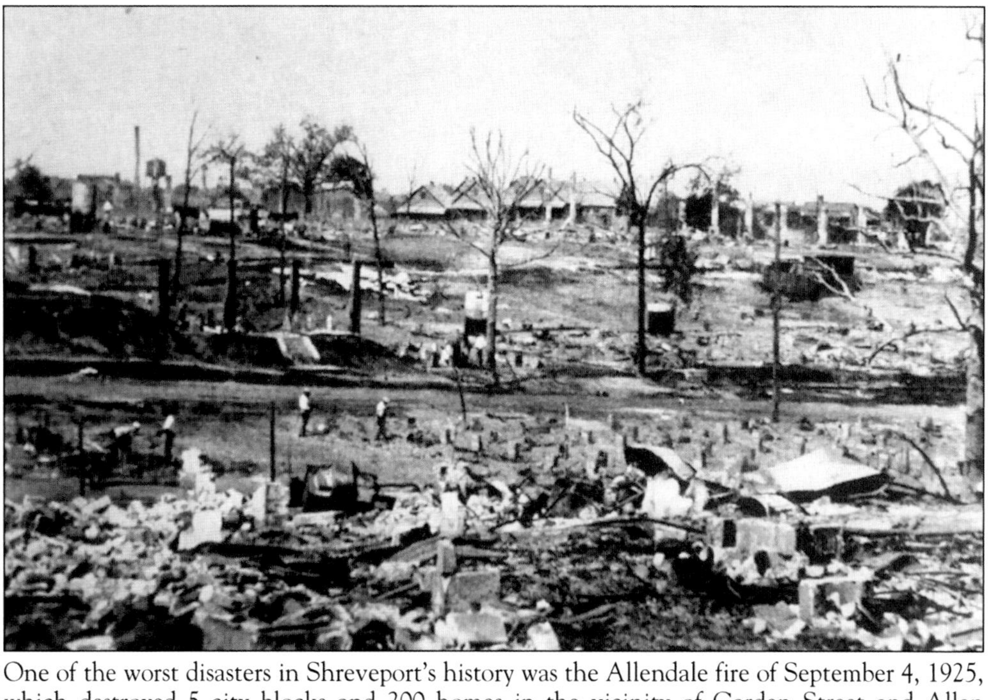

One of the worst disasters in Shreveport's history was the Allendale fire of September 4, 1925, which destroyed 5 city blocks and 200 homes in the vicinity of Garden Street and Allen Avenue. Few photographs of the ruins and none of the actual conflagration exist.

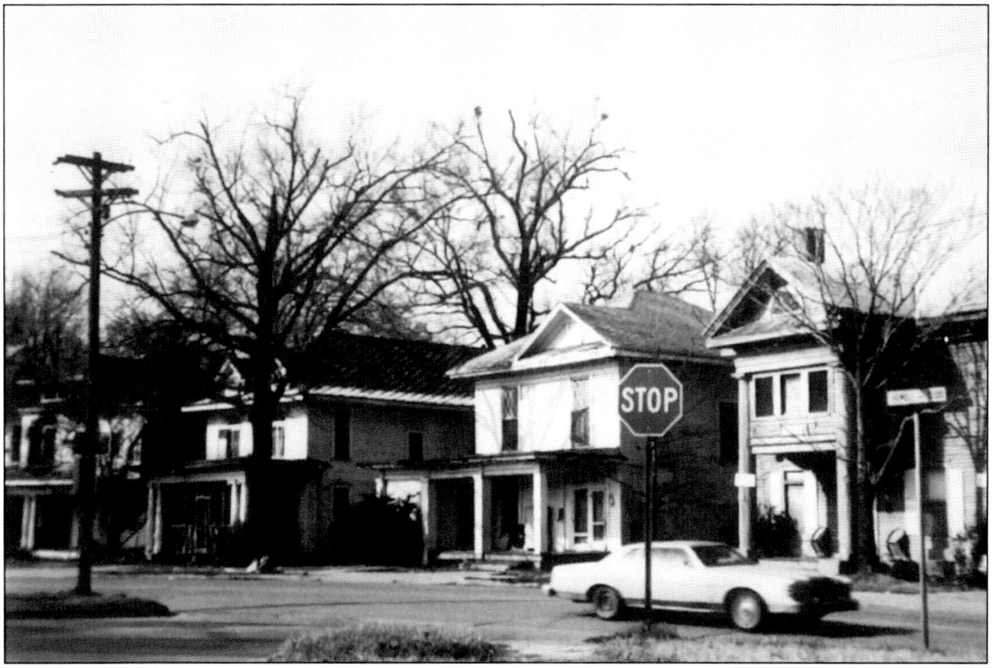

Fairfield Hill, where Fairfield Avenue met Howell Street, was once an area of fine homes, some dating to the 1850s. By the time this photo was taken, the area's heyday had passed and the homes were soon to be sacrificed to the construction of Interstate 20.

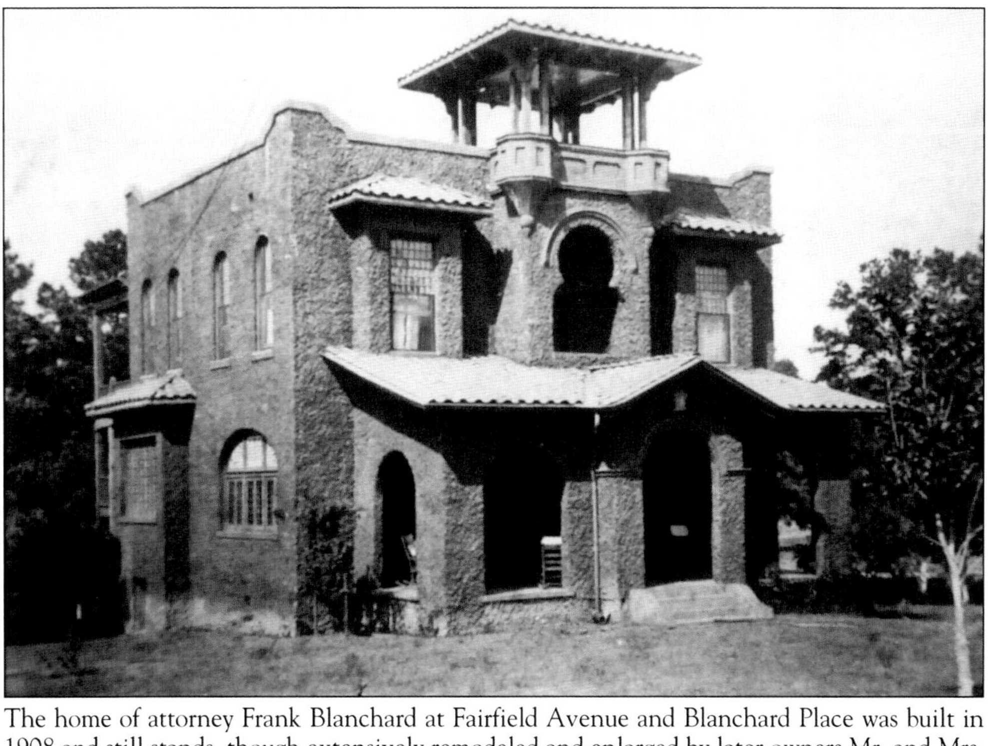

The home of attorney Frank Blanchard at Fairfield Avenue and Blanchard Place was built in 1908 and still stands, though extensively remodeled and enlarged by later owners Mr. and Mrs. Justin Querbes Sr. Its architect was Clarence W. King.

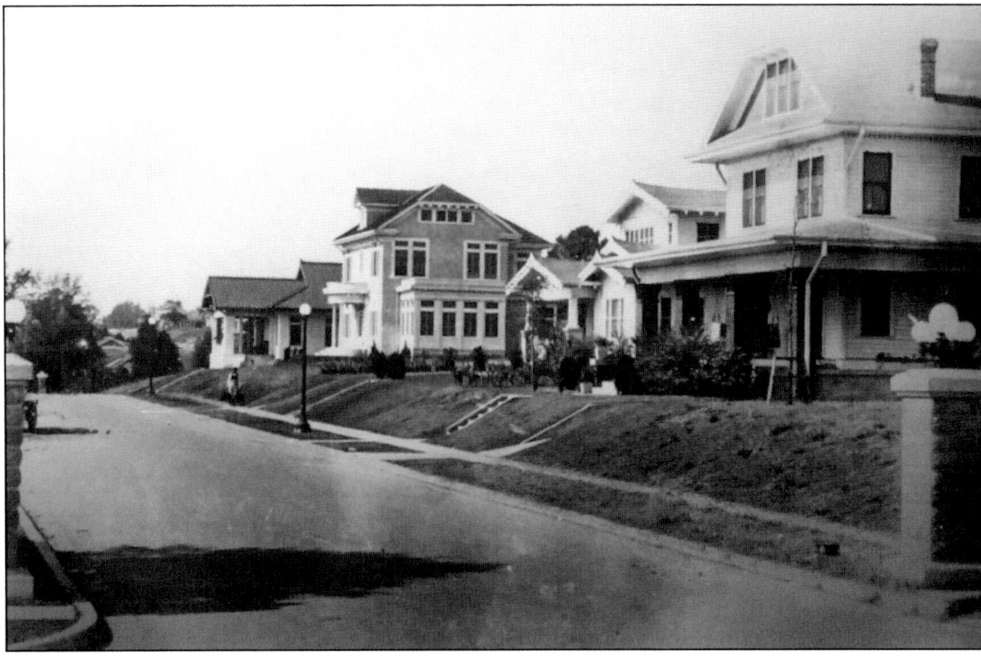

Shown here is a 1920s Grabill photograph of the 500 block of Atkins Street looking west from Highland Avenue. Several of the houses shown still stand, though the first two from right are gone.

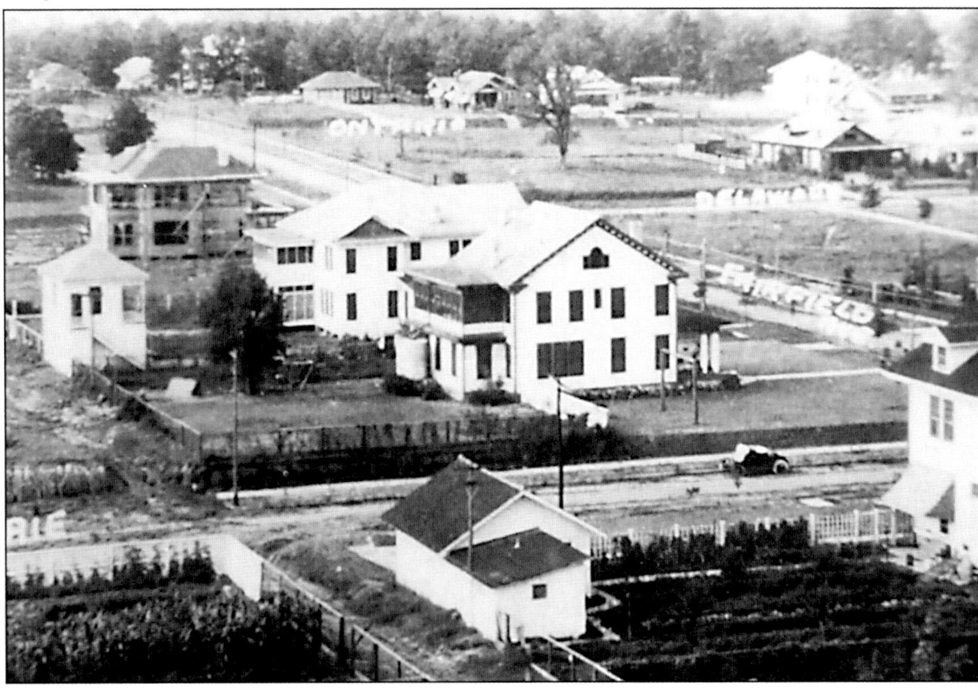

A view from the South Highland water tower by Burch Grabill in 1920 shows Fairfield Avenue at Erie Street with the 900 block of Delaware and Ontario Streets in the background. The village of South Highland was a residential enclave established by A.C. Steere in 1911. It was annexed to Shreveport in 1927.

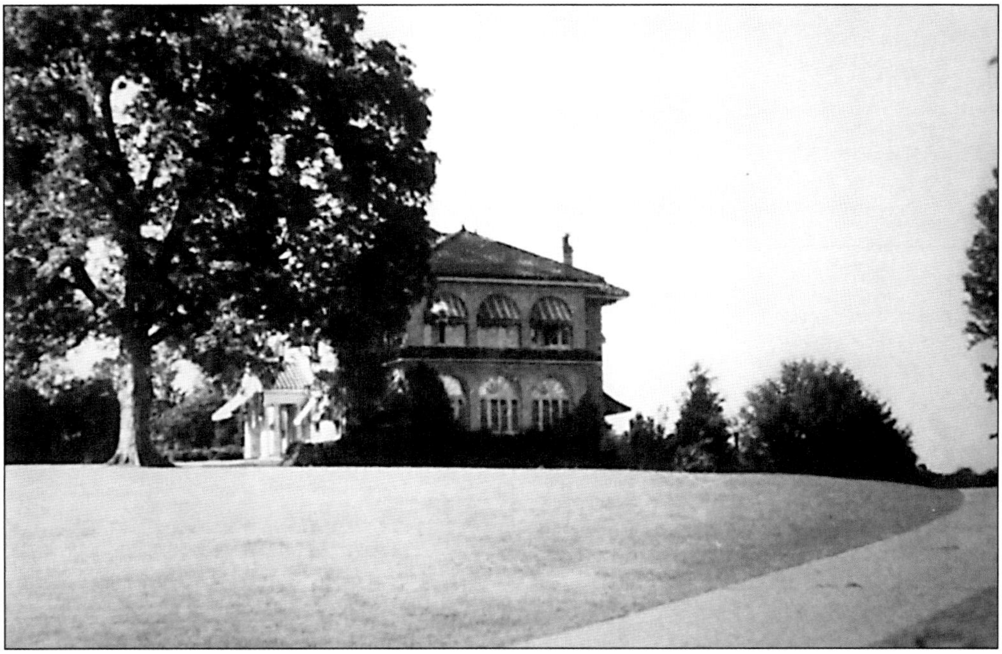

The Mediterranean Revival home of oilman Martin J. Grogan at 5801 Gilbert Drive originally sat on several acres of property laid out by Lambert Landscape Company around 1925. The house still stands, though the grounds today are greatly diminished in size.

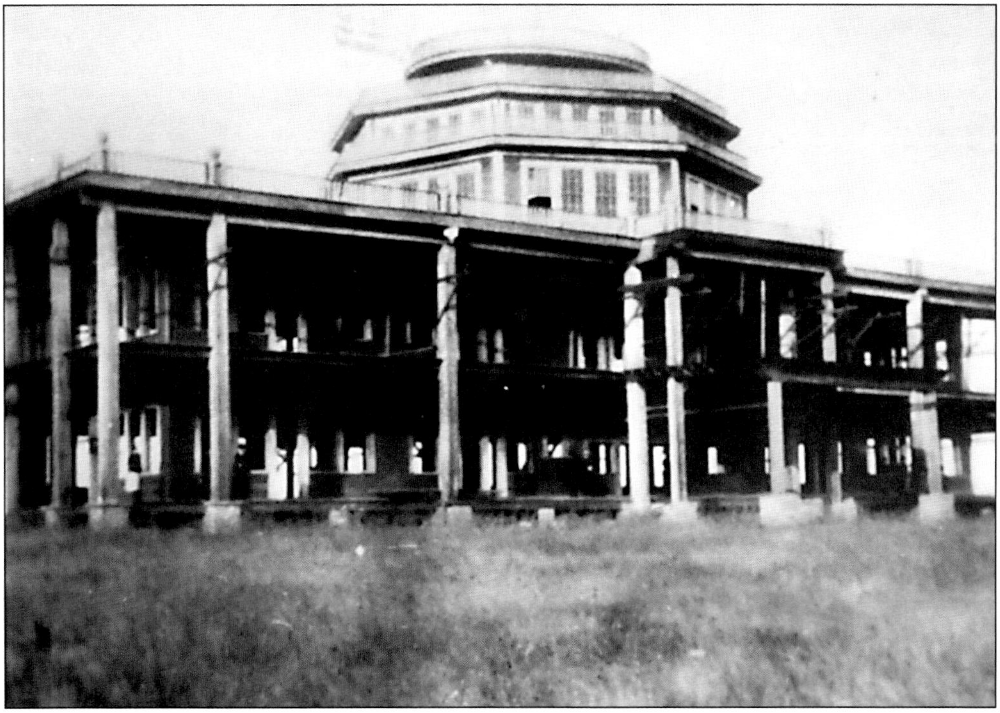

Page's Castle, a domed mansion begun in 1914 by planter Walter Page on Jefferson-Paige Road ("Paige" is a misspelling of Page), would-have been the area's largest residence if completed, but the death of Page's son in 1917 ended work on the house, which eventually was pulled down.

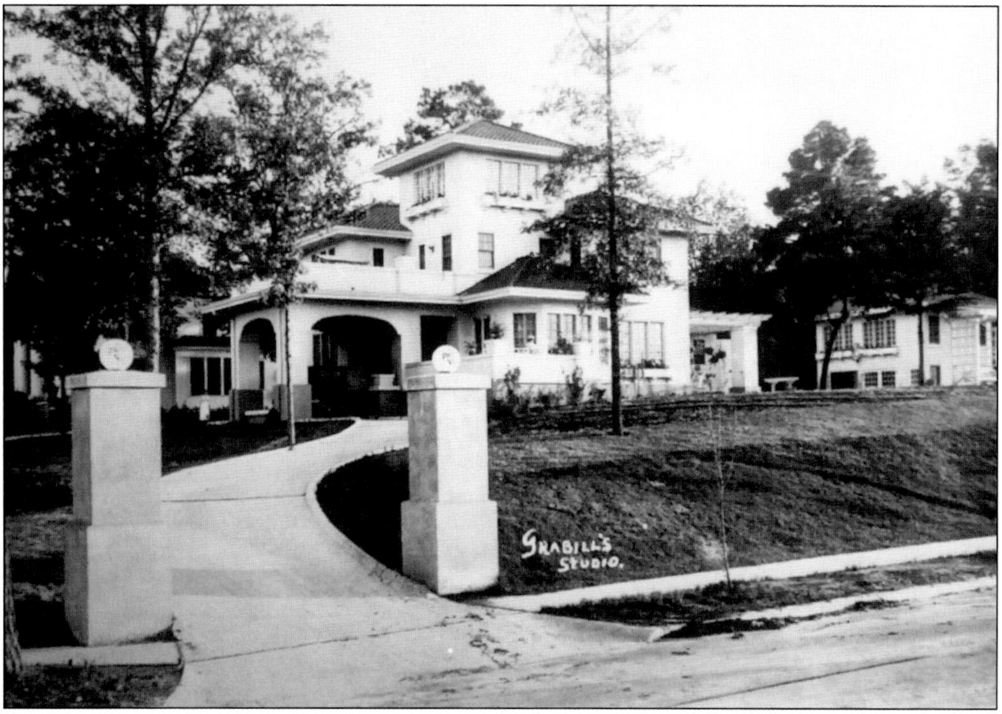

"Park Villa" at Centenary Boulevard and Kings Highway was built around 1918 for the Atkins family and later was home to the Alexander family, both prominent in the development of the Highland and Centenary areas of Shreveport. It still stands, though greatly altered.

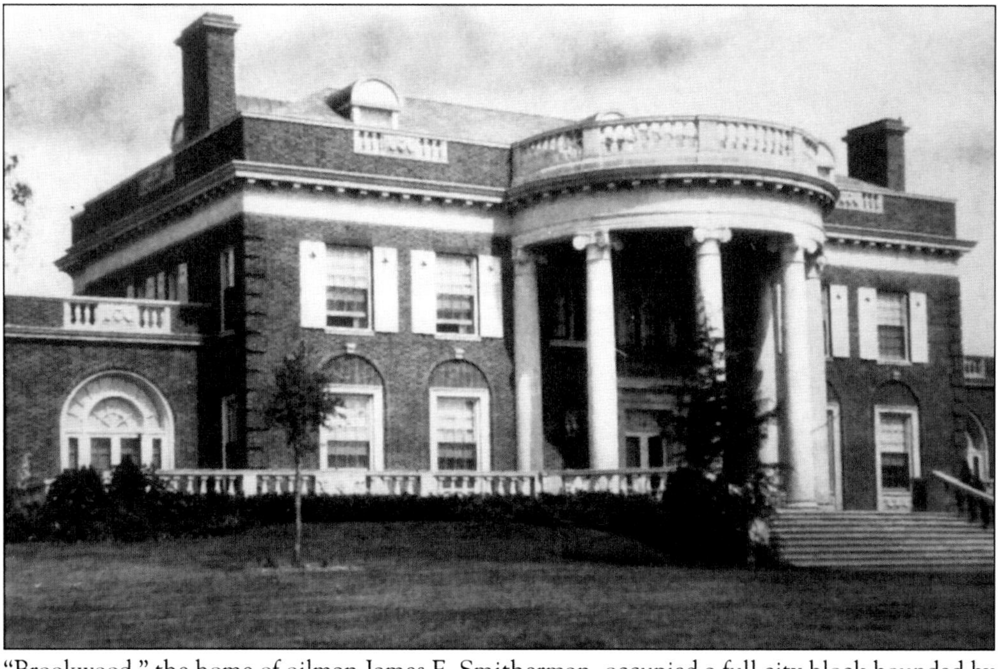

"Brookwood," the home of oilman James E. Smitherman, occupied a full city block bounded by Fairfield Avenue, McCormick Street, Line Avenue, and Dudley Drive when finished in 1925. The house still stands amid a sea of homes and townhouses built upon its former grounds.

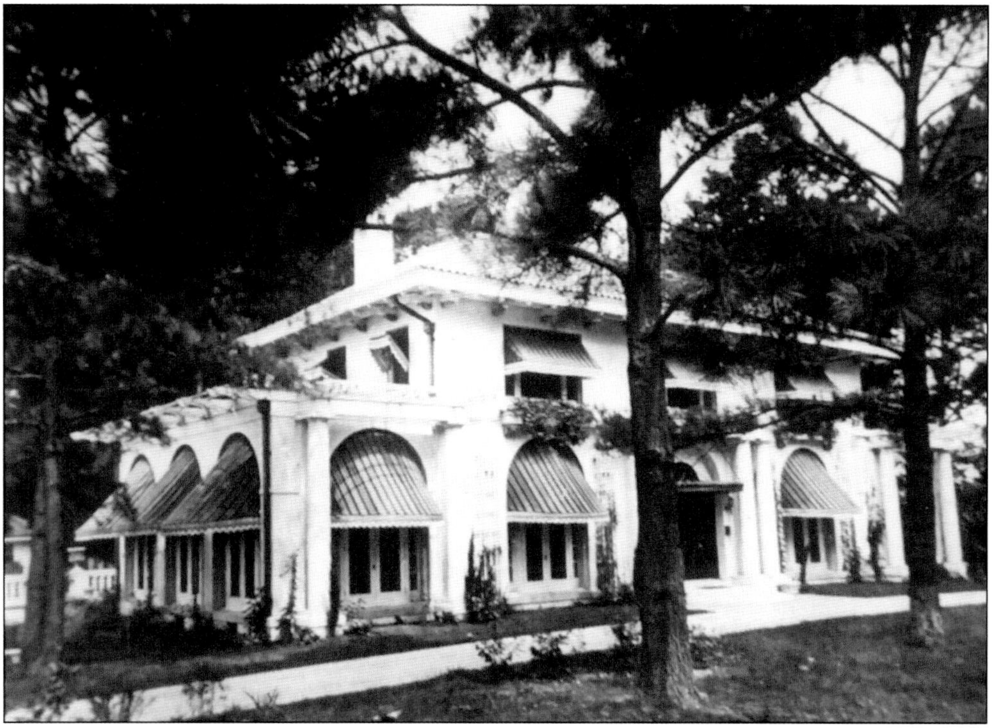

Shown here are exterior (above) and interior views of the Files house, built in 1921 at Fairfield Avenue and Wilkinson Street. The interior view (below) shows the solarium, or "sun porch," as it appeared when the house was new.

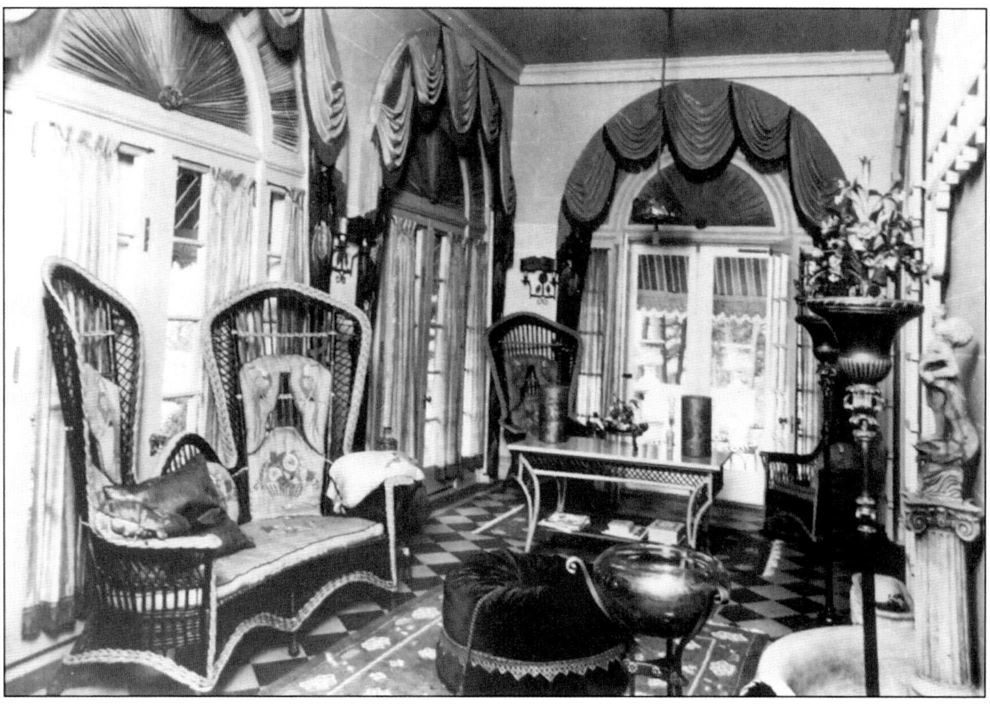

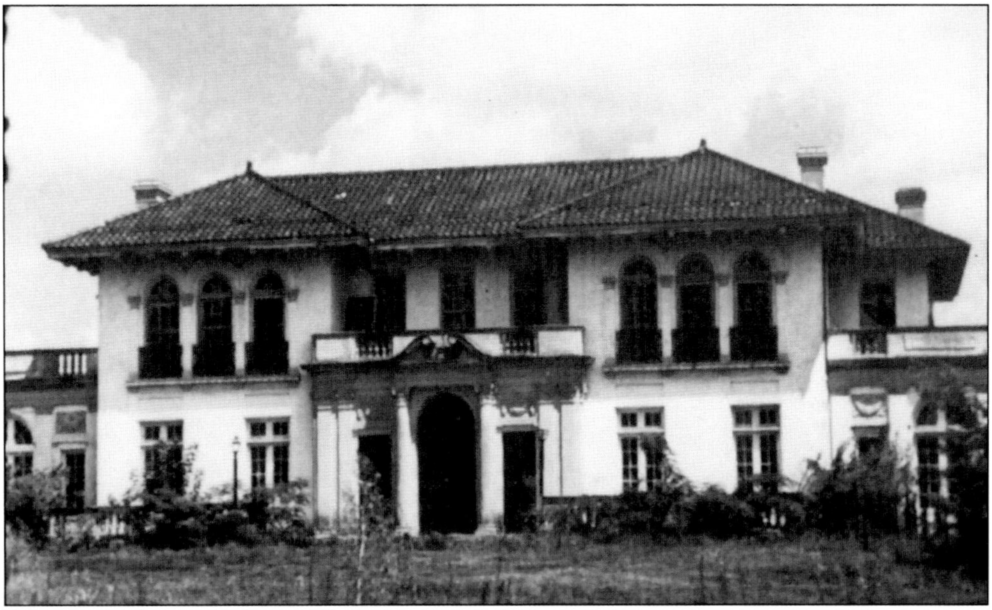

This mansion at 820 Jordan Street was built in 1922 by noted Shreveport attorney Sidney Herold, whose 1915 challenge to Louisiana's public school Bible-reading law had national ramifications. In 1978 the mansion was demolished.

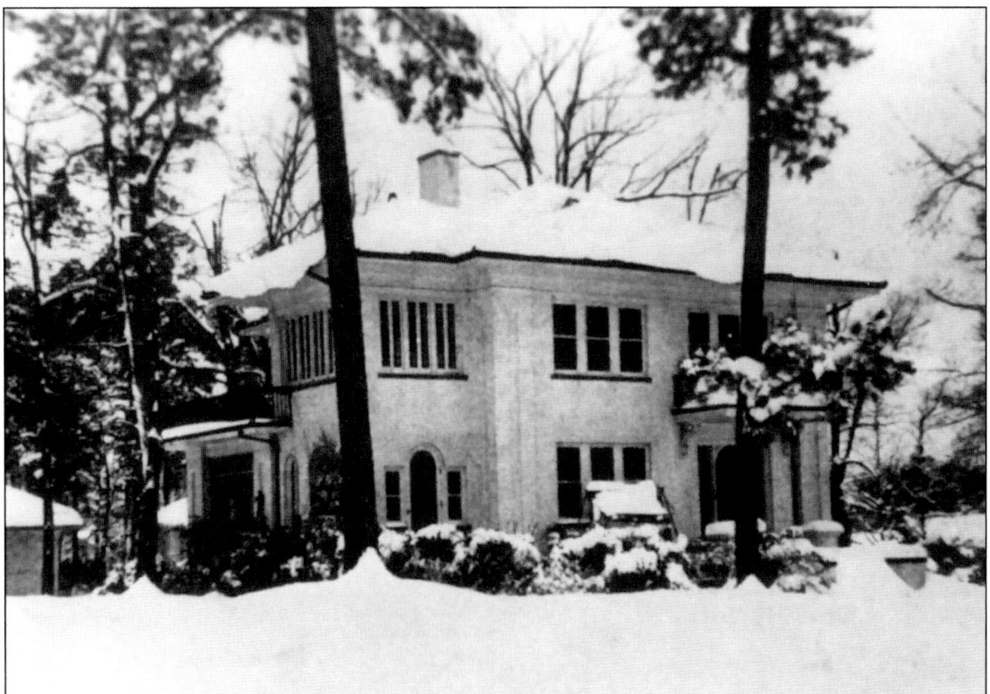

The residence of Governor Huey P. Long at 305 Forest Avenue was built in 1924. This photograph, made during a freak snowstorm in 1928, was used by the Longs on their 1929 family Christmas card.

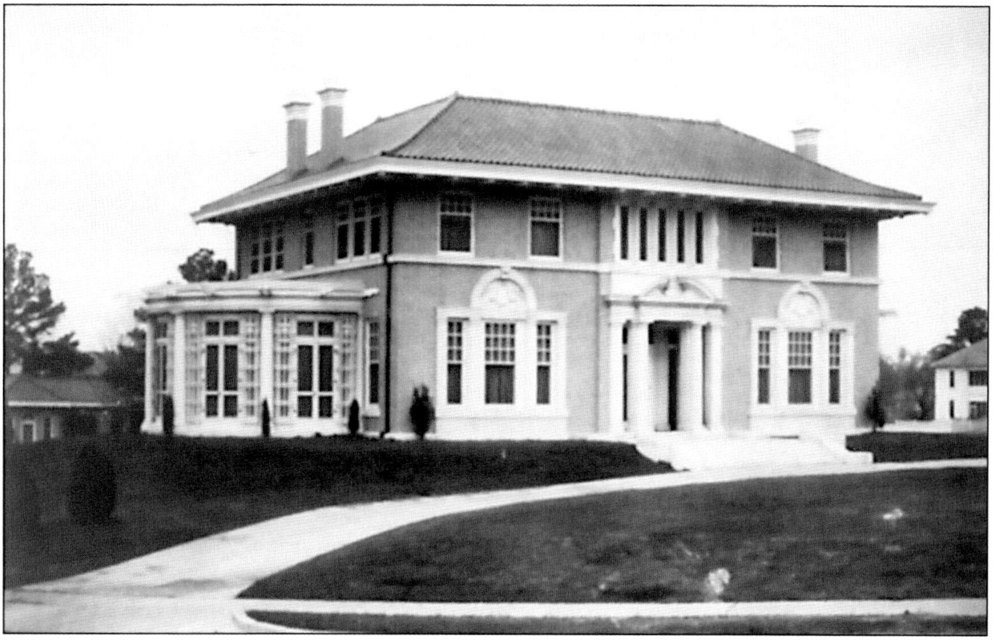

The home formerly at the intersection of Fairfield Avenue with St. Vincent Avenue and Kings Highway stood from 1928 to 1982. It was built by cottonseed oil manufacturer Sidney J. Harman, who was also in the ice and cold storage business.

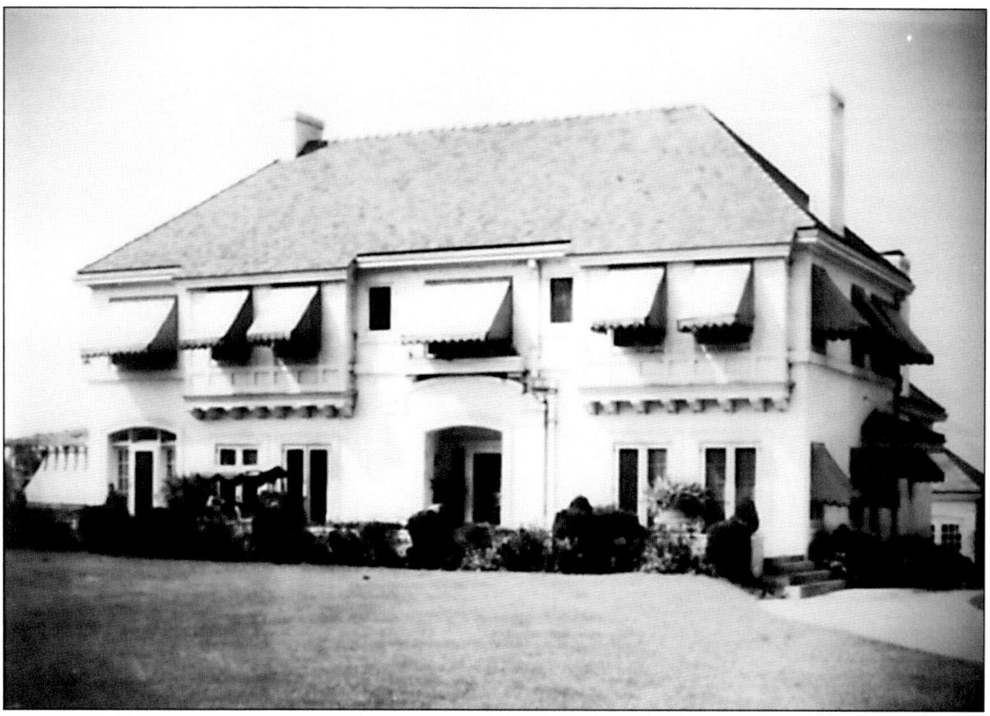

The Tudor Revival residence of oilman Ernest Ratcliff at Fairfield Avenue and Kings Highway was built in 1921 and still stands, though for many years it has been used as a medical clinic.

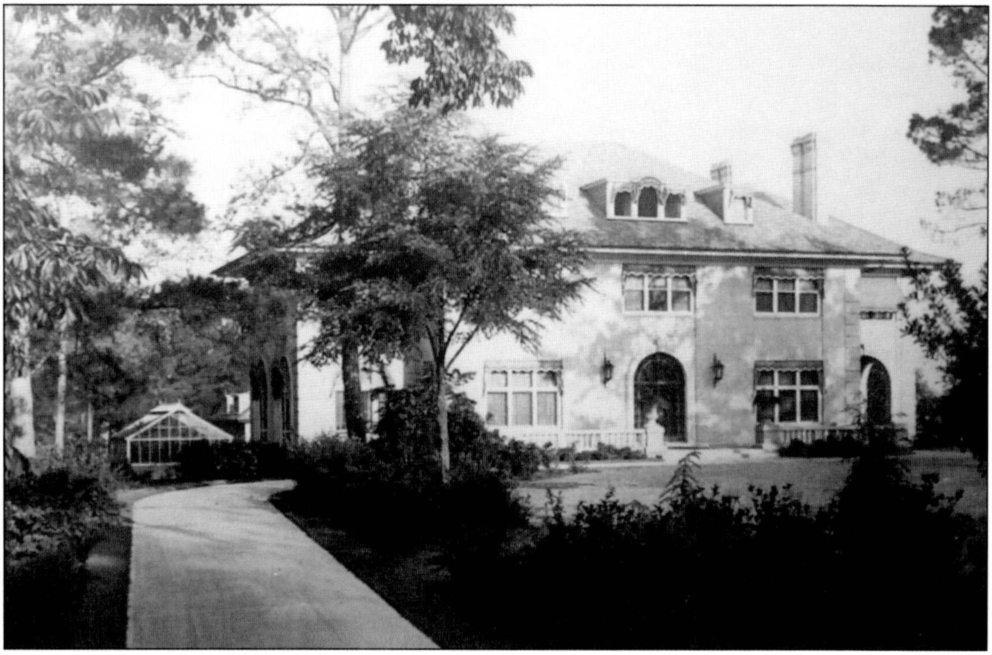

The Henry C. Walker Jr. home at 2610 Fairfield Avenue was built in 1925 and was designed by the architectural firm of Maritz and Young from St. Louis, Missouri.

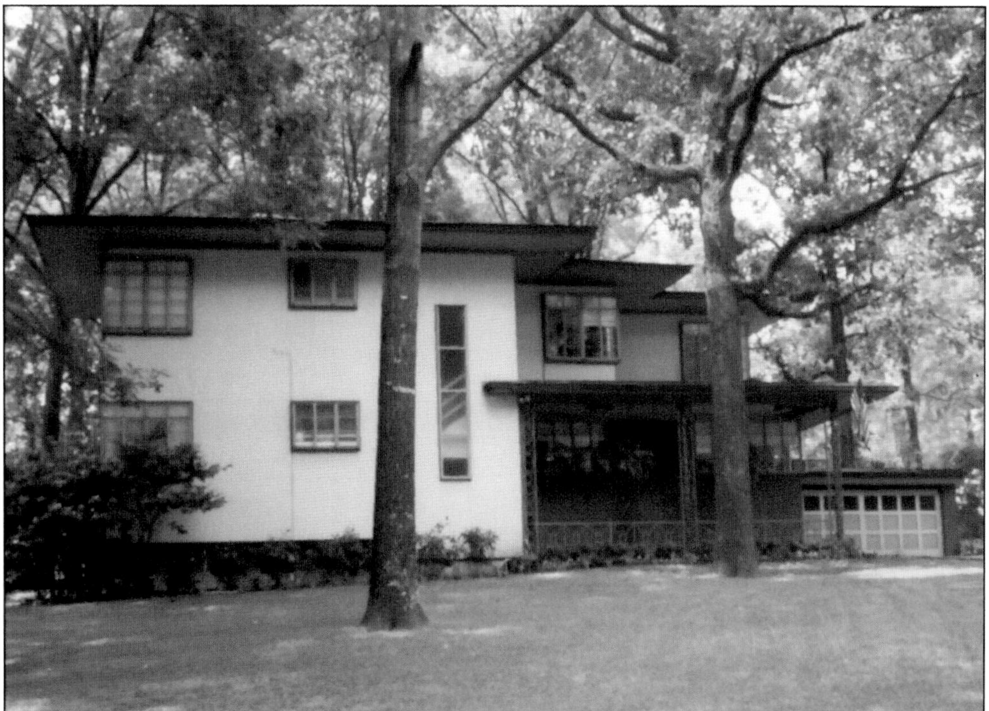

The David Flesh house on Sherwood Road, built in 1935 and designed by prominent architects Samuel G. and William Wiener, is one of the most important International Style homes in Shreveport.

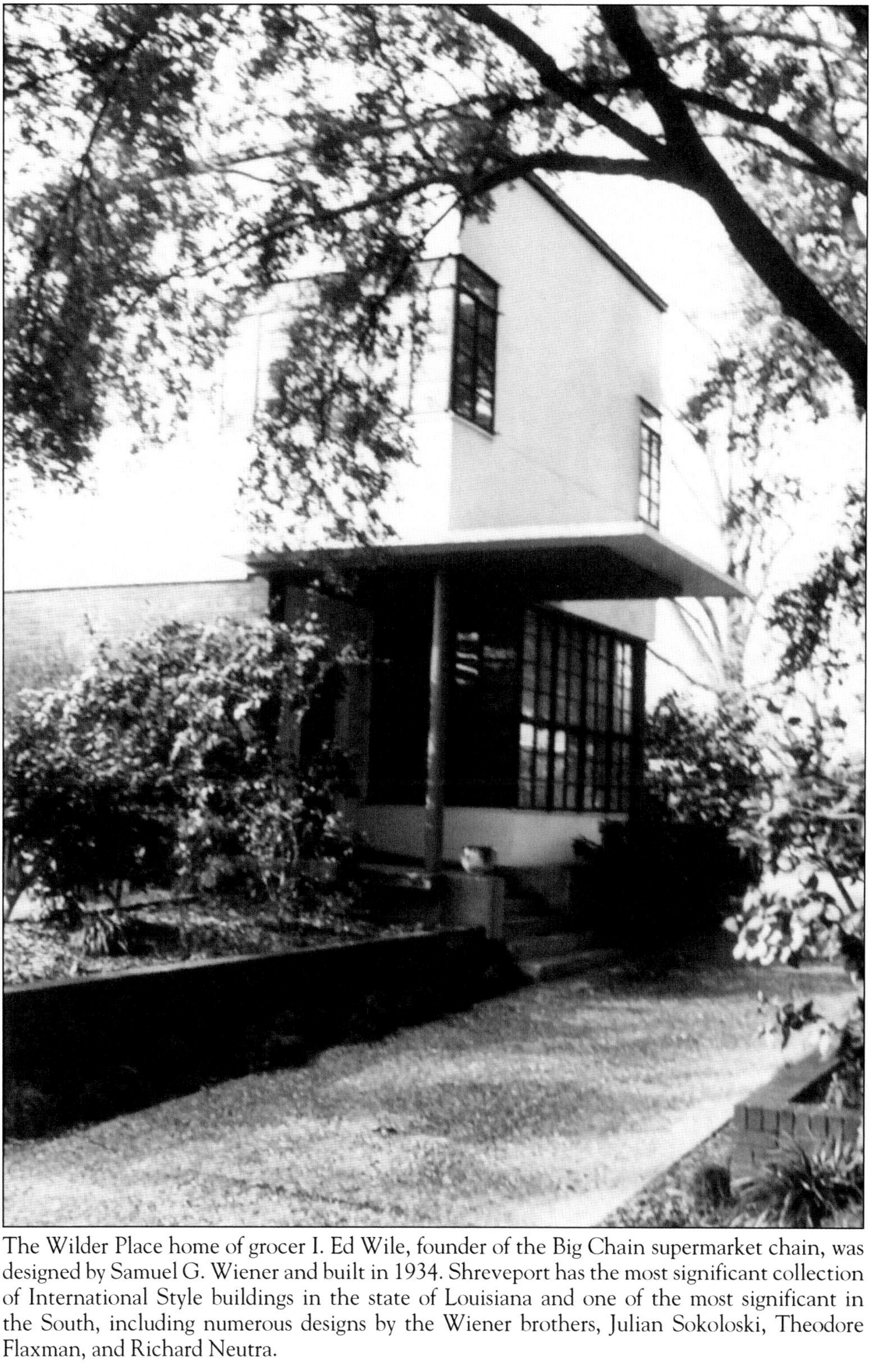

The Wilder Place home of grocer I. Ed Wile, founder of the Big Chain supermarket chain, was designed by Samuel G. Wiener and built in 1934. Shreveport has the most significant collection of International Style buildings in the state of Louisiana and one of the most significant in the South, including numerous designs by the Wiener brothers, Julian Sokoloski, Theodore Flaxman, and Richard Neutra.

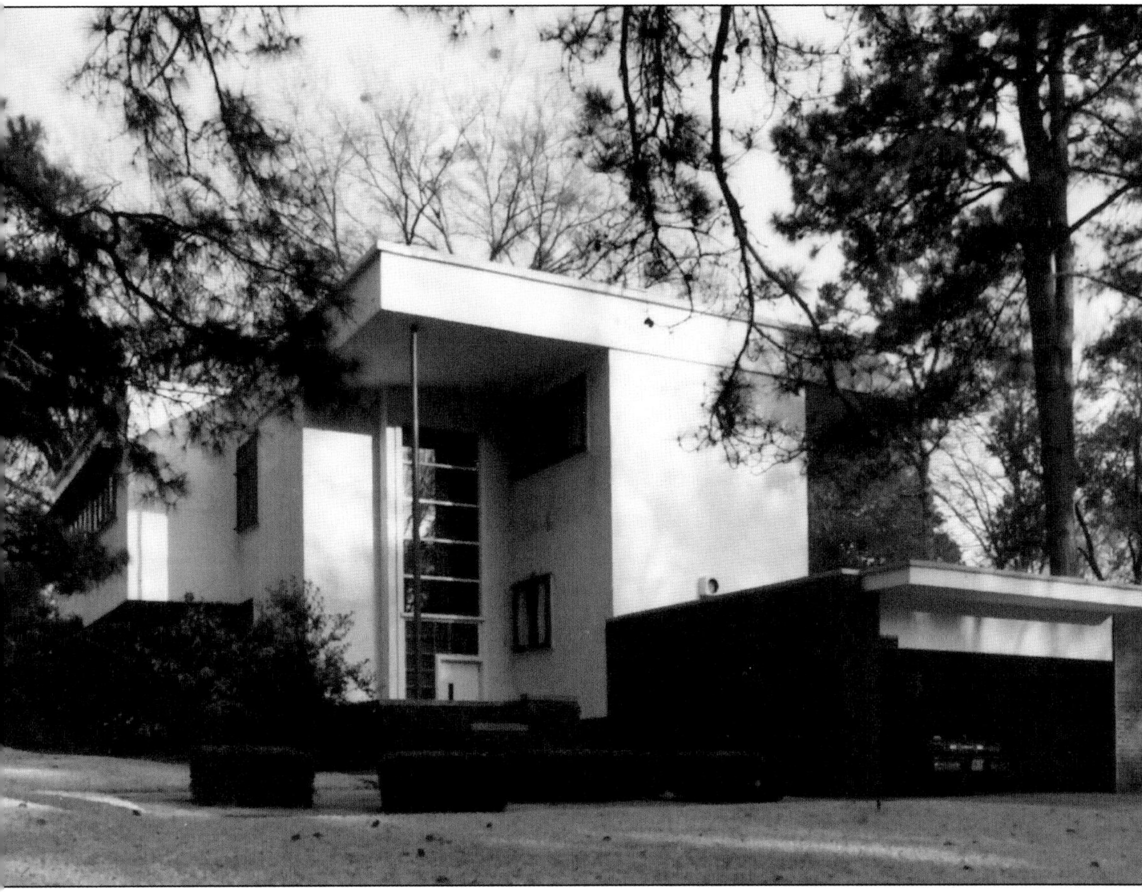

The residence of Samuel G. Wiener on Longleaf Road, just off Creswell Road, was built by the architect in 1937 for himself. It is one of the most important, early International Style residences in Louisiana.

Five

Churches, Schools, and Cemeteries

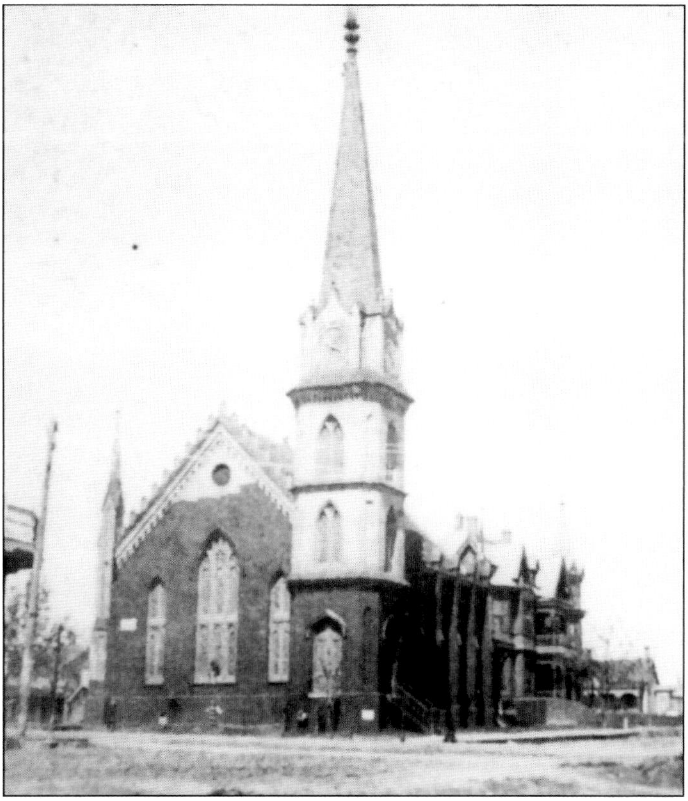

The First Baptist Church stood at the northwest corner of Texas and McNeill Streets from 1879 to 1907 and contained the first public clock in the city. Designed by architect N.S. Allen, the church contained brick from the Shreveport University, a Baptist institution which closed after the yellow fever epidemic of 1873.

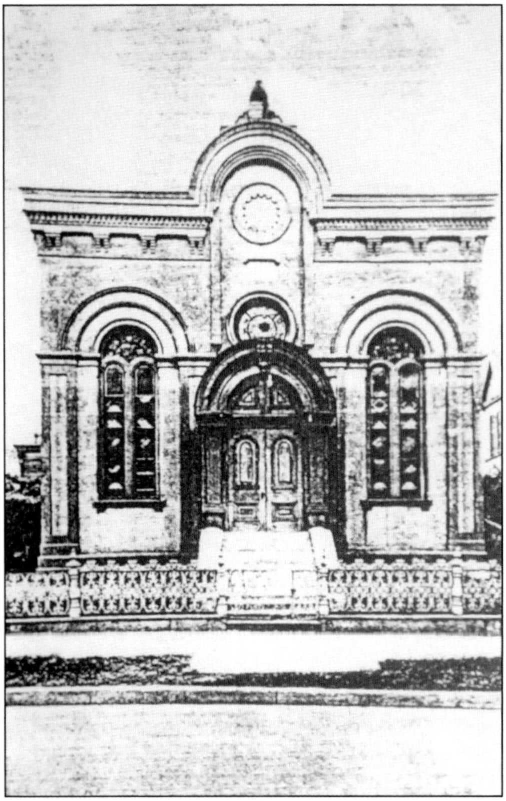

This is the first permanent home of B'nai Zion Temple, built in 1869 at 320 Fannin Street. Founded in 1859 as Congregation Har El, the synagogue became a Reform Jewish temple in 1867. Designed by architect Benjamin Harrod of New Orleans, the synagogue remained in use until 1915. It was later the Christian Science Church and was torn down in 1929.

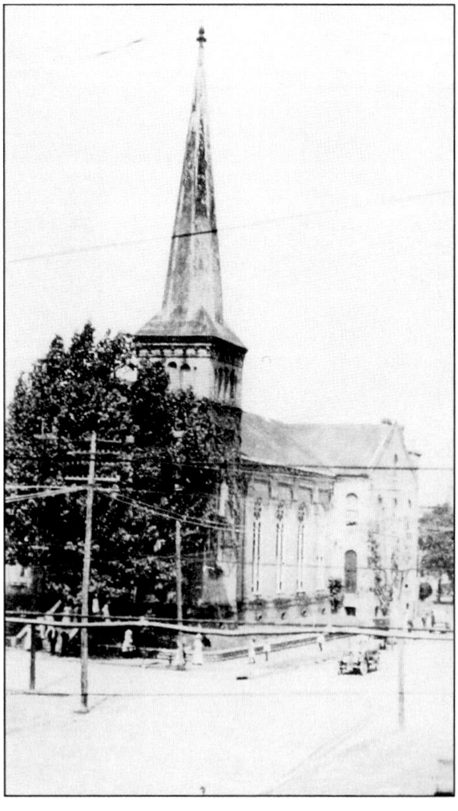

The First Presbyterian Church, founded in 1845, was located at 400 Travis Street from 1870 to 1926. In its later days the church building was home to the YWCA, which removed the church's steeple. In 1956 it was demolished to make way for the Beck Building.

St. Mark's Episcopal Church was located at 300 Fannin Street, at the corner with Market Street, from 1859 to 1905. It was designed by noted English-American architect Frederick Clarke Withers and dedicated in 1860 by Bishop Leonidas Polk, who conducted Shreveport's first religious service in 1839.

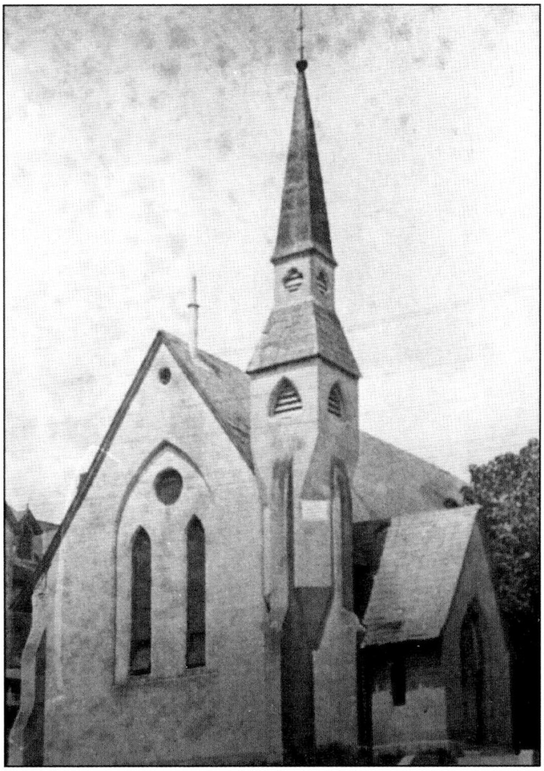

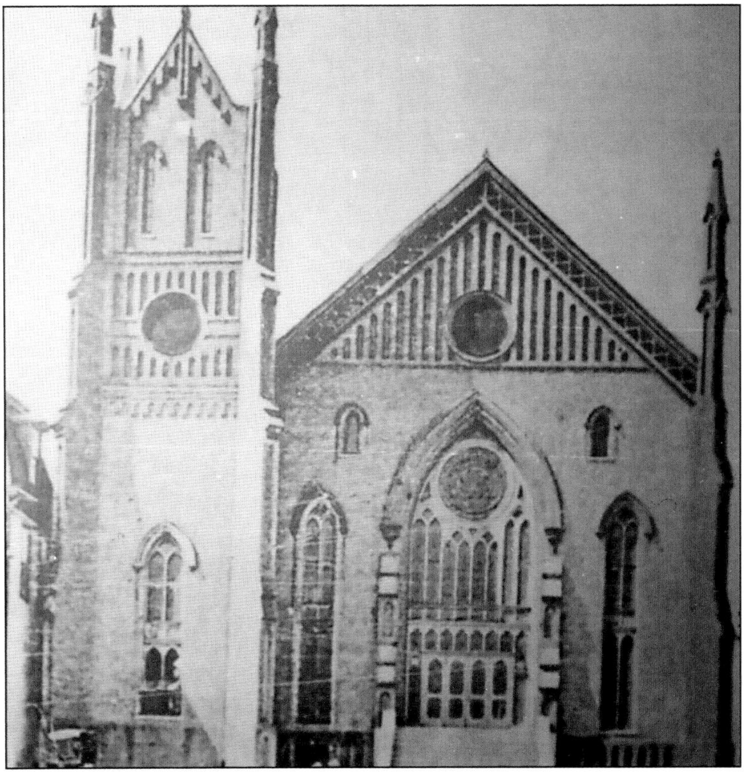

The Gothic Revival Style First Methodist Church, built in 1883 at Common and Texas Streets, stood until 1912, when it was razed to build the present church. Founded in 1845, the church was first located at Market and Fannin Streets.

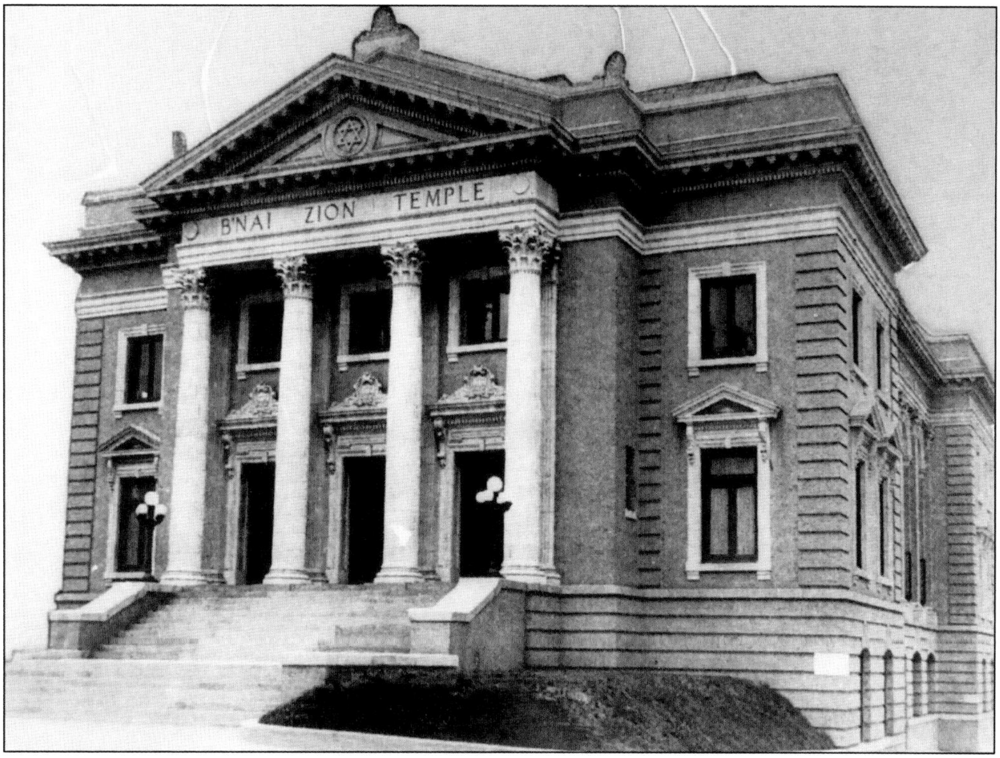

B'nai Zion Temple's second synagogue was located at Cotton and Common Streets from 1915 to 1956. The building, designed by architect Edward F. Neild, still stands, though long vacant.

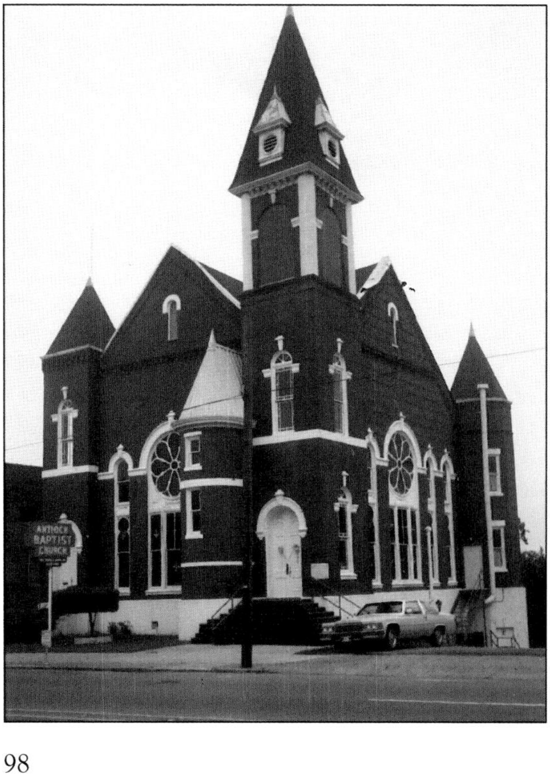

Antioch Baptist Church was founded in 1866 as the First Colored Baptist Church. In 1902 the present church, designed by architect N.S. Allen, was built at Texas Avenue and Lawrence Street.

The St. Paul African Methodist Episcopal Church, Shreveport's first black Methodist congregation, was established in 1865 and was located at 620 Caddo Street until 1926, when it moved to Looney Street at Pierre Avenue. It is now the St. Paul United Methodist Church.

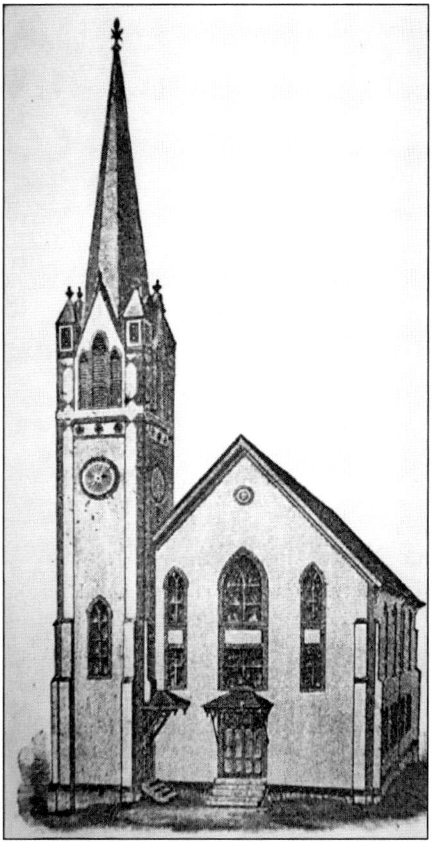

The First Baptist Church was located at Travis and McNeill Streets from 1907 to 1963. Founded in 1845, the church was first located at Travis and Market Streets. Dr. M.E. Dodd, pastor from 1912 to 1950, was one of the most influential Baptist evangelists in the nation, partly due to his early use of radio.

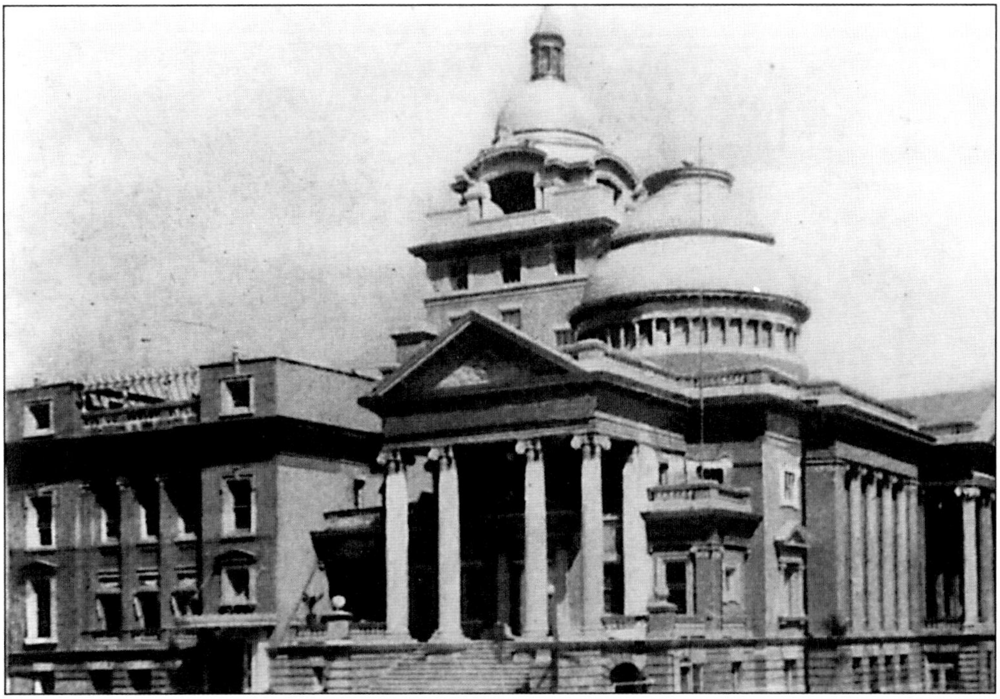

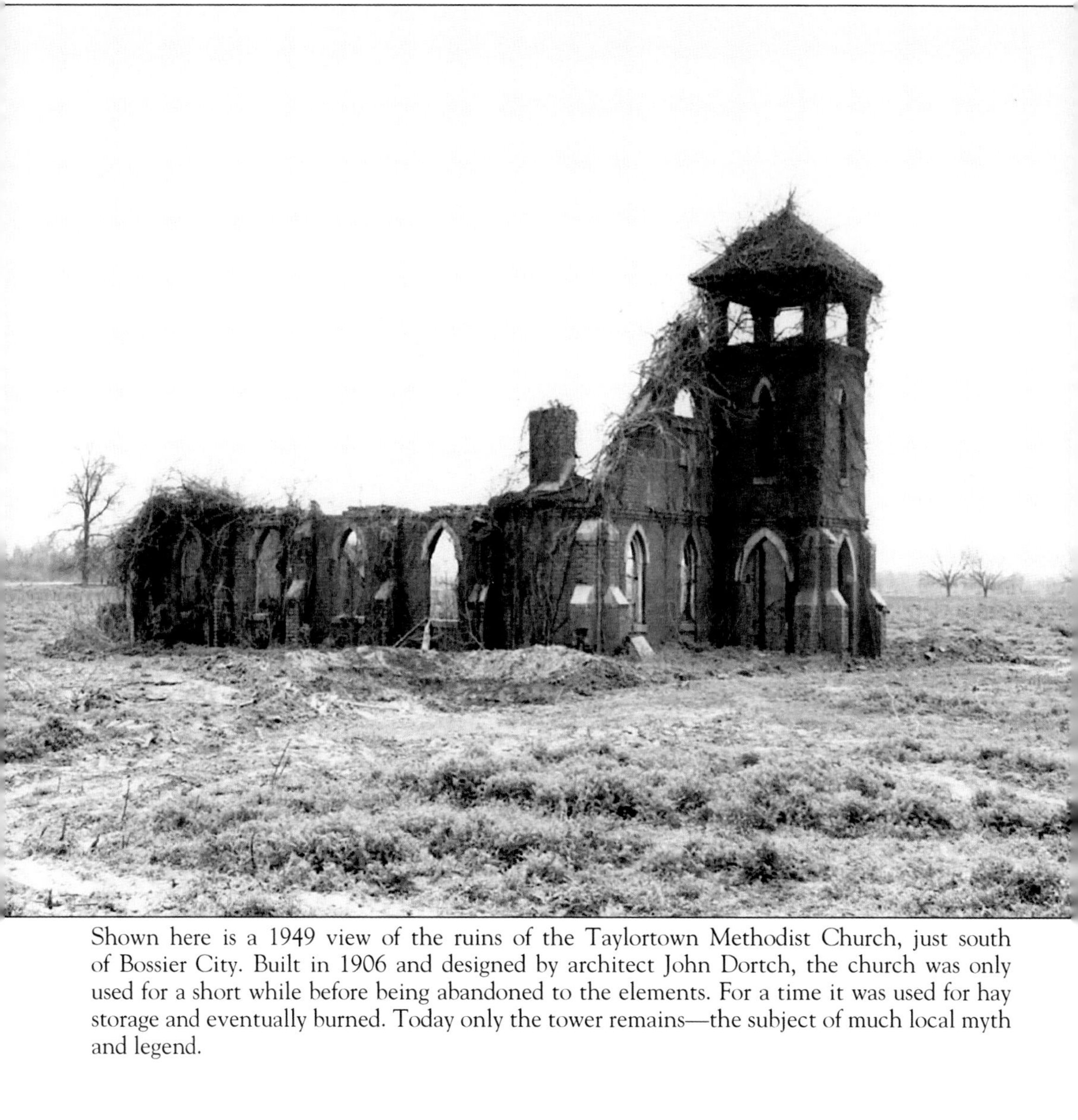

Shown here is a 1949 view of the ruins of the Taylortown Methodist Church, just south of Bossier City. Built in 1906 and designed by architect John Dortch, the church was only used for a short while before being abandoned to the elements. For a time it was used for hay storage and eventually burned. Today only the tower remains—the subject of much local myth and legend.

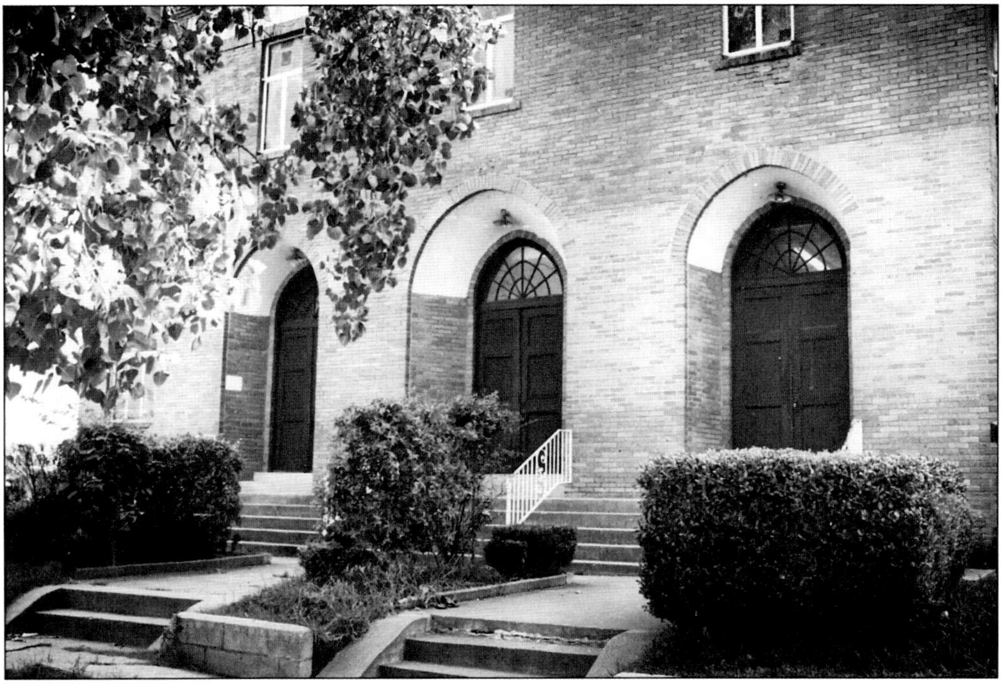

The old Galilee Baptist Church, located at Williamson and Snow Streets, was the scene of addresses by Dr. Martin Luther King Jr. in 1958 and 1962. Plans to desegregate Caddo Parish's school system were launched here. The church was founded in 1877 and this building built in 1917. The old church building is now part of the City Hall complex.

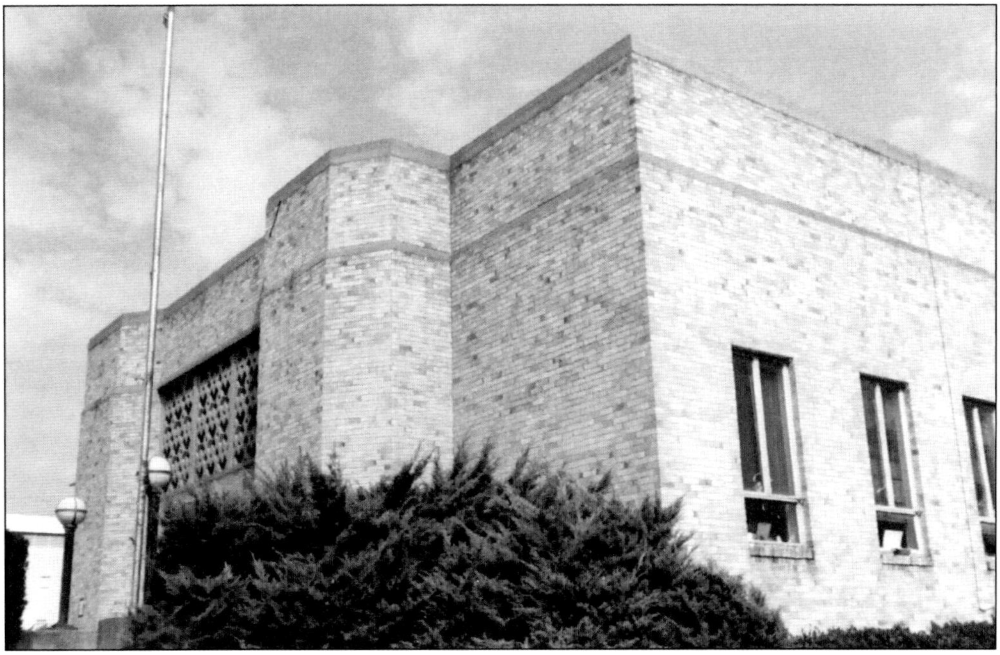

Congregation Agudath Achim was founded in 1902 and was first located at Fannin and McNeill Streets. From 1938 to 1980, the Orthodox Jewish synagogue was located on Line Avenue at Margaret Place. It was designed by Shreveport architect Seymour Van Os.

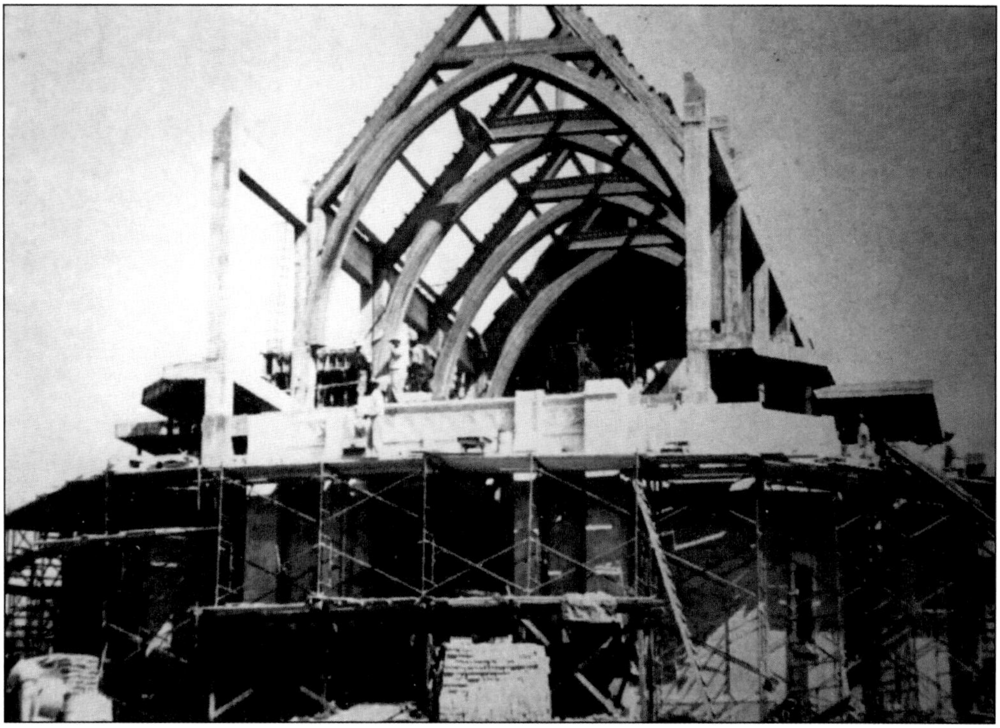

St. Mark's Episcopal Church, now St. Mark's Cathedral, was photographed while under construction at Fairfield Avenue and Rutherford Street in 1958. Begun in 1957, the monumental Gothic Revival church was dedicated in 1959. St. Mark's was founded in 1839.

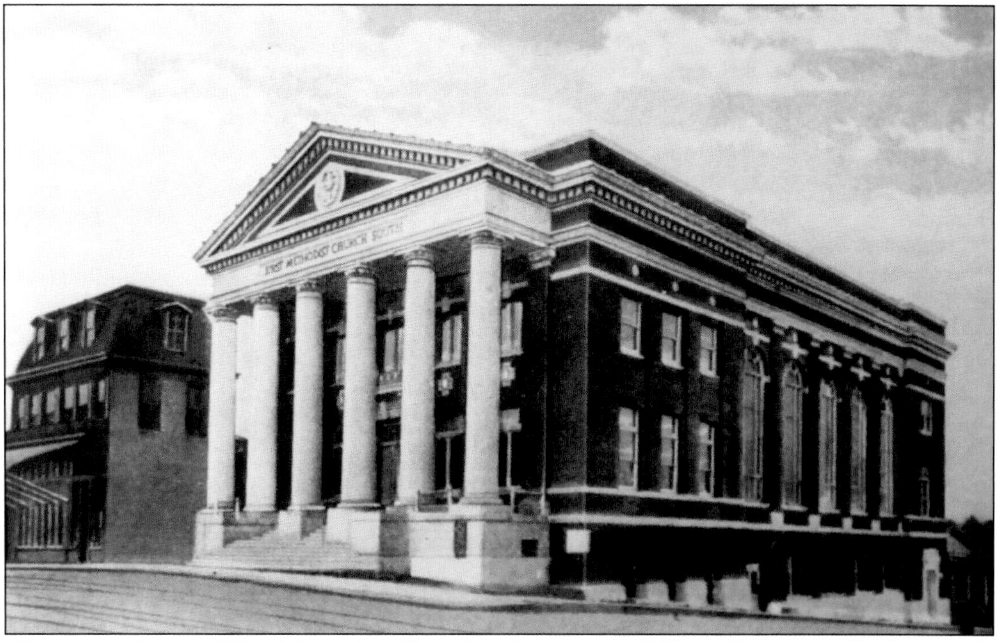

The present home of First Methodist Church at Common and Texas Streets was built in 1913, shortly before this photograph was made. In 1972 a Neo-Classical steeple was erected atop the church.

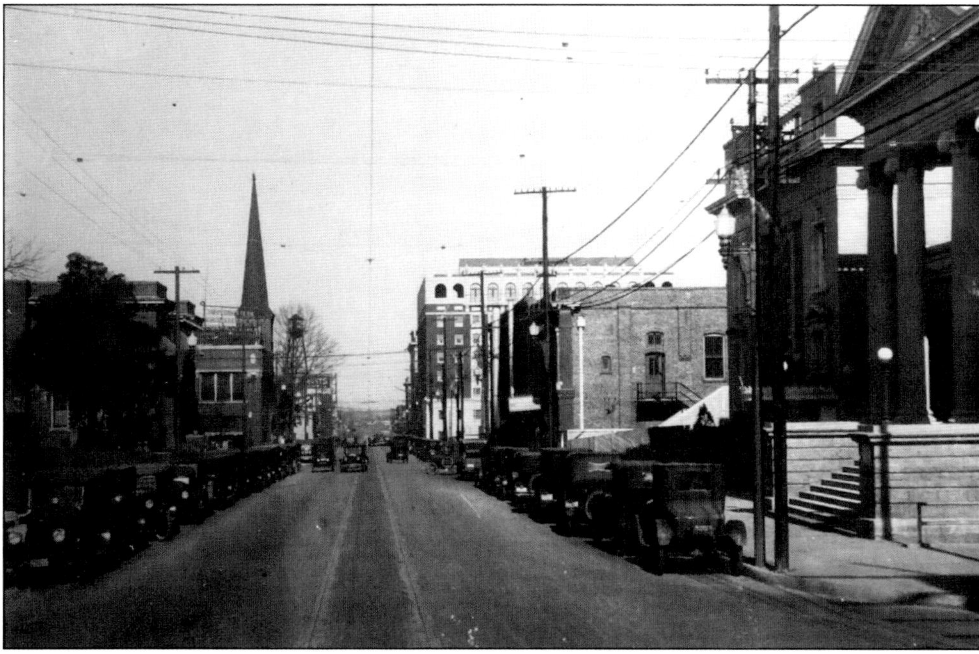

This photograph of Travis Street looking east from McNeill Street was taken in 1923. At right is the First Baptist Church. The steeple at left is atop the First Presbyterian Church.

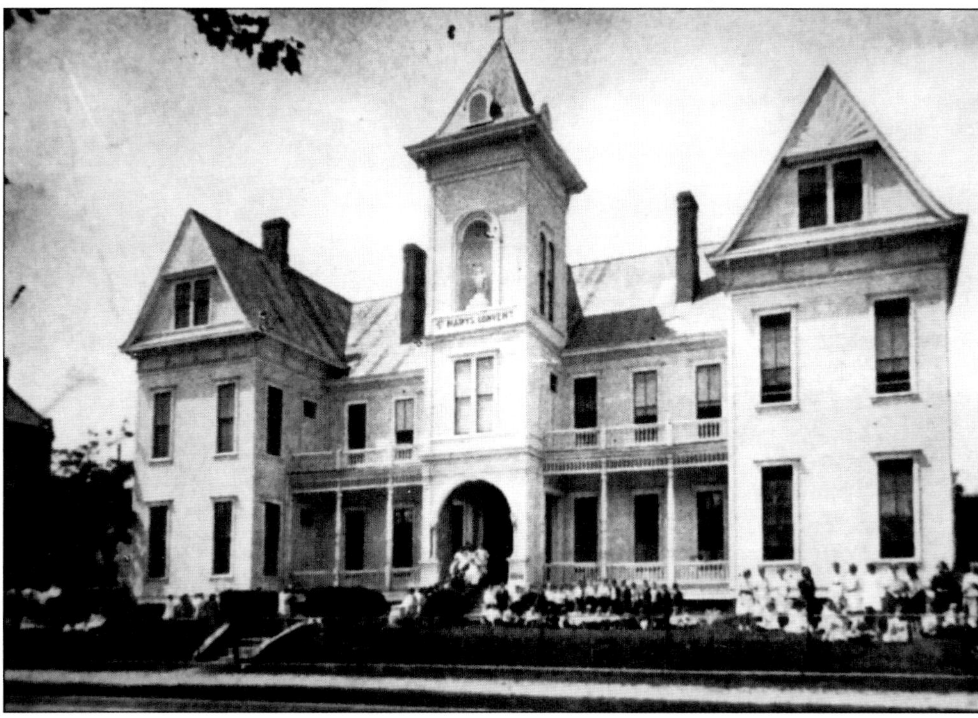

St. Mary's Convent and School, founded in 1860, was located in this building at Edwards and Fannin Streets from 1888 to 1955. Next door was Holy Trinity Church, built in 1896 and still in use. The Catholic presence in Shreveport dates from the founding of Holy Trinity parish in 1856.

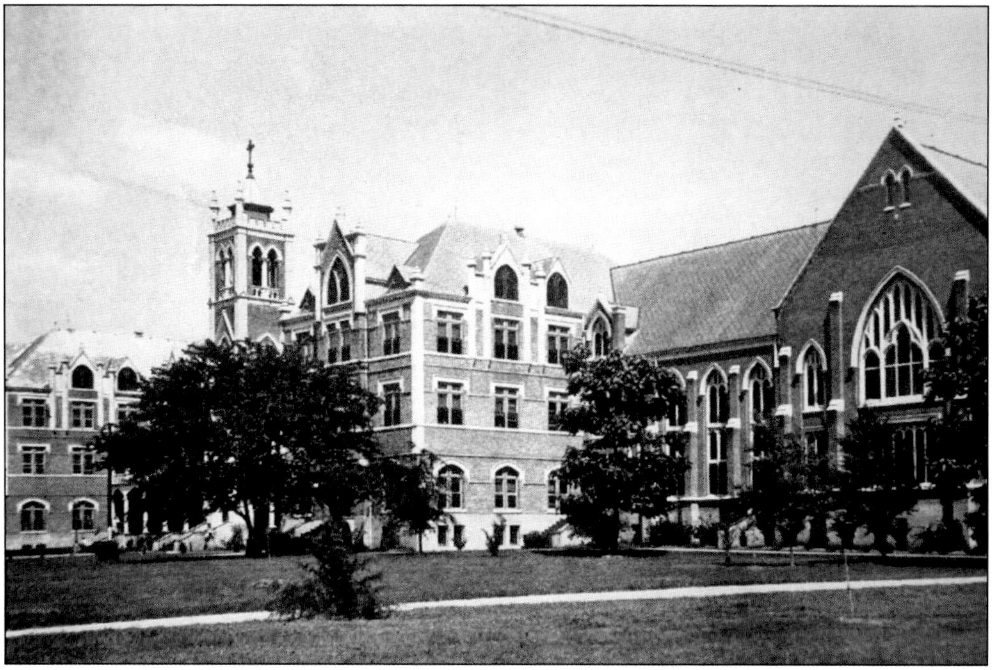

St. Vincent's Convent and Academy was founded in 1868 by the Daughters of the Cross, a French order of nuns. In 1906 the original building, a remodeled plantation house, burned and was replaced by the buildings above. In 1973 the site was cleared for Mall St. Vincent.

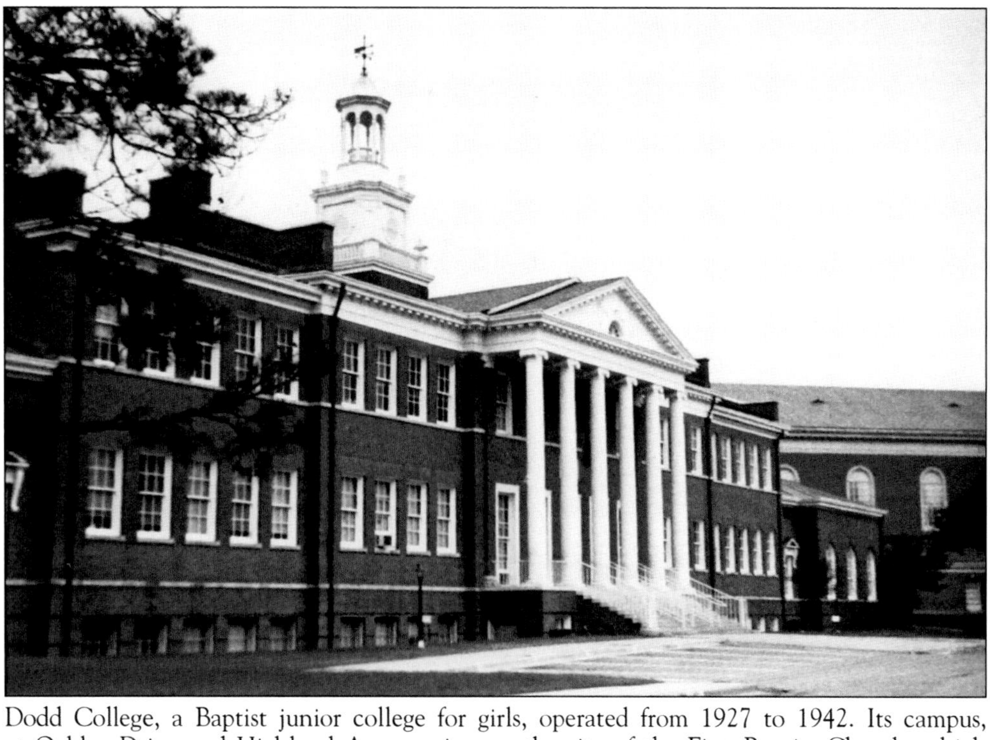

Dodd College, a Baptist junior college for girls, operated from 1927 to 1942. Its campus, at Ockley Drive and Highland Avenue, is now the site of the First Baptist Church, which incorporates the school's old buildings.

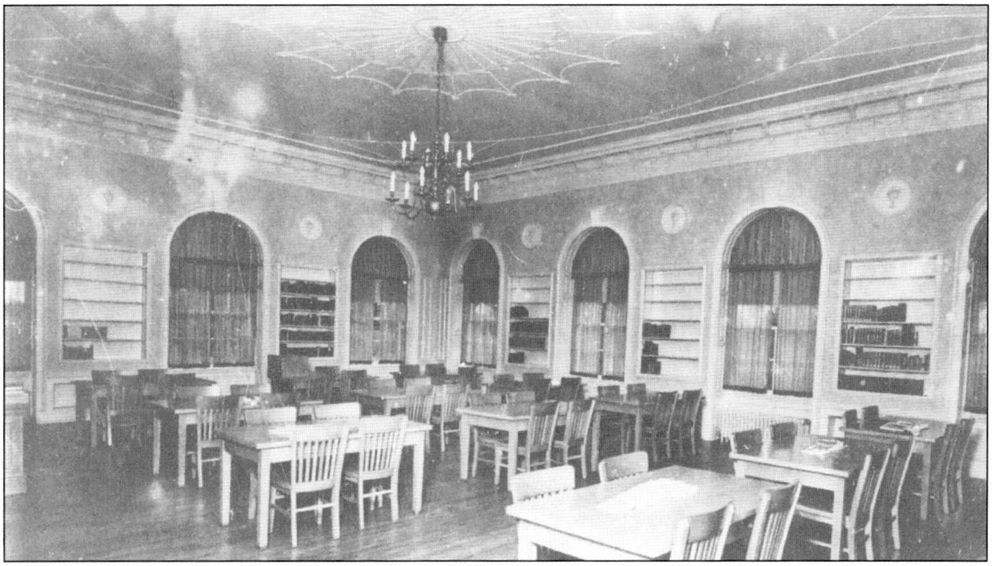

The library of Dodd College was housed in the east wing of Shreveport Hall. Now called Dodd Hall, the building houses the First Baptist Church School, a private school established in 1973. This view is from the 1920s.

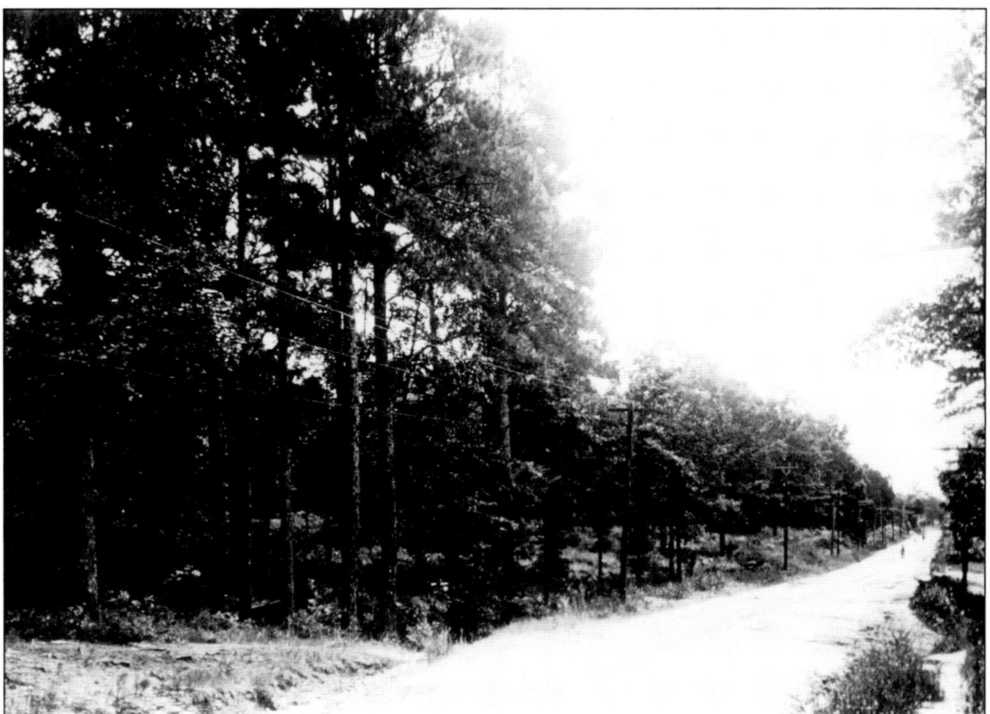

Shown here is Centenary Boulevard at Kings Highway in 1906. In 1908 Centenary College of Louisiana cleared this land for its campus. Centenary, founded in 1825 at Jackson, Louisiana, is the state's oldest institution of higher learning.

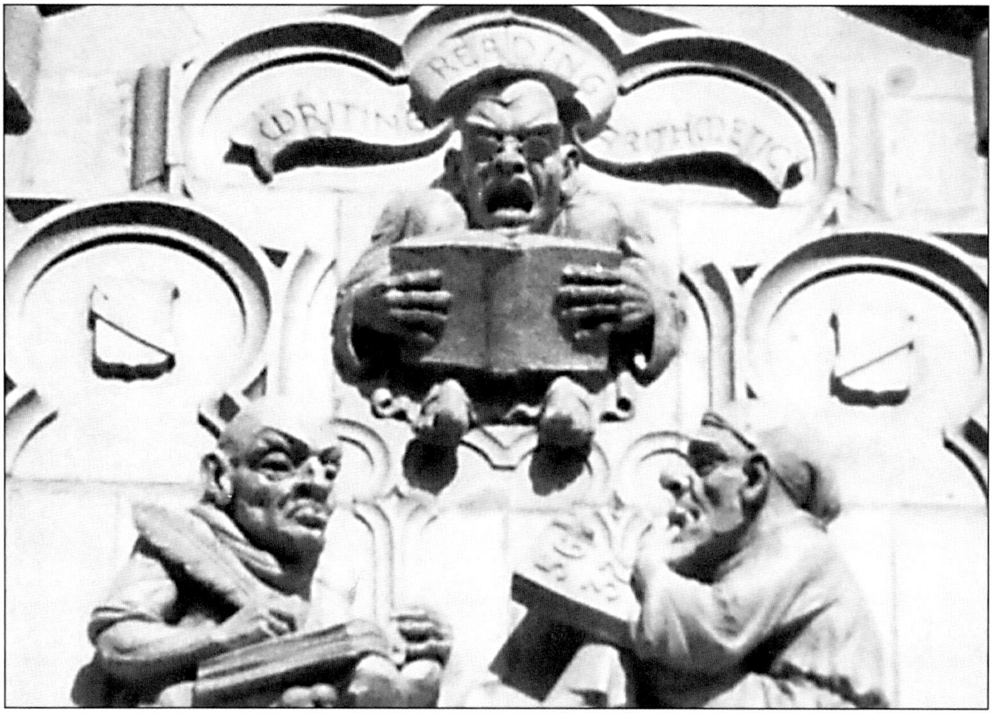

Allegorical figures of "Reading, Writing, and Arithmetic" decorate the Fairfield Elementary School, built in 1923 as part of a major school building program by the Caddo Parish School Board that lasted through the 1920s.

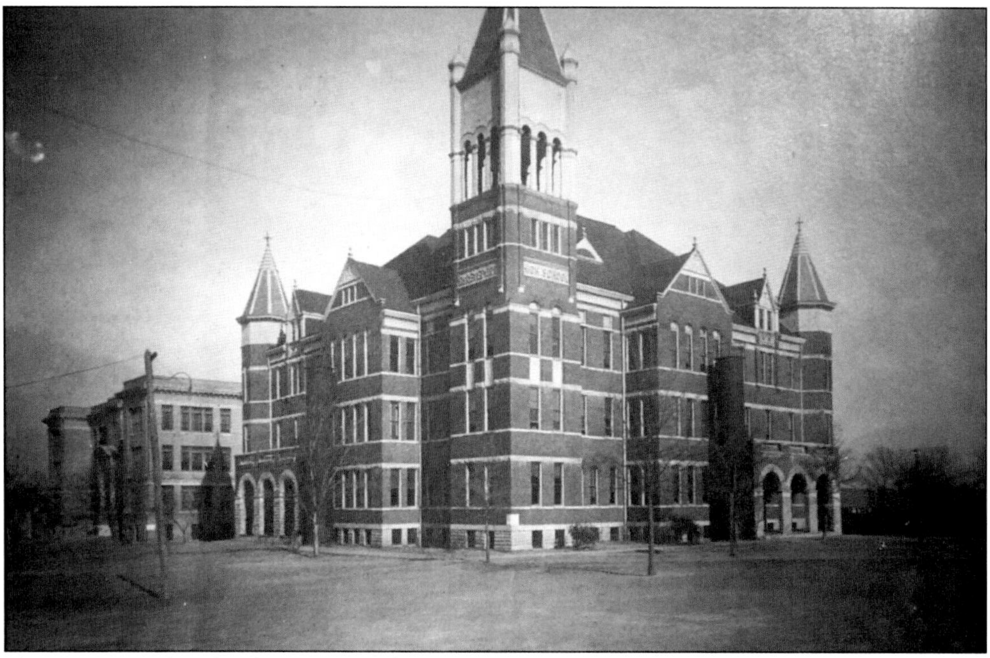

Shreveport High School at Hope and Snow Streets was the largest public school in Louisiana when opened in 1899. Expanded in 1910, it closed in 1925 when Byrd High School was opened on Line Avenue.

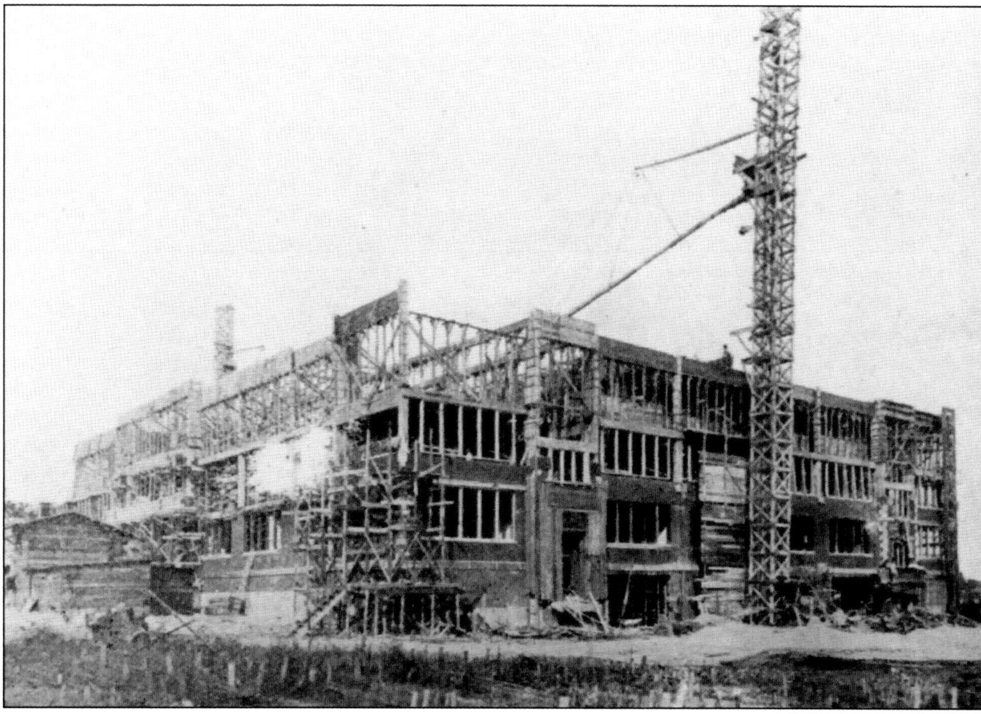

This is the only known photograph of the construction of Byrd High School (above) at Line Avenue and King's Highway, 1924. The school, named for Prof. Clifton Ellis Byrd, father of Shreveport's public schools, opened a year later. The sculpture above the entrance (below) is a Baroque rendition of the state seal.

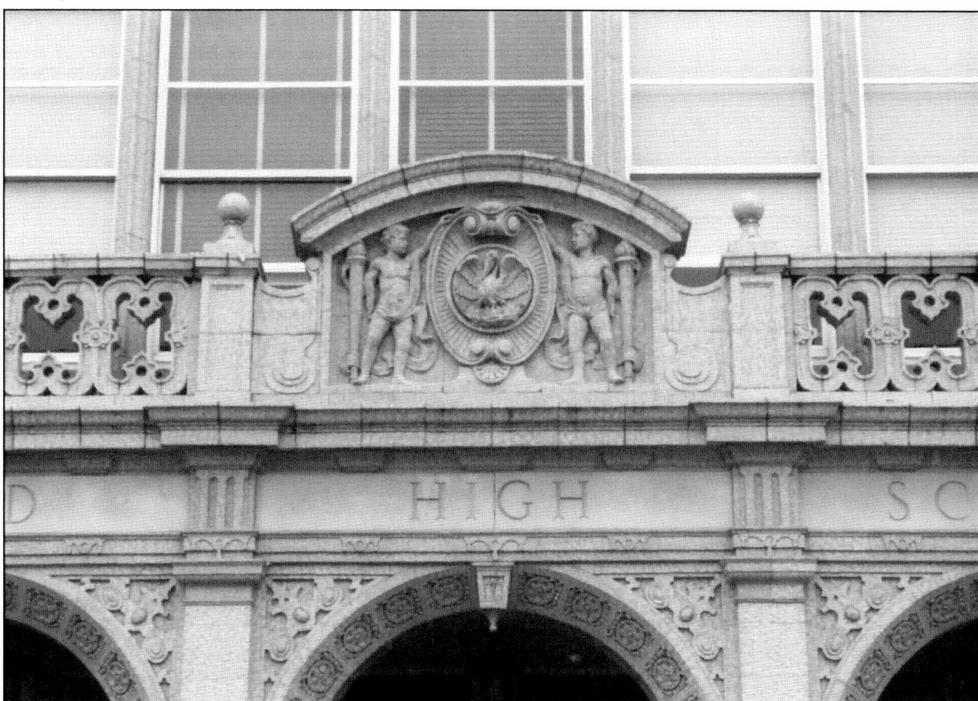

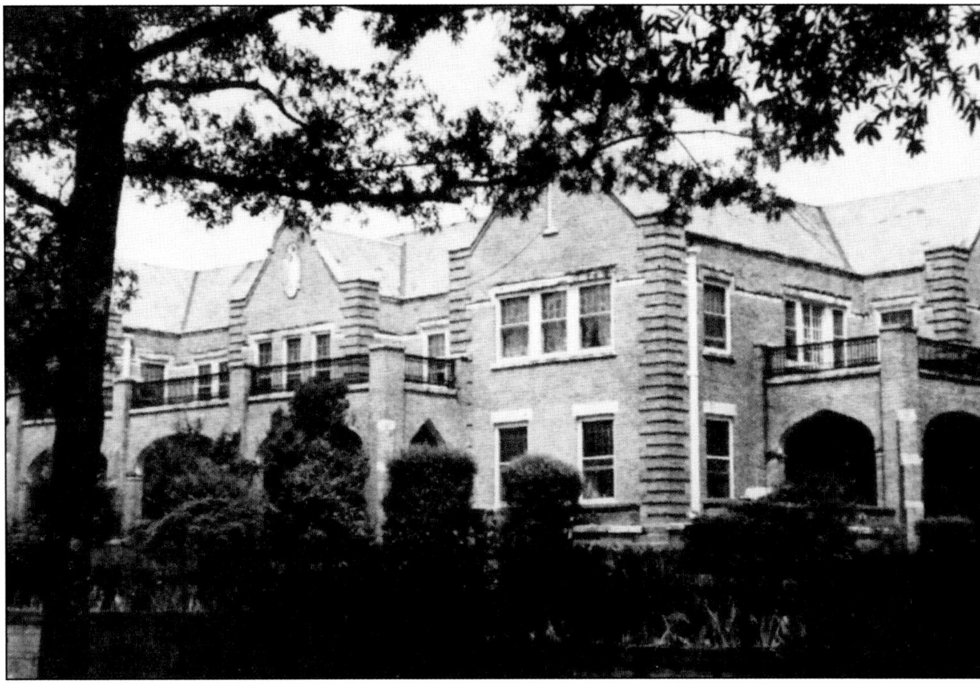

The Genevieve Orphanage, founded in 1889, stood at Olive and Elizabeth Streets from 1907 to 1960. Its successor, the Center for Families, today occupies newer facilities at the same address.

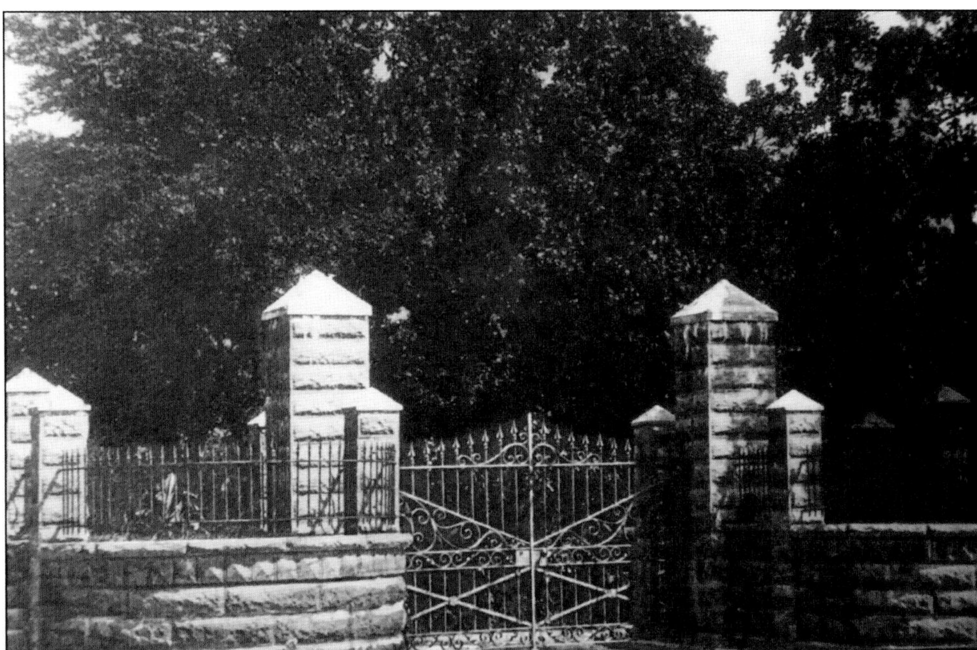

Oakland Cemetery, Shreveport's oldest municipal burial ground, opened in 1847, though the oldest burial dates to 1842. Located at Milam Street and Grand Avenue, its main gate, shown here, was built in 1905.

A view of Oakland Cemetery (right) shows some of its magnificent Victorian monuments. In the nineteenth century the cemetery played a significant role in the spiritual lives of citizens, for whom death was always near. All faiths are represented here. The Jewish section (below) opened in 1858 and was the fifth Jewish cemetery in Louisiana.

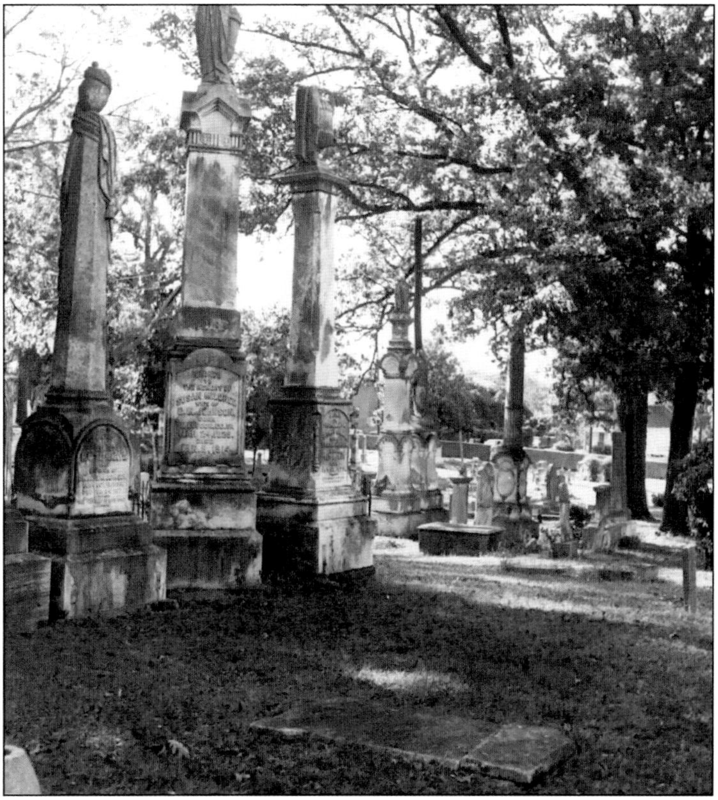

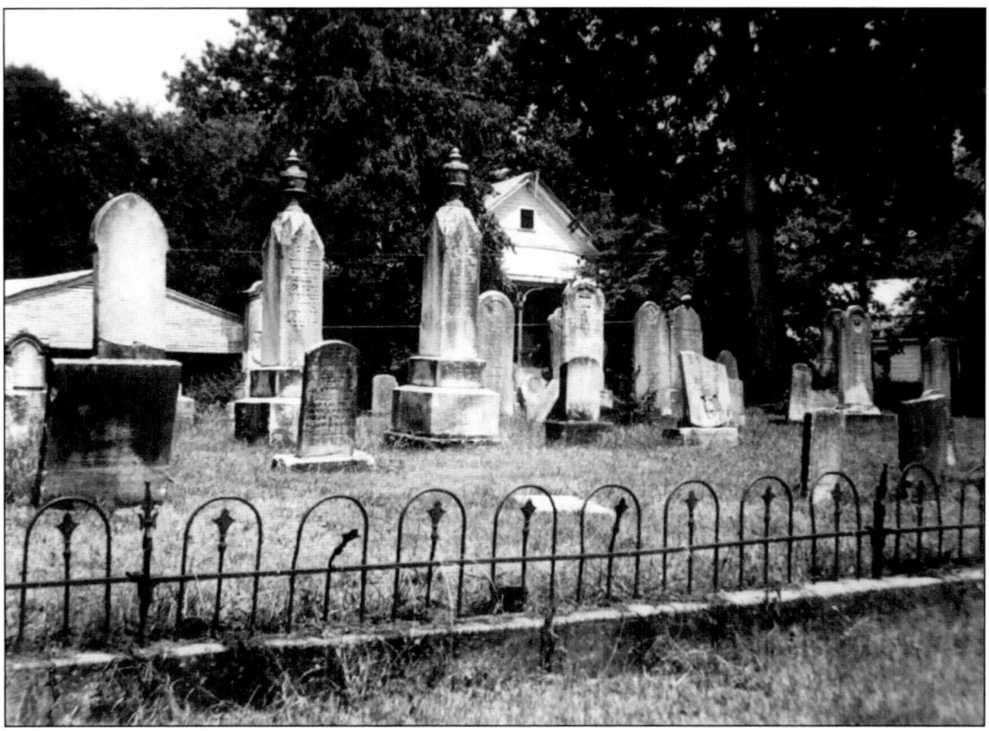

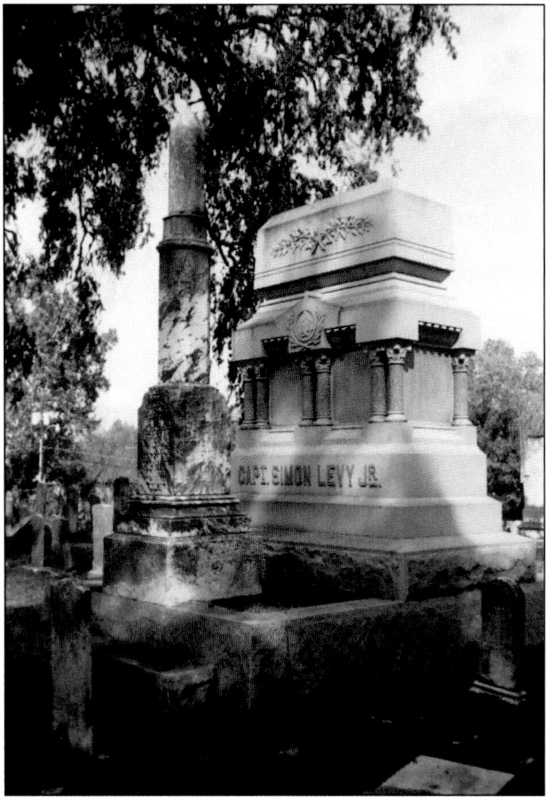

The tomb of Captain Simon Levy Jr. (see p. 62) and his wife, Henriette Bodenheimer Levy (1850–1878), is one of the most imposing at Oakland Cemetery (left). Other historic cemeteries containing interesting monuments include Hebrew Rest, Greenwood, Forest Park, and St. Joseph's Catholic Cemetery (below), located on Texas Avenue. Established in 1882, it contains many above-ground tombs.

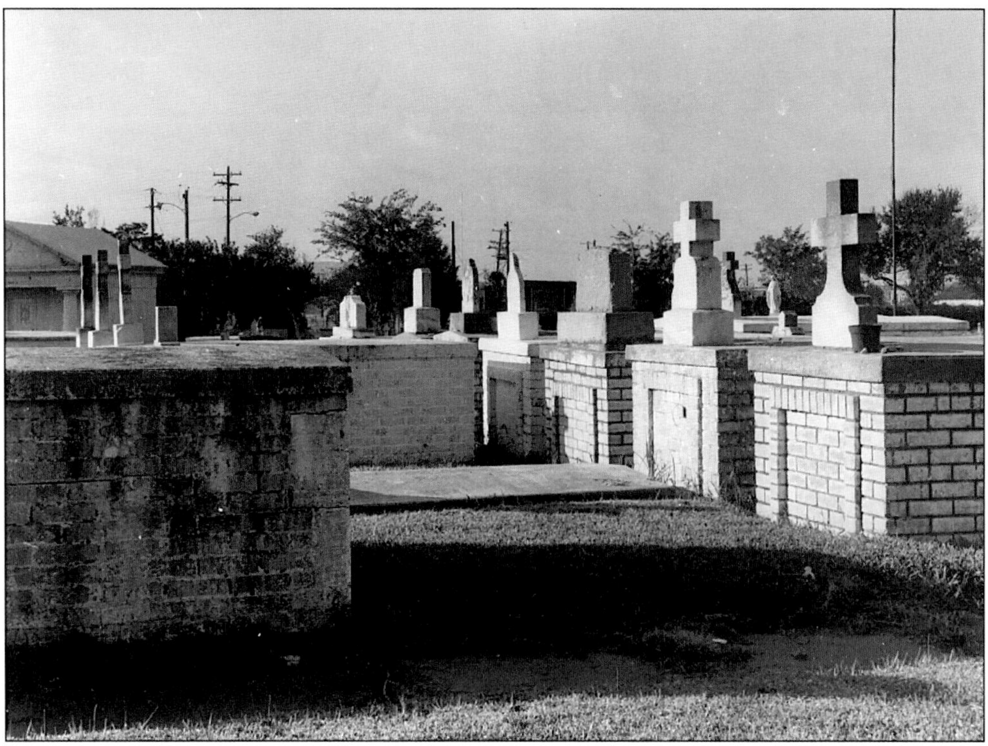

Six

Life, Culture, and Entertainment

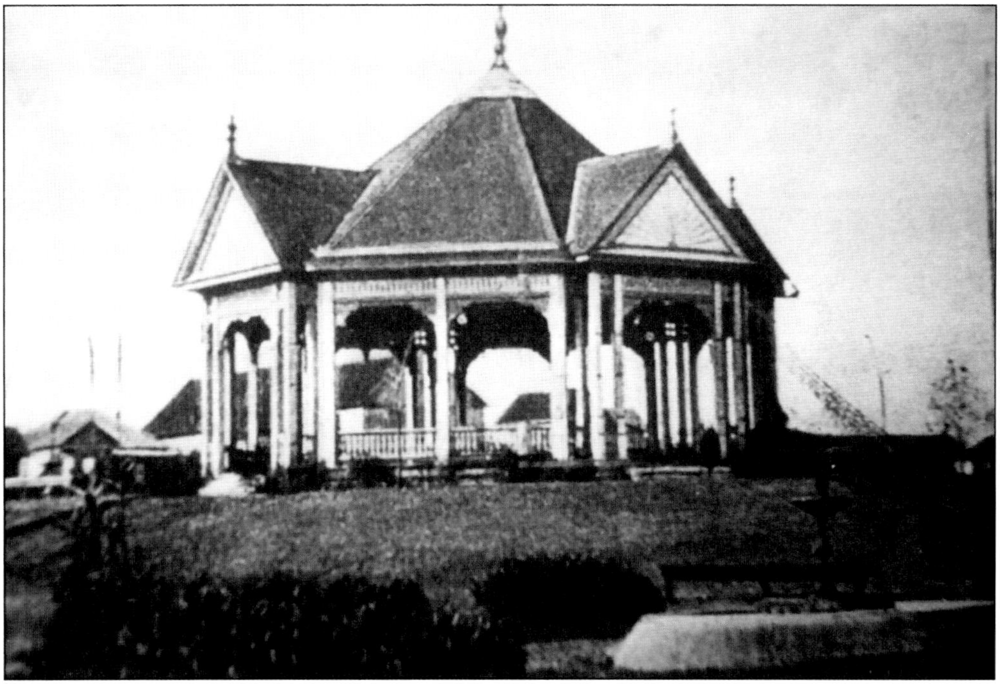

Pictured here is the pavilion at Princess Park. Shreveport's first public park was Oakland Cemetery, but in 1895 an effort by a group of Shreveport women organized the City Park Association, which raised funds to build a city park at Common and Howell Streets. Named for Gertrude "Princess" Ardis, who led the association's efforts, the park is the oldest of many city parks in Shreveport today. The site of the pavilion is now occupied by the offices of the Shreveport Regional Arts Council.

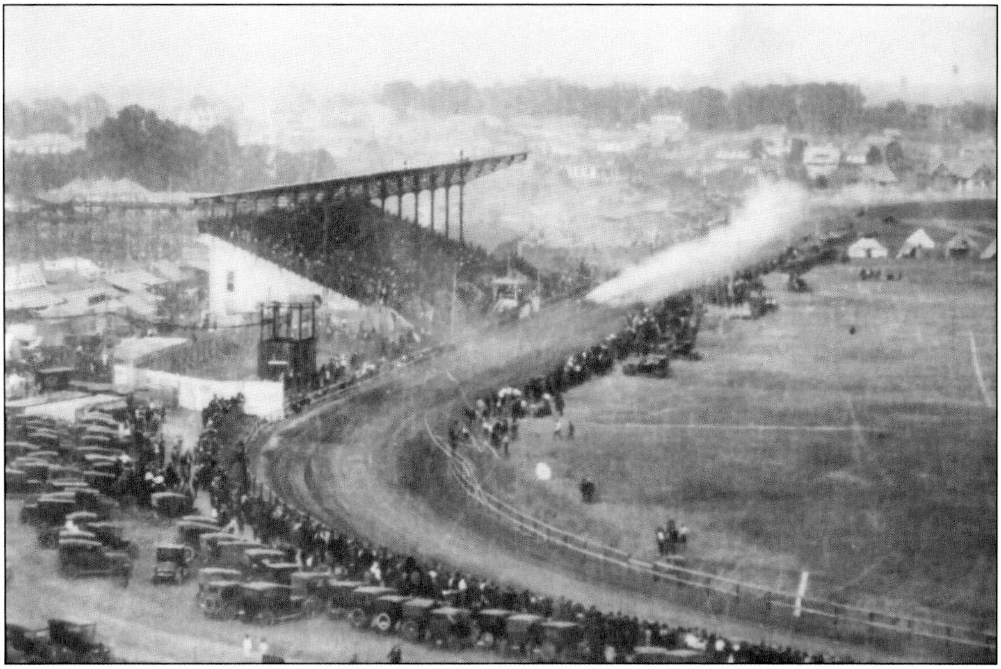

The State Fair Grounds on Greenwood Road were laid out in 1906. Above is a 1920s view of the racetrack, where first horseraces and later auto races were held. The track remains, though the grandstand was razed in the 1980s. Below is State Fair Stadium, built in 1924. Remodeled and enlarged several times through the years, it has been known as Independence Stadium since 1976.

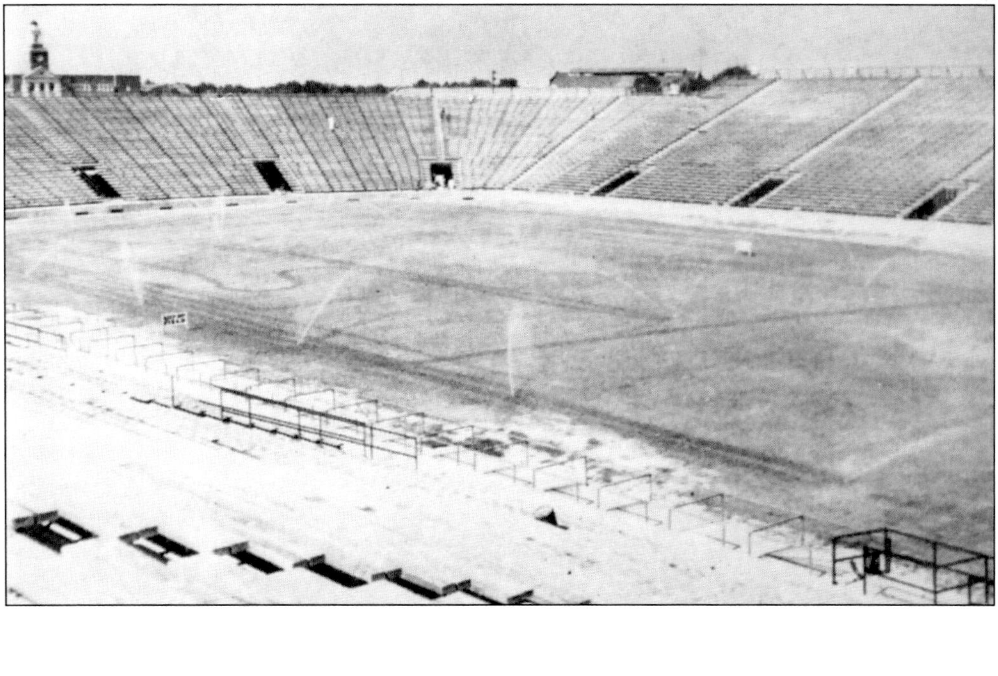

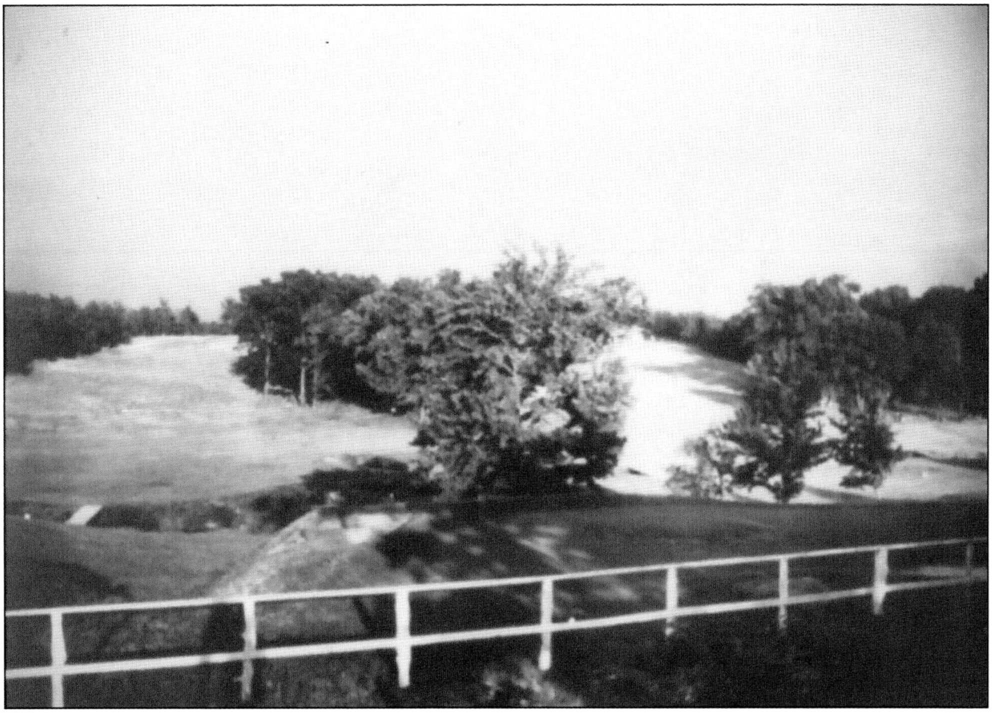

The Shreveport Country Club was founded as the Pelican Golf Club in 1901. In 1913 its present course was first laid out (above) at the end of Esplanade Boulevard, off Greenwood Road. That same year the club built the city's first swimming pool (right). In 1952 the present clubhouse replaced the one shown in this 1920s photograph.

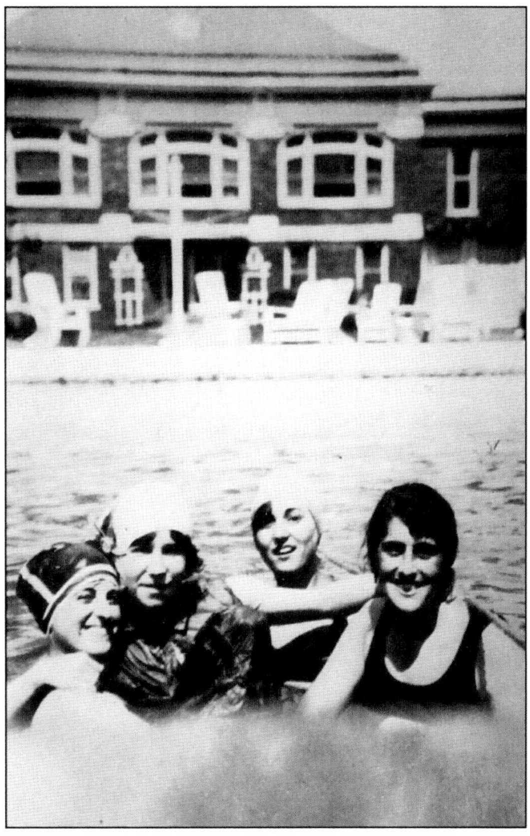

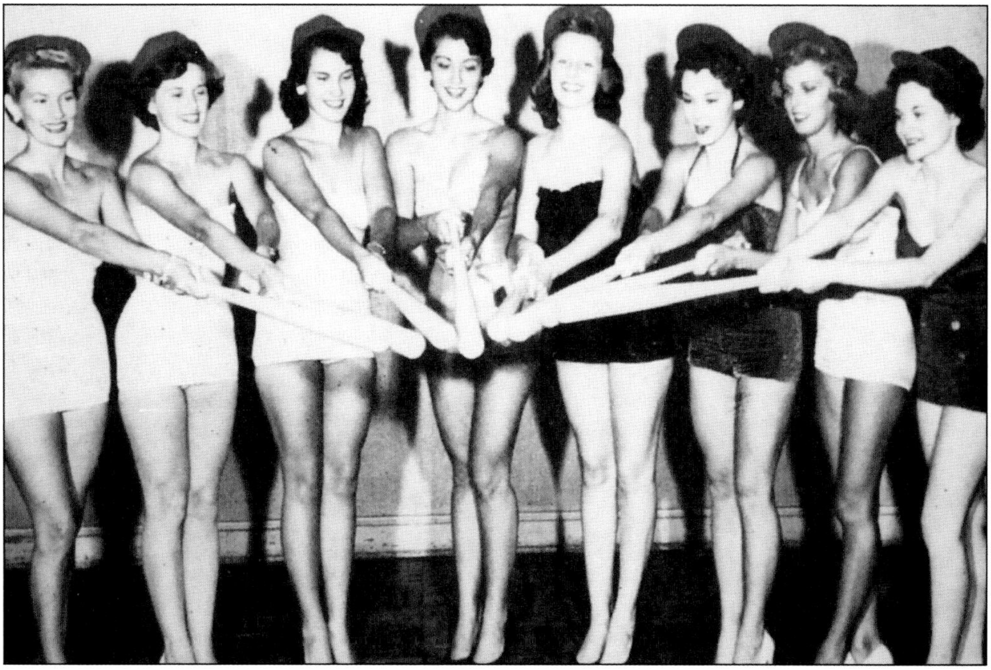

Professional baseball has been a part of Shreveport since 1895, when the city first fielded a team in the Texas League. In the 1910s and 1920s such teams as the New York Yankees, Brooklyn Dodgers, and St. Louis Browns held their summer camps here. At top is a 1952 photo of finalists in the Texas League's "Queen of Baseball" contest. Below is a view of the Shreveport's old ballpark, located at Park Avenue and Gary Street from 1921 to 1985.

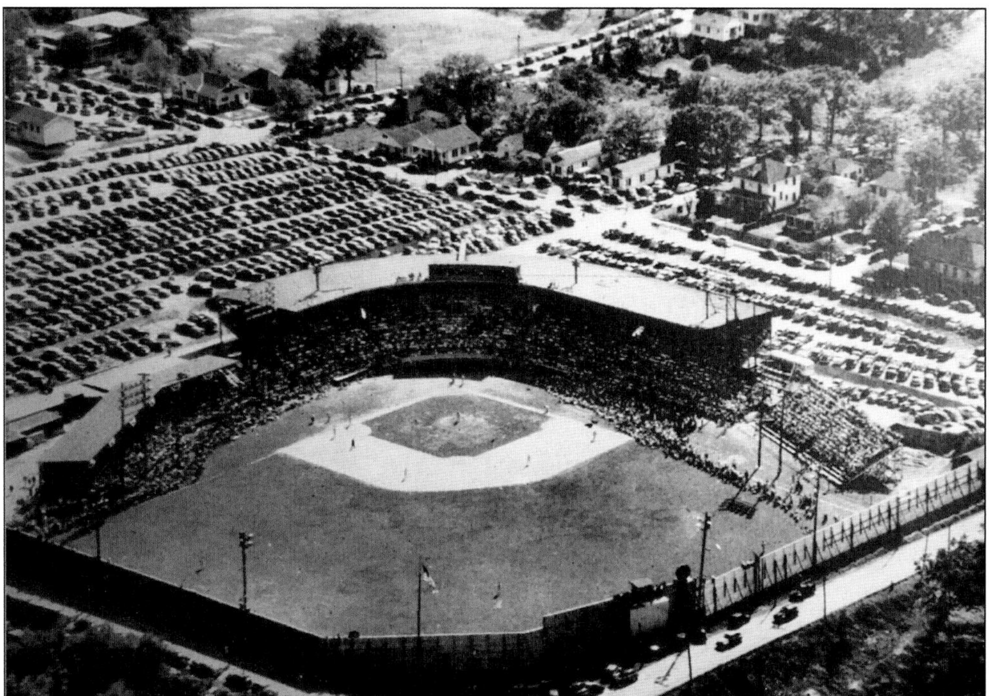

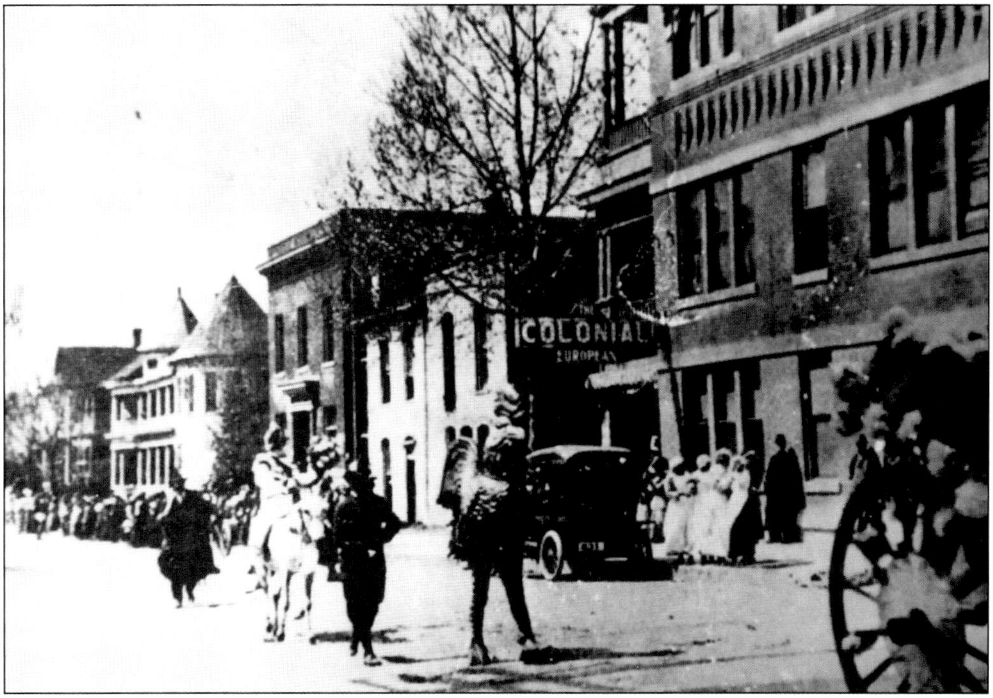

Mardi Gras was first celebrated in Shreveport in the 1860s, though its largest parades (excepting those held today) came in the period from 1890 to 1927. Above is a view of the 1900 Mardi Gras parade in the 300 block of Milam Street. Below, a crowd of revelers gathers on the Courthouse Square in 1926.

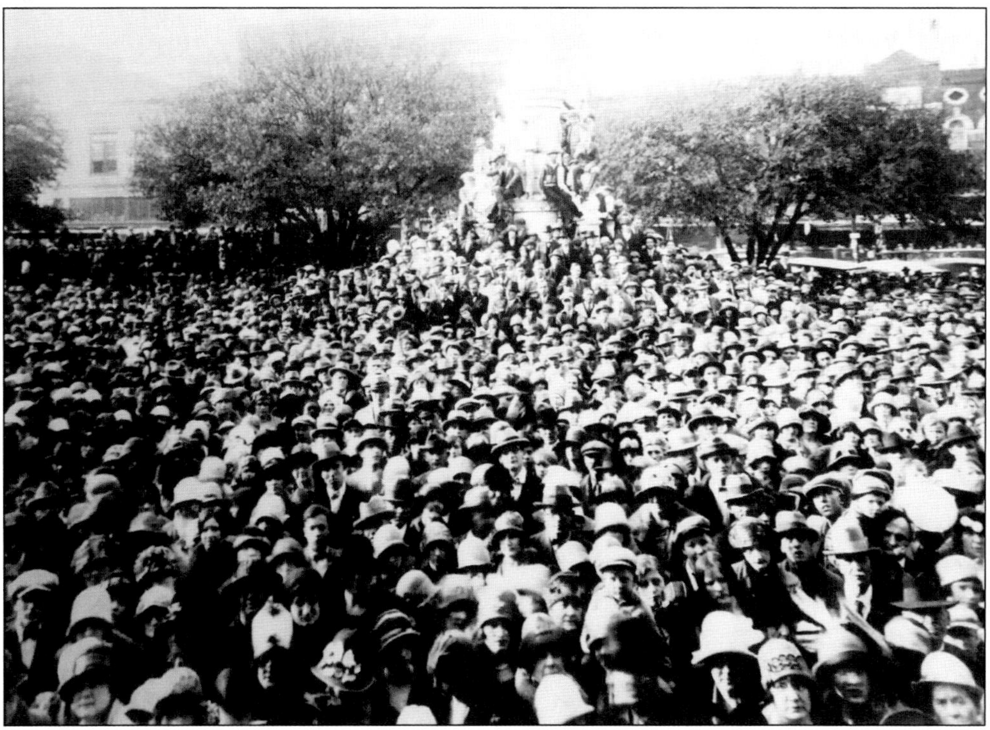

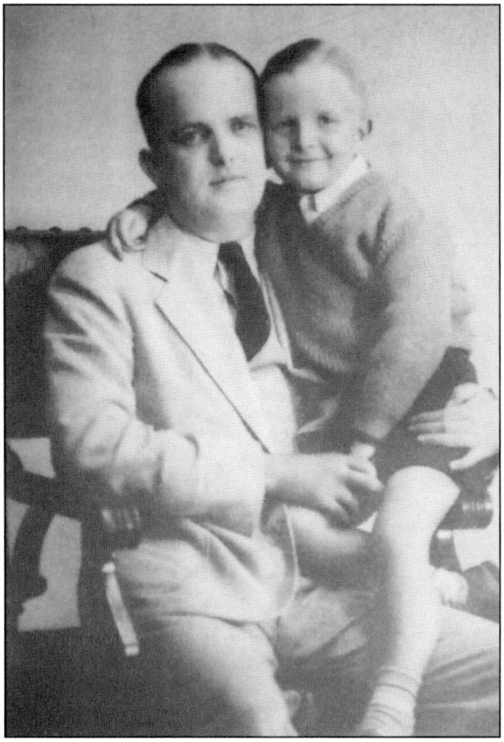

Author Truman Capote (1924–1984) sits on the lap of his father, Shreveporter Arch Persons (1897–1981), as a child. Born Truman Persons in New Orleans, Capote later took his stepfather's surname. His father was a lifelong Shreveport businessman and is buried at Forest Park Cemetery on St. Vincent Avenue.

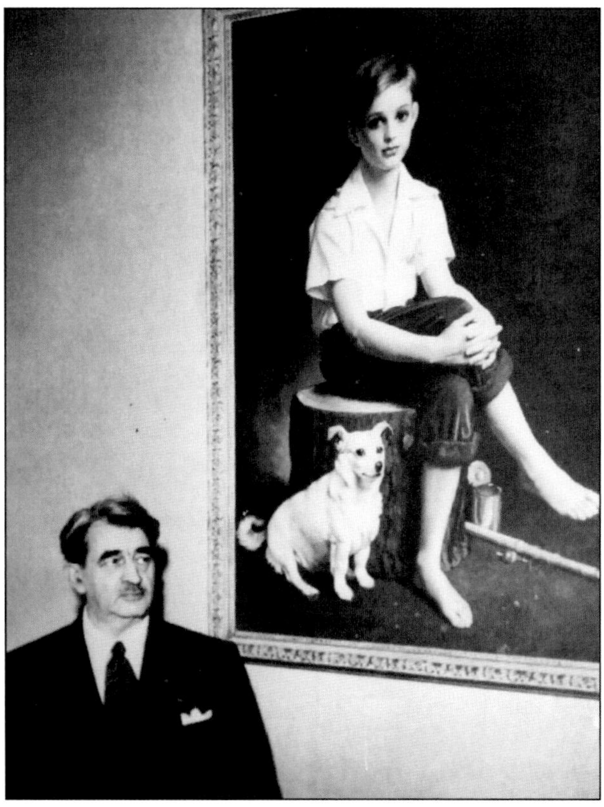

Painter Jean Despujols (1886–1965) made Shreveport his home for many years and is buried at Greenwood Cemetery. Educated in France and Italy and an acclaimed artist in his native France, Despujols chronicled Indochina for the French government in the 1930s. Here he poses by a portrait of Shreveporter Camille Despot. Many of his works may be seen at Shreveport's Meadows Museum.

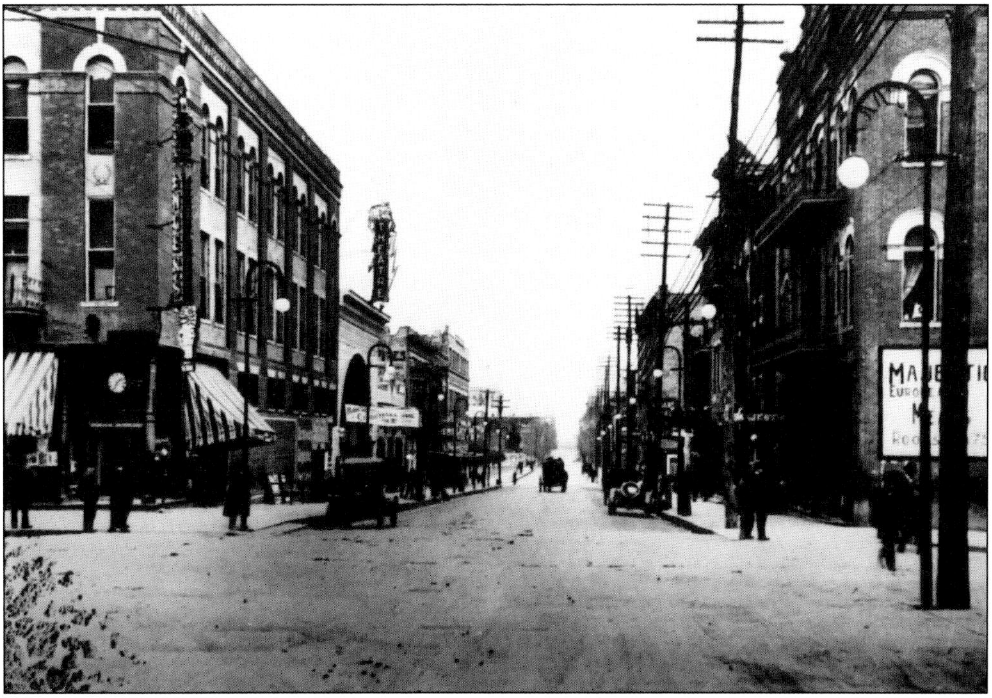

This is a view of Milam Street looking east from Louisiana Street, about 1920 (above). At left is the Saenger drugstore, and behind it, the Saenger Theatre, both belonging to Julian and Abe Saenger, sons of Rabbi Israel Saenger of Shreveport. In 1924 the brothers built the Strand Theatre (below) a block away. It became the headquarters for their chain of vaudeville houses and cinemas that stretched across the South.

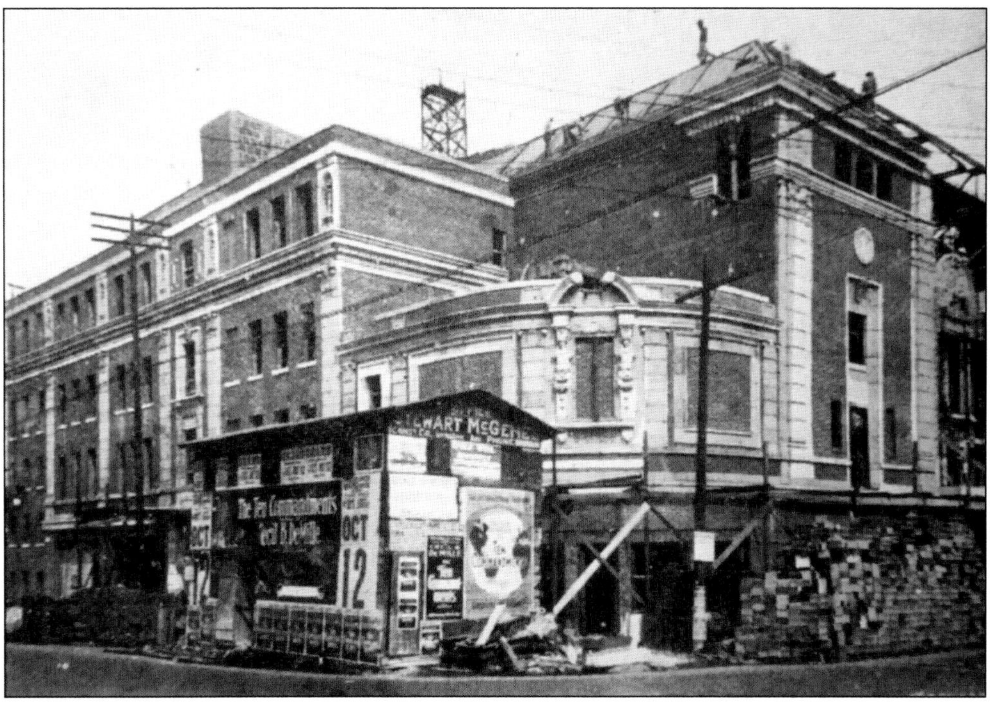

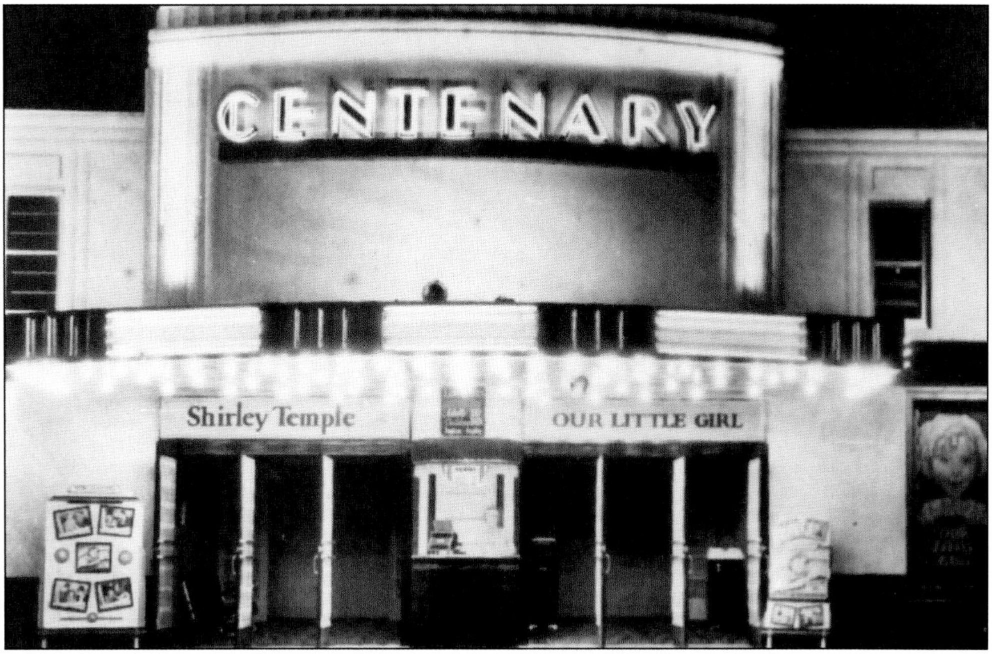

By the 1930s Shreveport had numerous cinemas found in every part of town. Pictured here is the Centenary, located on Centenary Boulevard at Wilkinson Street. The structure still stands, though altered almost beyond recognition as an office complex. Few early area cinemas survive at all and none retain their original use.

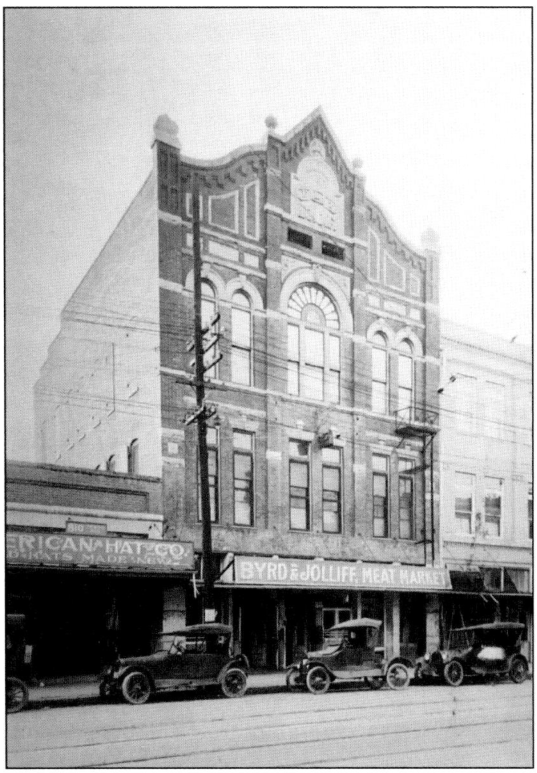

From the city's earliest days fraternal societies such as the Freemasons and Odd Fellows were an important part of the lives of many Shreveporters, especially during the nineteenth and early twentieth centuries. Shown here is the Neith Lodge of the Independent Order of Odd Fellows, which stood at 806 Texas Avenue.

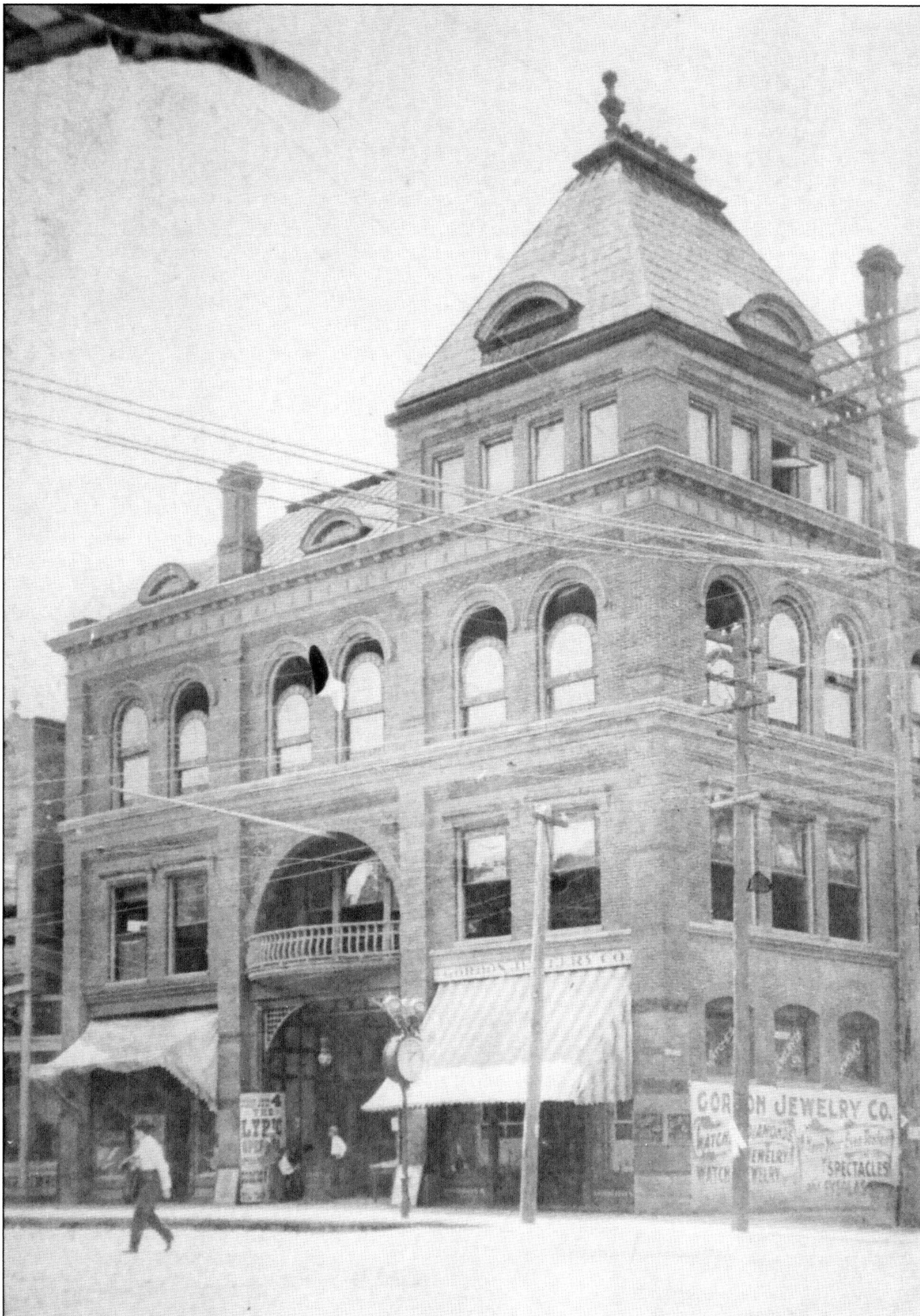

The center of entertainment for many years in Shreveport was the Grand Opera House, built in 1887. Such noted performers as Sarah Bernhardt, Paderewski, Edwin Booth, Modjeska, and others graced its stage. It was demolished in 1927, and today the site is the address of the Bank One Tower, formerly the First National Bank Tower, at Texas and Edwards Streets.

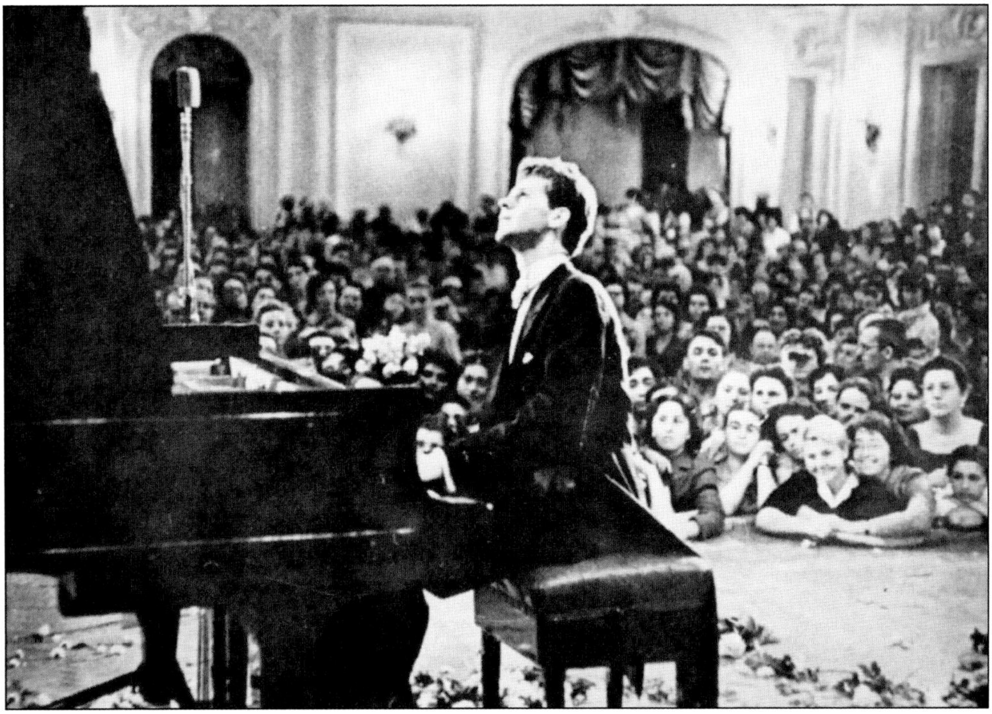

Shreveport native Harvey LeVan Cliburn, born in 1934, is one of the nation's premier pianists. Although his family moved to Texas when he was a child, Van Cliburn has always kept close ties to his home city, where he still maintains a home.

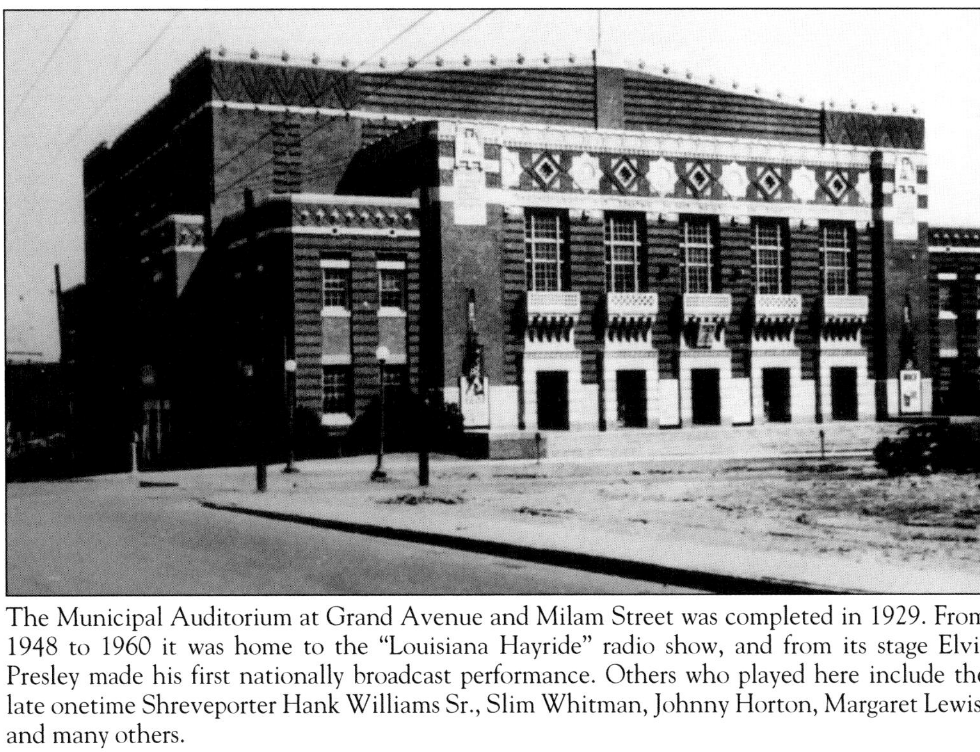

The Municipal Auditorium at Grand Avenue and Milam Street was completed in 1929. From 1948 to 1960 it was home to the "Louisiana Hayride" radio show, and from its stage Elvis Presley made his first nationally broadcast performance. Others who played here include the late onetime Shreveporter Hank Williams Sr., Slim Whitman, Johnny Horton, Margaret Lewis, and many others.

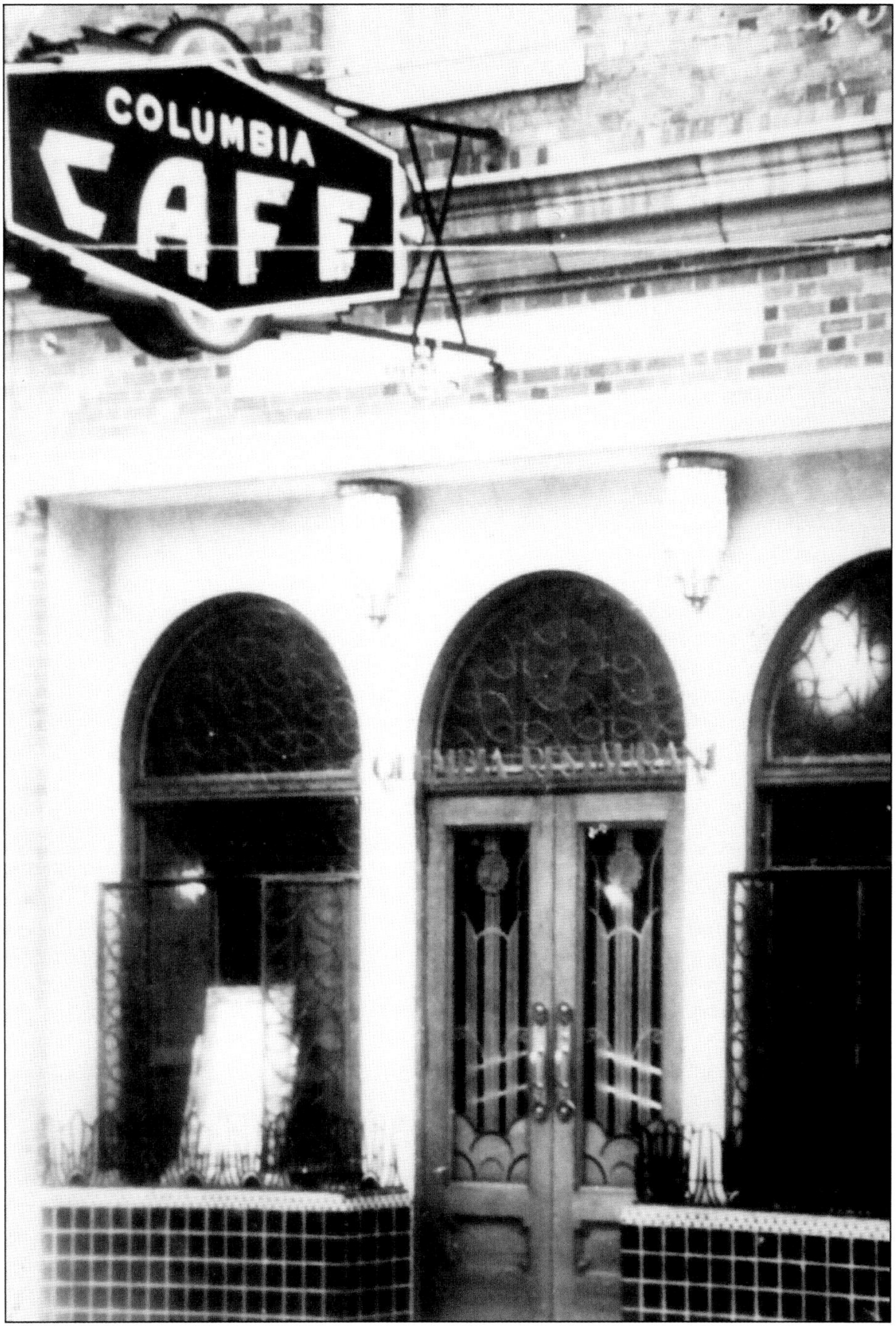

Shreveport's premier restaurant from 1899 to 1971 was the Columbia, located at 521 Market Street. During the oil boom it is said that some of the deals that resulted in the region's greatest fortunes were struck there. The Columbia was also the first air-conditioned restaurant in Shreveport. A German chef, Emanuel Mahne, is thought to have opened the city's first true restaurant in the 1840s. Today the oldest operating restaurant in Shreveport is Brocato's, established in 1924.

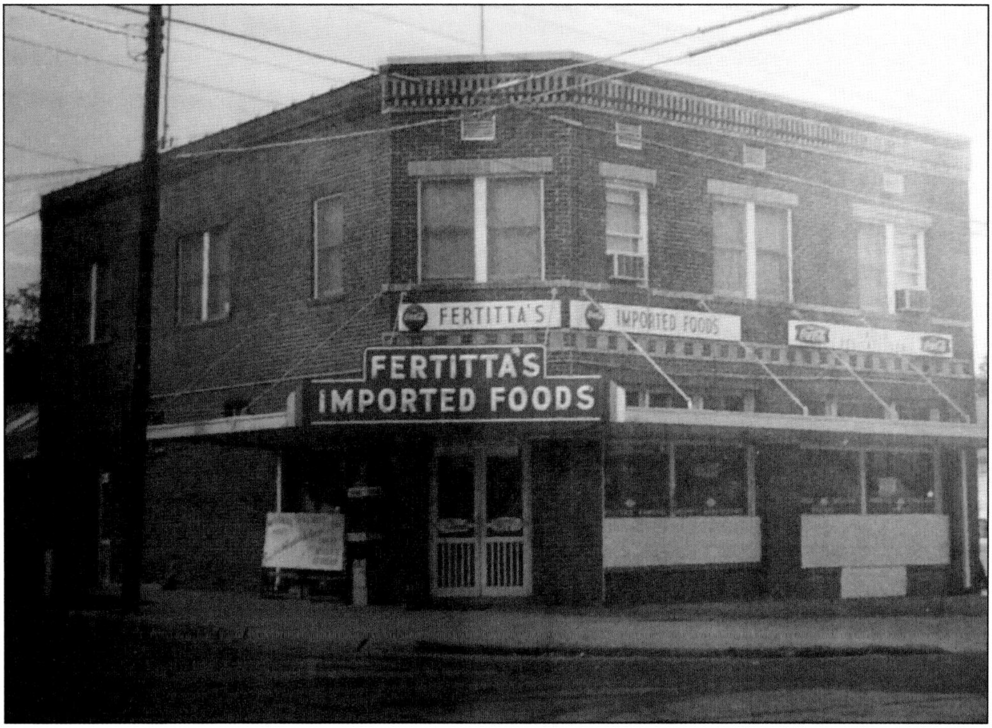

The oldest restaurant to continually operate at the same location is Fertitta's Deli at Fairfield and Christian Streets. Opened in 1927, it is now run by the third generation of the same family. This view is from the 1950s, though little has changed since then.

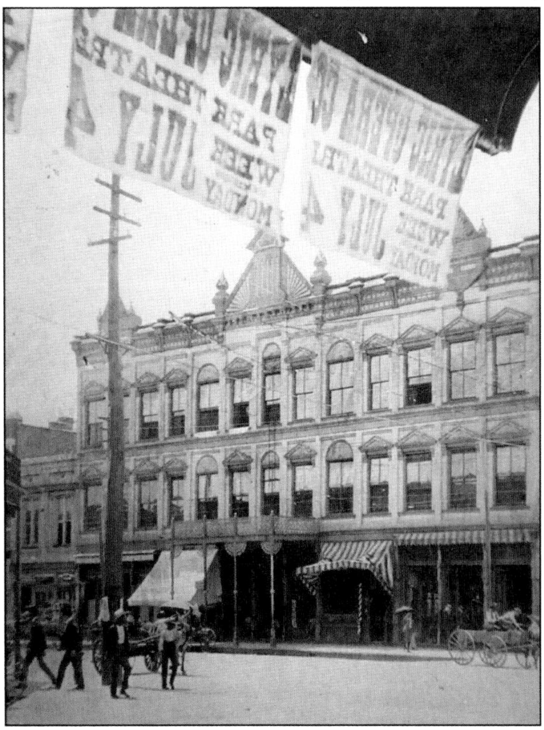

The Phoenix Hotel, built by Peter Youree in 1887 at Texas and Market Streets, was the city's finest hotel for many years. Shown here in 1904, it contained a restaurant, grill, bar, shops, and provided a livery stable for its guests.

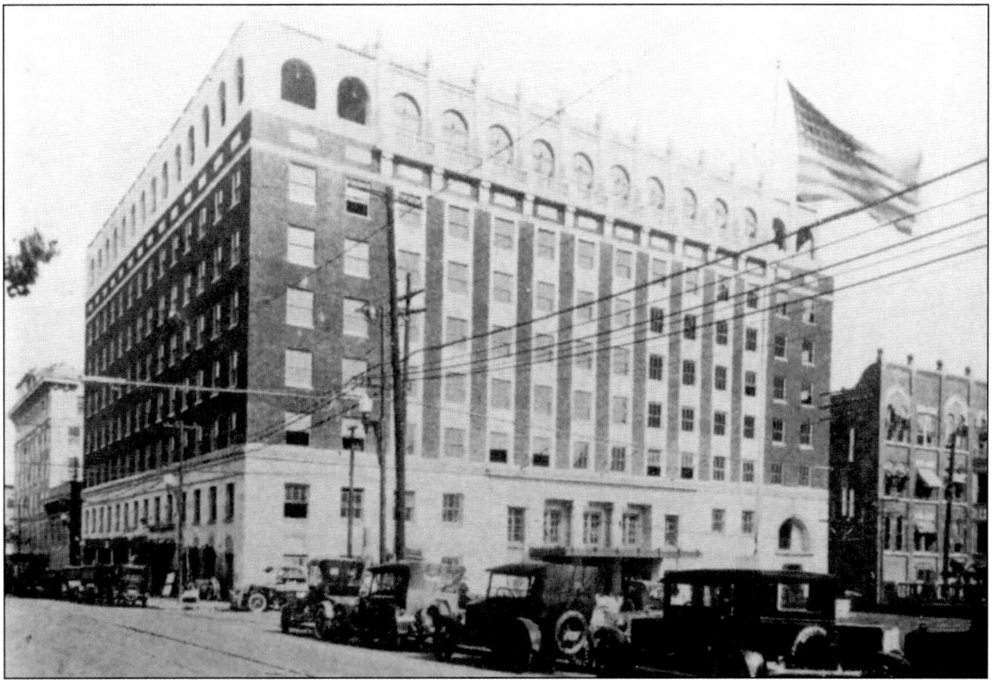

The Washington-Youree, occupying three-quarters of a city block with entrances on Edwards, Market, Travis, and Texas Streets, incorporated the Phoenix, Youree, and Washington Hotels from 1922 until its demolition in 1980. At its height, it had seven restaurants and a multitude of shops and other amenities. Above is the Edwards Street facade, and below is the marble lobby, designed by St. Louis architect Holden Brock Sr.

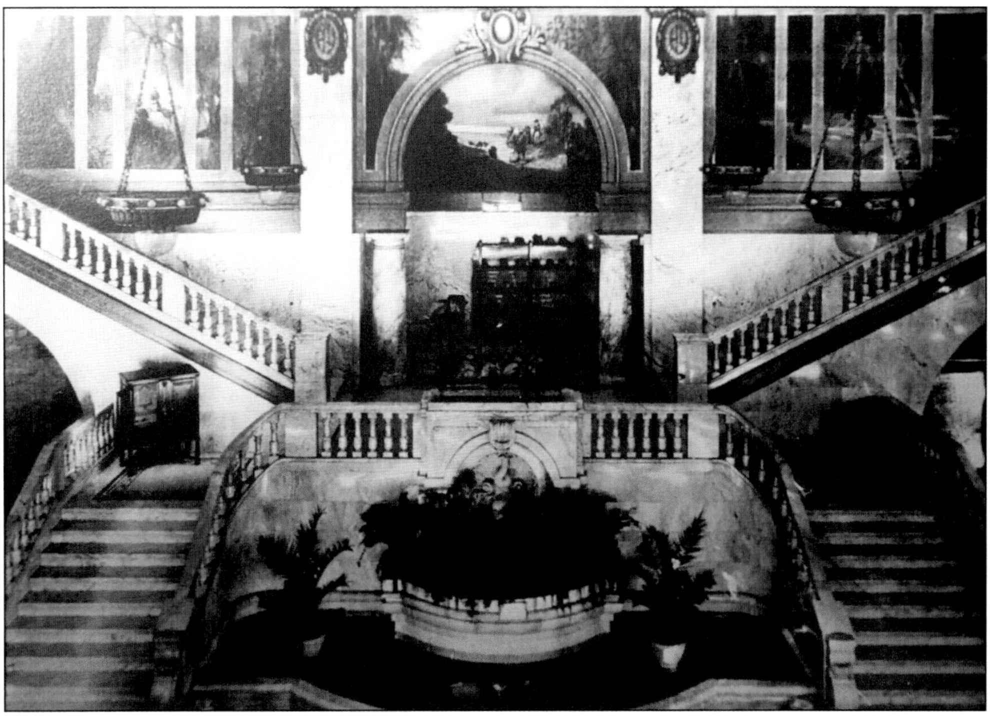

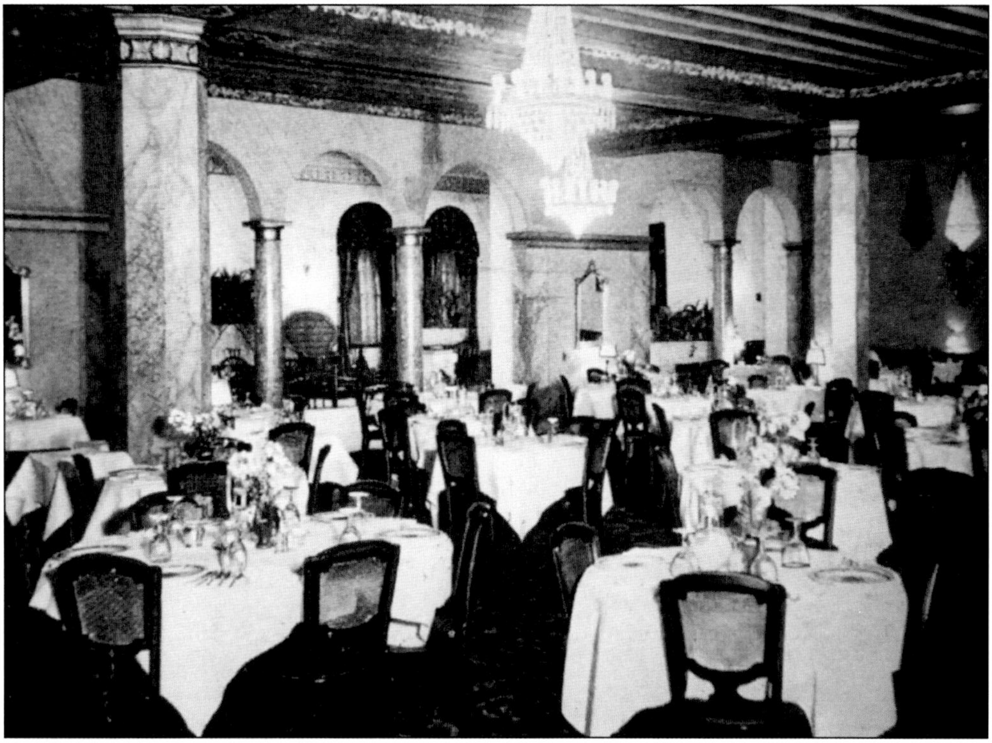

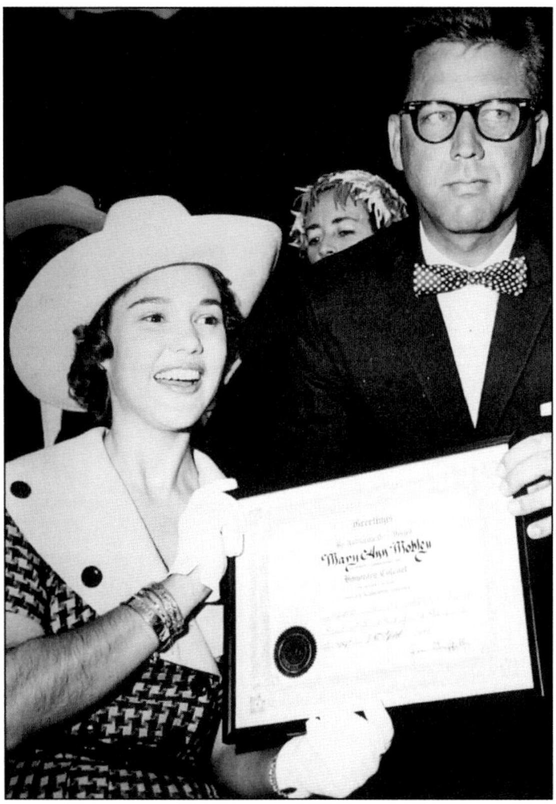

This is the main dining room of the Washington-Youree Hotel as it appeared in the 1920s. The dining room is remembered as having served some of the finest cuisine in the region. Additionally, the hotel once housed the Shreveport Club and the Petroleum Club.

Miss America Mary Ann Mobley receives a citation from Holiday-in-Dixie president Jim Griffith in 1959. The Holiday-in-Dixie festival, began in 1949, is the city's annual springtime celebration, and its cotillion ball is Shreveport's foremost society event. Once held at the Washington-Youree's ballroom, it is now held at the Municipal Auditorium.

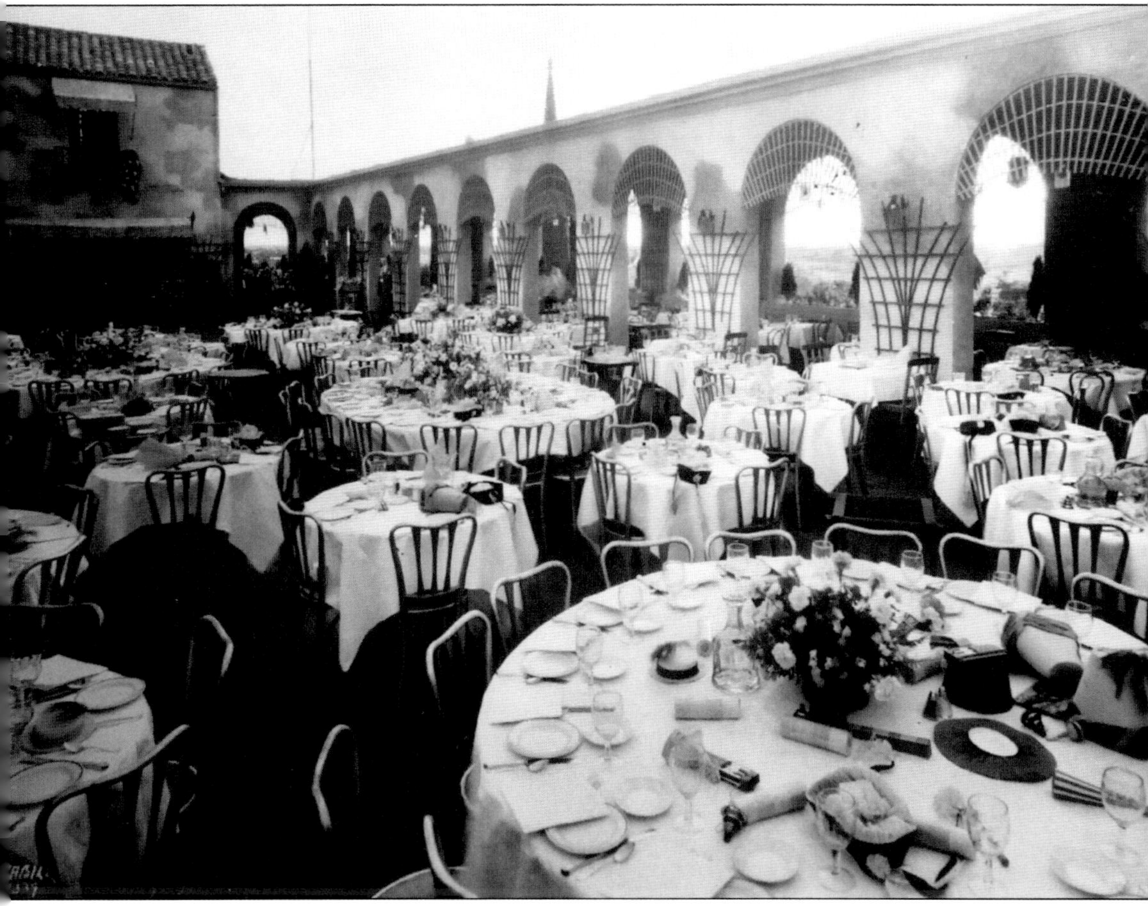

Here is the Washington-Youree roof garden with tables set for a party in 1924. For years dinners here included performances by big-band leaders such as Shreveporter Jan Garber and his orchestra. Perry Como made his radio debut from here.

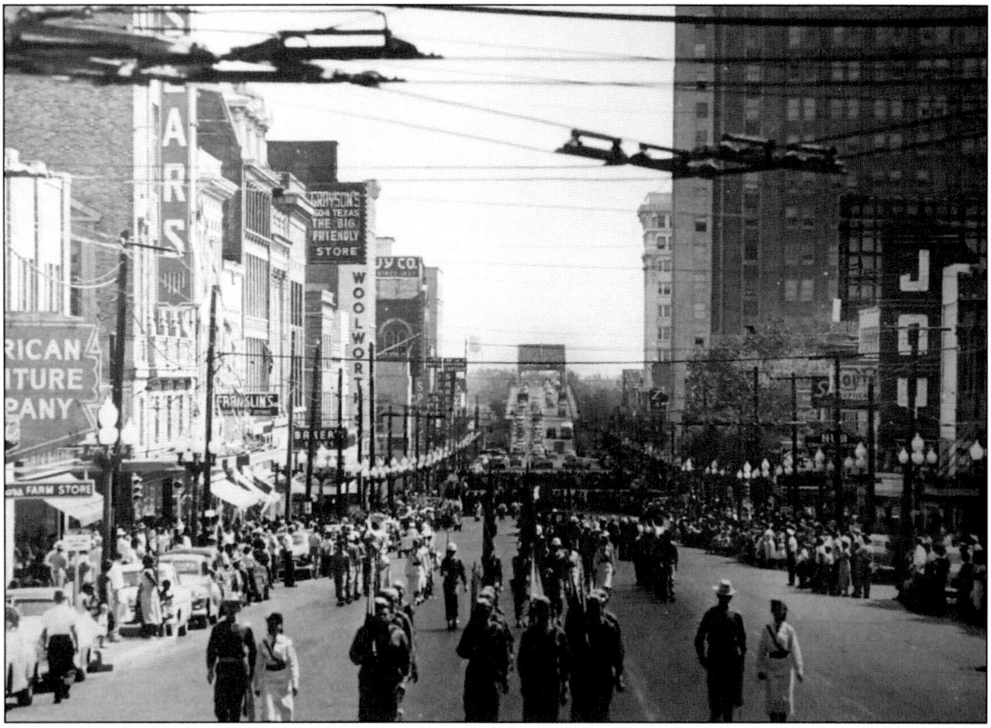

Since 1949 one of the major events of Holiday-in-Dixie has been its Classic Parade. Above is a view of the parade on Texas Street as seen from Common Street, 1955. Since 1962 the Holiday-in-Dixie Ambassadors Club has brought numerous noted figures to the city during the festival. Below, President Gerald R. Ford speaks at Barksdale Air Force Base during the 1976 festival.

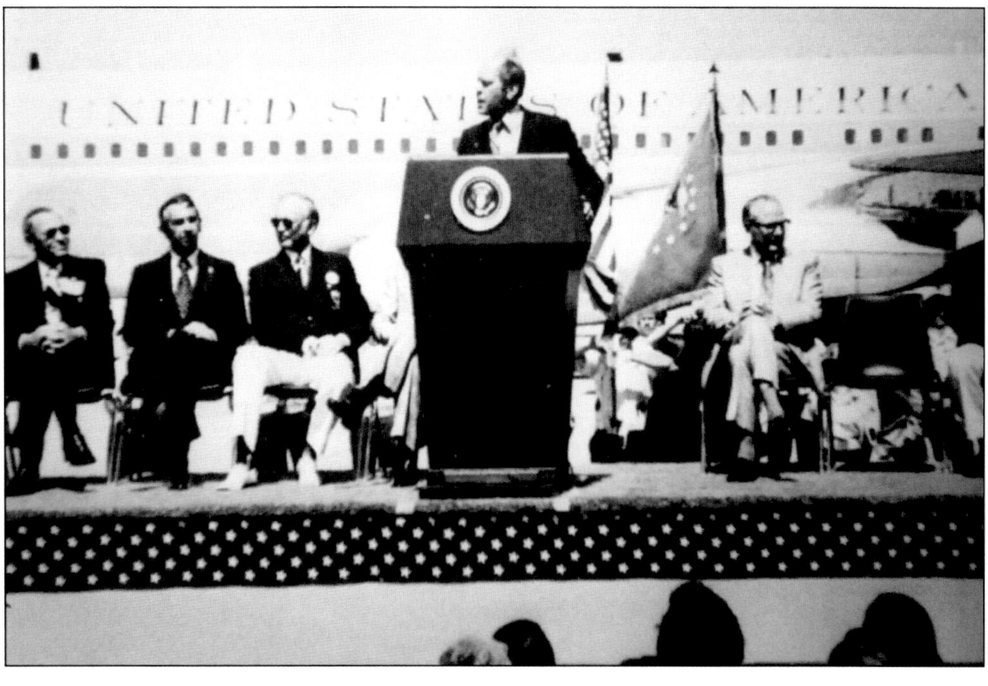

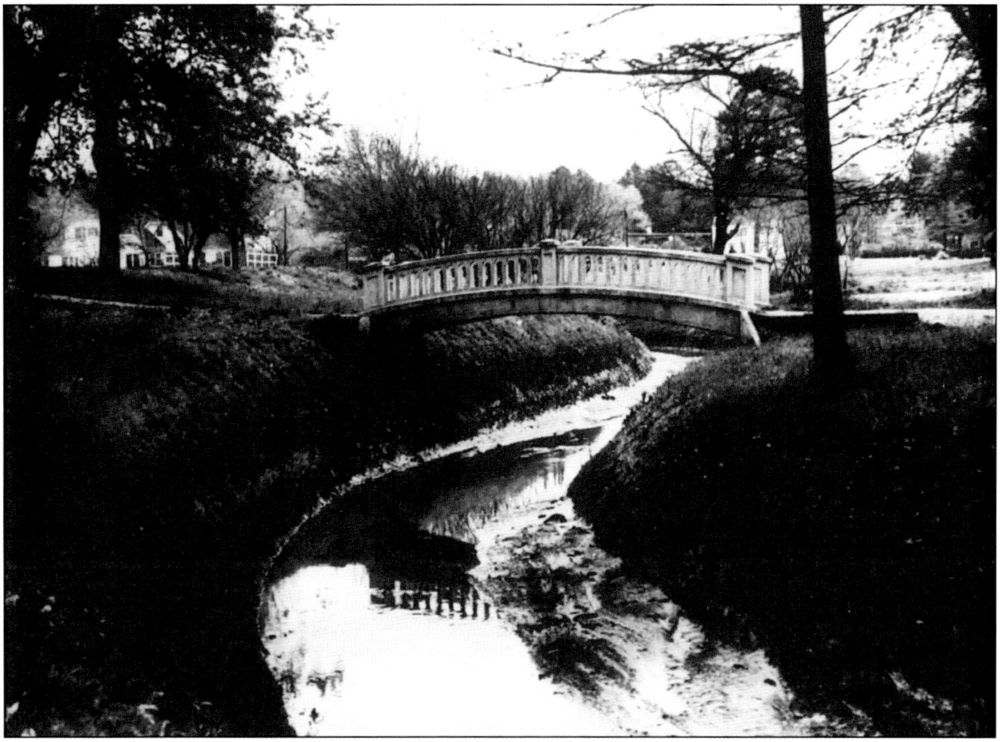

This 1920s view of Betty Virginia Park in the South Highlands area typifies the natural beauty of Shreveport. In every season the city is filled with beautiful, lush foliage and tranquil scenery.

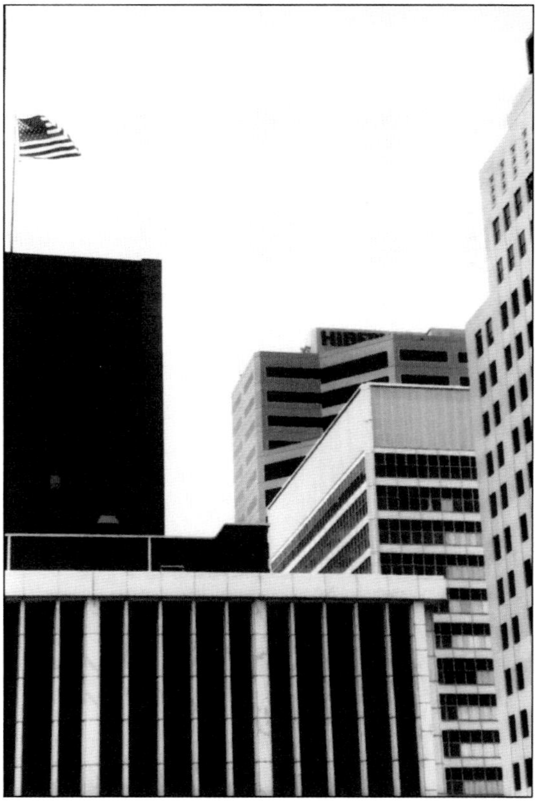

Shreveport is also the modern, busy center of a substantial metropolitan area that includes over 200,000 people in the city itself and over 350,000 in its vicinity. Downtown, where the city began in 1836, remains the heart of Shreveport both spiritually and economically.

Acknowledgments

Many sources were relied upon in assembling the material in this book. As in my newspaper columns and other writings, I have depended upon as many primary documents as possible, as well as secondary materials wherever required. People ask me where I get my information and my only reply is "everywhere." This is because there is no one source of data. The job of the historian is to find as many sources as possible, compare them, glean from them all that can be gleaned, and report them. Sometimes he must interpret them, sometimes apply them to some larger picture, but always he must do his utmost best to be thorough and accurate—above all to be accurate.

Of course, there are many pitfalls on the treacherous path of historical research. Misinformation sometimes tends to be repeated by so many sources that finally it becomes difficult to separate the myth from the fact, and often when one does, the hostility of those whose time-honored legends have been disputed must be dealt with.

Oral history is an important source of information, though it is never one to be taken on its own without verification of the facts. Memory, no matter how excellent, has a way of unintentionally rewriting history as time passes. Old newspapers, city directories, and other published sources from the time being researched are also of great value but, again, must be checked against other sources to assure accuracy. Least impeachable are court records, property records, wills, marriage and death records, cemetery records, church records, and the like. Diaries and personal memoirs, when they are available, are of enormous value as well.

In the preparation of this book, in addition to the above-noted primary sources, the standard collection of secondary sources on Shreveport history has been consulted. Among these are the following: *Biographical & Historical Memoirs of Northwestern Louisiana* by J. Fair Hardin (1937), *Chronicles of Shreveport & Caddo Parish* by Maude H. O'Pry (1928), *Shreveport: A Photographic Remembrance* by Pat Meador and Bailey Thompson (1986), *History of Shreveport and Shreveport Builders* by Lila McLure and J. Ed Howe (volume 1, 1937; volume 2, 1951), and *Historical Profile: Shreveport 1850* by Katherine Brash Jeter and Fredericka Doll Gute. Also, there are numerous church and synagogue histories, organizational histories, pamphlets of all sorts, and other books of local interest which were consulted but not necessarily used in this effort.

Shreveport's finest repository of historical materials is the Louisiana State University in Shreveport Noel Library Archives. The Archives and I have enjoyed a mutually beneficial relationship for many years, and I wish to thank that institution's wonderful, patient, and always helpful staff, especially archivist Laura Brown Street. Special thanks also go to Goodloe R. Stuck, Katherine Brash Jeter, Gary D. Joiner, Roland J. Achee, Arthur R. Carmody, and Neil Johnson, who first told me of the *Images of America* series.